EXIT

EXIT

The Endings That Set Us Free

SARA LAWRENCE-LIGHTFOOT

SARAH CRICHTON BOOKS

Farrar, Straus and Giroux   New York

Sarah Crichton Books
Farrar, Straus and Giroux
18 West 18th Street, New York 10011

Copyright © 2012 by Sara Lawrence-Lightfoot
All rights reserved
Distributed in Canada by D&M Publishers, Inc.
Printed in the United States of America
First edition, 2012

Grateful acknowledgment is made for permission to reprint an excerpt from "Getting Closer," copyright © 2011 by Steven Millhauser, from *We Others: New and Selected Stories* by Steven Millhauser. Used by permission of Alfred A. Knopf, a division of Random House, Inc.

Library of Congress Cataloging-in-Publication Data
Lawrence-Lightfoot, Sara, 1944–
    Exit : the endings that set us free / Sara Lawrence-Lightfoot. — 1st ed.
        p.   cm.
    Includes bibliographical references and index.
    ISBN 978-0-374-15119-5 (alk. paper)
    1. Farewells.   2. Separation (Psychology)   3. Manners and customs.
    I. Title.
GT3050 .L397 2012
390—dc23

                                                          2011042768

Designed by Jonathan D. Lippincott

www.fsgbooks.com

1   3   5   7   9   10   8   6   4   2

For my students
Carry it on

Contents

EXIT

Introduction

EXITS: VISIBLE AND INVISIBLE

I have always been fascinated by exits, endings, leave-takings—by the ways in which we say goodbye to one another, to the lives we've led, to the families we've been part of, to the children we've nurtured, to the organizations we've worked for, to the communities where we've belonged, to the identities that have defined us, to the roles that have given us purpose and status. My curiosity includes exits big and small, those goodbyes that are embroidered into the habits of our everyday encounters as well as those that are forever memorable and rock our worlds. Those that go unnoticed and underappreciated and those that are accompanied by elaborate rituals and splendid ceremony. I have been just as intrigued by the ordinary exits that punctuate our days—goodbyes at the door as our children leave for school each morning (I would always stand at the window, secretly watching the backs of my young children to see if they were determined and tall, if their postures tilted forward, if in their exits I could see the strength they would need to take on the world), hugs at the airport as we leave to go on a trip, farewells to our students at the end of the school term—as I am about the leave-takings that become the major markers of our lives: the rupture of a long friendship; the dissolution of a marriage; the death of a parent; the departure of our children for college; the decision to leave a lifelong career; the abrupt firing of a veteran employee; the exits from the "closet," the priesthood, our countries of origin.

I think there must be some relationship between our developing the habit of small goodbyes and our ability to master and mark the larger farewells, a connection between the micro and the macro that somehow makes the latter smoother and more bearable because one has successfully accomplished the former. I certainly believe that the art of attending to, practicing, ritualizing, and developing a language for leave-taking in the most ordinary moments and settings augers well for taking on the more extraordinary exits that life is sure to serve up.

This book explores the large and small stories of exit, the coexistence and layering of the micro-encounters of everyday experience and the long arc of macro-dramas that take shape across our lifetimes and within a larger cultural narrative. I am interested in the ways in which people leave one thing and move on to the next; the ways in which they anticipate, define, and reflect on their departure; the factors and feelings that motivate their leave-taking; the ways in which the exit both opens up and closes paths forward, offers new opportunities and unanticipated casualties, and feels like victory or defeat, or both. I am particularly curious about how people revisit and reconstruct their moments of decision making, the setting in which they make the decision to move on or have the epiphany that something is over and done. What actually happens—in the noise and the silences—that provokes the moment? What are the events that anticipate the climax and precipitate the exit? How is the decision communicated and to whom? What is the tone and texture of the encounter? Is there anger, sadness, relief, or resolution in the aftermath; ambivalence or closure; feelings of loss or liberation? Whom do people turn to for support, reassurance, and validation?

I believe that people's memories of these exit moments are

unusually vivid, colorful, and detailed; that their recollections are full of feeling and emotion, imagery, symbolism, and metaphor; and that the specificity, authenticity, and power of these moments speak to their significance in shaping life journeys, in taking new paths, in reconstructing one's sense of self. I also believe that these moments are pregnant with paradox—the counterpoint and convergence of vulnerability and toughness, inertia and movement, urgency and patience, chaos and control. I always imagine these moments in bold relief, standing out in Technicolor, refracted images reconstructed with complexity, subtlety, and nuance.

I am sure that one of the reasons that the topic fascinates me is because I have known such moments, and they stand as signposts of courage and treachery in my life, those moments when I said to myself—after months of deliberation, indecision, and ambivalence—"I'm out of here." The moment when confusion turned to certainty, doubt to clarity, hemming and hawing to tough resolve; when complexity and opaqueness seemed to become transparently simple; when I stopped making lists of the pros and cons, the opportunities and liabilities, and decided instead to take the leap of faith.

I recall the details of such exit moments—what I was wearing, what my breathing felt like, how my stomach cramped, what I said, the tears I shed, whom I rushed to for support, the place I went to calm down—when I pulled my son out of a fancy private school to which he was fiercely loyal but where he was unappreciated and marginalized . . . or when I decided to exit the traditional scholarly track and embark on a research project, imaginative and controversial in its methodology and design, that all my senior colleagues felt might threaten my becoming tenured at the university . . . or when I declared that a long and close friendship was finally over after years of tolerating my friend's chronic inattention, her unwillingness to share the responsibilities and burdens of sustaining our relationship . . . or when I decided to initiate divorce proceedings, after years of quiet suffering, earnest stints in couples therapy, and deepening fractures impossible to heal.

I recall feeling in all these instances that I had somehow failed—in my own eyes and certainly in the sights of others. Even as I recognized the rightness of the decision and the courage required to make it, there was some part of me that felt weak in giving up and moving on, something in me that questioned whether I might have stuck it out longer. I remember, in each case, searching for cultural rituals and social scripts, a set of protocols, ceremonies, or practices that might offer me support and guidance or bring me into community with others who were charting similar exits. And I remember the disappointment of finding myself without a compass or reference group. I am struck, as well, by how these big exit markers—those that are most vivid in my memory—are tinged with sadness, poignancy, a sense of defeat, even though they all, in the end, led to something better and brighter.

I find this idea of exit intriguing and worthy of deep exploration because I think there are few lessons—in our culture, in our schooling, in our socialization—in how to do it well, even gracefully. Our culture seems to applaud the spirit, gumption, and promise of beginnings. We admire the entry, the moment when people launch themselves into something new, plan and execute a new project, take on important work, get married, embark on an adventure. These are likely to be moments of hope, optimism, and expectation as we compose the next chapter for ourselves. We give kudos to someone who is entrepreneurial, who paves a path for himself, who has a plan for what's next and can plot the strategy to move from here to there. By contrast, our exits are often ignored or invisible. They seem to represent the negative spaces of our life narratives. There is little appreciation or applause when we decide (or it is decided for us) that it is time to move on. We often slink away in the night, hoping that no one will notice, that the darkness will make the departure disappear. If the entry recalls a straight and erect posture, a person who is strong and determined, then we imagine a person stooped, weakened, and despairing as he makes his exit.

This cultural regard of exit is particularly troublesome in a society where leave-takings are the norm, where, for example, more than half of the marriages end in divorce,[1] forcing tortured exits, publicly exposed and privately endured; where tens of thousands of immigrants flood into our country each day,[2] exiting the place where their lives and families have been rooted, leaving the continuity and familiarity of their pasts, rupturing their cultural traditions and practices; where demographers predict that our young adults, now in their twenties, will likely have ten careers[3]—not just ten jobs—and it will be crucial that they learn not just the art of beginning anew but also the grit and grace of good exits; where, in these tough economic times,[4] the agony of exits seems to be the dominant narrative, as everyone knows someone in her family or among her close friends who has lost her job or is experiencing the painful assault of forced unemployment; and where the depleted job market forces young college graduates to move back home under their parents' roofs,[5] postponing the exits that were long planned and producing a developmental condition that psychologists have begun to describe—pejoratively—as a "failure to launch." And, of course, there is the inevitable and ultimate exit of death that, from my point of view, begs for more clear-eyed and respectful attention, more beautiful rituals, and more cultural honoring.

Our societal neglect of the rituals and purposes of exits is not only a puzzling contemporary phenomenon; it is also strange when we consider the history of our country—a history that has been primarily defined by leave-takings, departures, and journeys away from home. Except for Native Americans, who were our country's first inhabitants, or enslaved Africans, who were brought here against their will,[6] the history of the United States has been defined by exits. Albert Hirschman, whose book *Exit, Voice, and*

Loyalty (1970) remains the classic theoretical text on the subject, underscores its centrality in the American tradition and psyche even as he offers an economic framework and analysis.[7] After citing the seventeenth-century settlers fleeing European life, the American Revolution, and the westward expansion, Hirschman even paints the American idea of success—upward social mobility—as a sort of exit. He claims that the ideology of exit has been dominant and powerful in America:

> With the country having been founded on exit and having thrived on it, the belief in exit as a fundamental and beneficial social mechanism has been unquestioning . . . To most of its citizens—with the important exception of those whose forefathers came as slaves—exit from the country has long been peculiarly unthinkable.[8]

Not only has the American geographic and sociological map been defined by exits—chosen and forced—it is also true that exiting is a central marker and lever in our individual developmental journeys. I learned about the power and poignancy of exits most vividly as I became immersed in the research for my last book,[9] *The Third Chapter.* Witnessing and documenting the new learning of people between the ages of fifty and seventy-five—a time in life when demographers tell us that we are "neither young nor old"—I became keenly aware of the fragility and bravery associated with exits. It is difficult, sometimes excruciating and painful, to leave the places that are familiar, the roles that have shaped our identities and self-images, the work in which we have become skilled, knowledgeable, and authoritative, to do something that—at least initially—feels awkward and uncertain. More than half a century ago, when Erik Erikson, the developmental psychologist, charted the stages of lifelong development,[10] he envisioned each stage as a conflict between progression and regression—an inevitable tension between staying put and moving on, between sticking with the familiar and moving toward the strange. At the center of the contrary weights moving us forward and pulling us back is, of course, the leave-taking, the exit.

In an earlier book of mine,[11] *Respect*, I also wrote about the ways in which exits—gracefully communicated, negotiated, and ritualized—were interpreted as signs and symbols of deep respect. The trust and rapport of respectful relationships were built on knowing that in the end, someone would not just disappear and walk away, but would find a way of recognizing the importance and visibility of good departures. Likewise, the symmetry and authenticity at the center of respectful encounters require that we navigate the boundaries of restraint and connection, balancing coming together and moving away from one another. One of the protagonists in *Respect* is a hospice worker, psychotherapist, and Episcopal priest who speaks about "attention"—gentle, generous, and undiluted—as the most important dimension of respect. As he sits and talks with dying patients, he waits for them to take the lead and let him know what they need and want; he asks them questions others are too afraid to ask, about things they are dying to talk about. He is openhearted and unafraid, seeing the opportunities for growth and reconciliation in these final moments. He helps the dying person exit with dignity and grace.

Visual reminders of exit surround us each day of our lives, guiding our moves, anticipating our turns, flashing directions to us. We follow the exit arrows to find our way out of the parking garage; we notice the neon signs in the dark movie theater showing us where to go in case of an emergency; the flight attendant points out the exit doors in her instructions to us before we take off. It is one of the first words kindergartners learn as their teachers line them up single file before heading out to recess or as they practice their efficient formations during fire drills. The exits become signifiers of efficiency, safety, orderliness, and protection. Bloodred exit signs, like beacons in the hallway.

We drive along the highway tracing our fingers over the map or listening to the fake voice coming out of our GPS, and we count the exits, moving to the right lane in preparation for the turn that will get us to our destination. Or we travel the familiar highway to work and back and hardly need to attend to the exits that we know by heart; our mind is in automatic pilot mode. The exits—glowing white letters on green metal—mark distance, time, effort, belonging . . . how many exits until we get there, how many until a rest stop, how many until we merge onto a new road, how many until we can breathe more freely. We are pissed off when we miss them. Exits also hold memories. Exit 2, just before the Tappan Zee Bridge, takes you to our second cousin's house, where we used to go for their big July Fourth bash . . . the smell of barbecue, cold beers, dips in the pool, lazy days, and laughter. Exit 13 off the Palisades Parkway is coming back home to the place where I haven't lived for fifty years, where my ninety-seven-year-old mother still waits for me.

We also hear the language and metaphors of exit all around us. Exit visas must be applied for weeks before our departure, giving us legal permission to leave the country. In preparing for a theater performance, a director blocks out scenes with his actors onstage, noting the place where the playwright indicates they should exit, stage left. Accepting the fate of a lousy hand, a poker player "folds," walking away from the table, exiting on his own terms. Television newscasters, quoting police reports, give an account of a lurid crime and describe the survivor's "exit wounds." How did the bullet pass through the body? How did the knife slice through the flesh? What organs were nicked, impaired, destroyed? What arteries gushed blood? The emergency-room doctors must act quickly to close up the hole, sew back the edges, fuse the muscle fibers back together—to regenerate despite the injury. Exit wounds are for survivors; the ones who took the bullet or the knife, barely escaped death, and now feel the pain of living. The pain is a beautiful reminder of their survival, their proof of being alive.

Exits, therefore, are ubiquitous, marking the physical landscapes we inhabit, embedded in our language and metaphors, embroidered into the historical narrative of our country, braided into the sequence and arc of our individual development, shaped by the contemporary scene of our economic crises and global mobility, and laced into the intergenerational tensions and discourses in our families and communities. Perhaps it is the very ordinariness, familiarity, and ubiquity of our experiences of exit that make them invisible to us. And perhaps it is our overvaluing of the launch, the promise of entry, and the hopefulness of beginning, that render our exits ignoble by contrast.

Another interesting twist to the paradoxical ubiquity and invisibility of exits—big and small—is the way in which technology has reshaped our sense of connectedness and community,[12] our very identity; the ways in which our global access to one another through cyberspace channels has changed the pace and texture of our discourses and redrawn the boundaries between our public and private lives, remapped the edges of intimacy, even redefined the very meaning of friendship. In this fast-emerging context of technological advancement, beginnings and endings take on a different pace and meaning, exits are less clearly drawn, and entanglements seem easier to undo but harder to escape. Freshmen experiencing their first year of college text their parents several times a day, seeking and resisting advice on the courses they should enroll in, their dating life, and the pounds they've put on since eating cafeteria food. Moms and dads of summer campers receive daily videos recording their children's swim meets, canoeing trips, and group sings around the campfire at night. Young adults heading for the Peace Corps in Samoa or Namibia stay in close touch with their family and friends back home even as they try to build new relationships with the exotic strangers they are seeking to serve. The boundaries of exit become attenuated and eroded, yet another sign of their invisibility.

For two years I sought out and listened to people tell their big and memorable stories of leaving. As we talked together, some were in the midst of composing their exits, anticipating and planning their departures, anxious and excited about moving on. Others had exited long ago and used our dialogues as an opportunity for reflection—revisiting the ancient narratives that had changed the course of their lives, discovering new ways of interpreting and making sense of their journeys. Some interviewees told tales of forced exits; others spoke about designing and executing their planned departures. Still others found it hard to determine whether the impetus for their exits came from within—a decision motivated by them, within their jurisdiction and control—or whether their leave-takings were a response to subtle pressuring from friends and families, covert warnings from bosses, or influenced by the social prescriptions, norms, and rhythms deemed appropriate by our institutional cultures.

In all our conversations I followed the lead of my interviewees as they decided where to begin their stories, chose the central arc of their exit narratives, and rehearsed the major transformational moments of their departures. I listened carefully to the talk and the silences, the text and the subtexts of their narrations. I was attentive to those revelations that surprised them, to those discoveries that disoriented them, to the places where they feared to tread. I pushed for the details of long-buried memories. I stopped my probing when I felt myself crossing the boundaries of resistance and vulnerability. We took breaks, went for walks, and drank lots of water to hydrate us through what one storyteller called "the desert of my despair." For many—in fact, most—these were emotional encounters, filled with weeping and laughter, breakthroughs and breakdowns, curiosity and discovery.

There were some who at first found it hard to compose stories focused on "endings," after a lifetime of being taught—as one of my interviewees put it—"that stories have a beginning, a middle, and an end . . . and you begin at the beginning." For a few of my interviewees, I was fortunate enough to observe the public ceremonies and occasions marking their departures, listen to their impassioned and teary farewell speeches, and hear the gush of adulation and applause that honored their leaving and legacies. For others, we combed through personal diaries and journals, tracing the meanderings of their interior dialogues as they relived the maze of decisions and choices that preceded their exits. Some people showed me photographs that spurred detailed reflections of their leave-taking.

Although all the insights from my dozens of interviewees resonate in the themes, analysis, and arc of this book, I have chosen to write the narratives collected here because of their richness and variety, their subtlety and complexity. Like all good ethnographic inquiries, these stories help us see the strange in the familiar, the exotic in the ordinary, the visible in the invisible. Individually and collectively—in their similarities and differences, their harmony and dissonance—these tales offer a counterpoint to our usual exit narratives, challenging our cultural views and presumptions, helping us see the exits in our lives differently, and offering us intriguing metaphors and language for interpreting their meaning. And, like all stories, they allow us to glimpse the universal in the particular.

They tell of a gay man finding home and wholeness after exiting the closet; of a sixteen-year-old boy forced to leave Iran in the midst of the violent civil war; of a young boy who, after years of enduring terrifying bullying in school, finally discovered the exit that would set him free; of a woman who, after twenty-five years of building and nurturing a small nonprofit, decided it was time to leave, only to discover the loss, disorientation, and emptiness that followed; of a Catholic priest who—after prolonged deliberation and painful ambivalence—leaves the church he has always been devoted to, the life he has loved, and the work that has been deeply fulfilling; of a psychotherapist who helps her patients shed the painful haunts of ancient traumas and exit the abusive relationships that have left deep scars, at the same time as she prepares them for their successful "termination" from therapy; of an anthropologist who carefully stages her departure from the "field" after four years of research and understands, for the first time, the respect, trust, and truth telling that are critical to exiting well; of a woman who fulfilled her promise to her dying husband that his final months would be filled with abundant and luminous living.

In these stories, exit is not only the central subject and focus, the phenomenon under study and scrutiny; it also becomes the light, the lens, that allows us to understand other things—like home, like a parent's love, like the price of freedom, like the meaning of grace, like the living in dying—more deeply. The structure of this book, in fact, follows the light, illuminating those dimensions of our life stories that we are able to see—newly and differently—through the lens of exit.

Ultimately, it is my hope that the wisdom, insights, and perspectives found in this book will help create a new conversation, a bold counter-narrative illuminating the power and possibilities of exits. They will help us discover how we might accomplish our exit journeys with purposefulness and dignity, how we might see the movement away from the old as the productive prelude to entering the new, even when it may feel like failure or retreat. How might we find ways of reframing our exits, giving them the attention and significance they are due? Are there steps to take, routines to be practiced, discerning questions to be posed to make our departures more bearable, revelatory, and generative? Are there rituals we might invent to light a clearer path toward the exit? Are there in-

stitutional arrangements and norms, ceremonial events, a new language and way of seeing that would encourage a different approach
and attitude toward leave-takings?

This book, then, examines the cultural, developmental, relational, and organizational dimensions of these exit moments in
all their emotional, intellectual, and spiritual manifestations, in all
their colorful and textured detail—seeking to capture their importance in the productive propulsion of next chapters and new journeys; hoping to discover the lessons they hold for guiding and
helping folks to muster the energy, master the steps, and weather
the chaos of their departures; and searching for ways to challenge
and reframe our cultural expectations and priorities that have for
too long exalted the hope of beginnings and diminished the power
and value of exits.

One

HOME

When most of us think about *home*, we picture a physical place: the house where we grew up, the address we learned by heart in case we got lost, the room we painted hot pink when we turned eight and our parents allowed us to choose the color, the crack in the third flagstone step leading to the front door, the way no one used the front door anyway, since everyone came in through the back door right off the kitchen. Or our vision of home might be of the house where we now live with our children, where we make the mortgage payments each month and pay the electricity and oil bills, where we have set up a basketball hoop in the driveway for the kids to practice for the big games on Friday night up at the school, where we have barbeques for the neighbors on hot summer evenings, where the traffic and chaos of kids and dogs and busy schedules and homework are both comforting and exhausting. Our vision of home, whether it is the home of our childhood or the home we are creating as adults, has a location, an address, a mark on the map. It is a physical, tangible place. We have photo albums that chronicle our growing family over the years, everyone lined up on the front steps in the same pyramid arrangement—parents on top, kids on the bottom—with smiles that stay the same even as the bodies get bigger and bulkier.

Home is also the place where life is most familiar, where we fall into old patterns, where our roles become scripted and predictable, where there is a fine line between the bonds that bind and constrain. It is also a place where we live by secret codes and allusions that outsiders—even intimate outsiders—don't understand or appreciate. In her beautiful essay "On Going Home" (1961), Joan Didion speaks about the power and pull of home.

> I am home for my daughter's first birthday. By "home" I do not mean the house in Los Angeles where my husband and I and the baby live, but the place where my family is, in the Central Valley of California. It is a vital though troublesome distinction. My husband likes my family but is uneasy in their house, because once there I fall into their ways which are difficult, oblique, deliberately inarticulate, not my husband's ways. We live in dusty houses ("D-U-S-T," he once wrote with his finger on the surfaces all over the house, but no one noticed it) filled with mementos quite without value to him (what could the Canton dessert plates mean to him? How could he have known about the assay scales, why should he care if he did know?) . . . [1]

Home, here, is defined as much by those who are outsiders—who have no real clue of what is going on, where signals seem opaque and oblique—as by those who have the inside track, who know the secrets and shadows, the habits and artifacts, the history of the family that lives in this house. Home is made more vivid by the contrasts that get drawn between the outsider's discomfort and cluelessness and the insider's ancient and intuitive understandings.

In his biography of the poet Wallace Stevens (1968), Robert Pack echoes Didion's portrayal of going home, drawing the connection between the intimacy and belonging that home represents and the intimacy with his readers that Stevens achieves through his poetry. Stevens translates the language, rhythm, and cadence from his childhood home into his verse, capturing the themes of family and the feelings of familiarity with which we can all identify. Writes Pack:

> Home is the place where one understands the routine, knows the secret rhythms of family activity and communication, and feels the fullness of the presence of the familiar objects. It is this sense of intimacy that Stevens seeks with the world, and it is this sense of order a poet achieves that makes this intimacy possible.[2]

Here we get a sense of home as the place where we learn to interpret the noises and the silences, the texts and the subtexts of our lives, where the layers and subtleties of our communication are inscribed in our hearts and minds, our bones and bodies, eventually turning up—at least in Stevens's and Didion's case—in the form and texture of their art.

The novelist Paule Marshall takes us a step further into the auditory dimensions and cadences of home. In her autobiographical novel, *Brown Girl, Brownstones*, she offers an evocative and searing portrait of an immigrant family transplanted from Barbados to Brooklyn, and she speaks about home as the sound of the language of the Bajan women as they sit talking in the kitchen.[3] It is a language that Marshall herself heard as a child as she sat on the edges of the women's circle soaking up the gossip, the stories, savoring the rhythms and poetry of their words. In "From the Poets in the Kitchen," a short essay published in *The New York Times*, Marshall speaks about the language of home—particularly the talk among the women in the kitchen—that carried with it beauty, wisdom, poetry, and culture, that survived the transplantation from the blue-green sea and open horizons of Barbados to the city streets and brownstones of Brooklyn.

I grew up among poets—whatever that breed is supposed to look like. Nothing about them suggested that poetry was their calling. They were just a group of ordinary housewives and mothers, my mother included, who dressed in a way (shapeless housedresses, dowdy felt hats, dark, solemn coats) that made it impossible for me to imagine they had ever been young.[4]

So whether we envision home as a place, a physical location on the map that we can now google for directions; whether we feel it in the familiarity, obliqueness, and intimacy of family; or whether we hear it in the language and poetry of our mothers, home is the place we return to. It is the place that forms us, that embraces and inhibits us, that shapes our identity. It is a place where our arrival is awaited.

The tales of exit found in this chapter reframe and transfigure the meaning of home. The two stories—of a teenage Iranian boy escaping the political strife and violence in his war-torn country to come to America, and of a middle-aged gay man reflecting on his long and brave exit from the closet—shape a view of home that is earned and discovered after the protagonists have traveled far away, literally and figuratively, from their family's place of origin, far away from the cultures and communities that nourished and raised them. The lens of exit in both narratives points to the emotional and spiritual construction of home as a hard-won place of comfort, safety, belonging, and love. Finding home requires leaving and searching, trials and tribulations, and many exits along the way.

HUNGRY FOR HOME

"I'll go."

It did not hit him that he was actually leaving—his family, his country, his life—until he arrived at the airport in Tehran, surrounded by his parents and siblings and a huge crowd of aunts and uncles, some of whom had traveled hundreds of miles to say goodbye. He was carrying one small cardboard suitcase, and his mother had sewn a zippered pouch into his underwear to hide the $3,000 he was taking with him. His father had had to sell a plot of land, use all of the family's savings, and borrow from his uncles in order to come up with the money that Bijan Jalili needed to travel to the United States.

Suddenly the fear swept over him, and he froze. How could he have said—in a moment of weakness—that he would go to school in America? How could he have committed to something that now seemed so scary and wrong? How could he leave all those he loved and the life he knew? This was unbearable. "Just then it hit me . . . What have I done! But it was too late to back out," says Bijan, his whole body shivering as he must have done on that fateful day. "I couldn't stomach it . . . my belly was burning. I was scared out of my gourd . . . I was like a child afraid of the dark . . . I felt like I was lost in the jungle, being swallowed up by dangerous creatures."

Bijan looked over at his father, whose head was bowed in prayer, his face washed in tears, a picture of agony and faith. His mother couldn't stop crying—huge, sobbing wails that echoed through the airport lounge—as she clung to him for dear life. Finally his plane was announced and the waiting was over. Bijan hugged everyone hard and kissed them each on both cheeks before beginning the long march down the ramp to the plane. "Leaving my parents behind was unbearable. My feet were like Jell-O. I could hardly move them. I thought that I would just collapse." Bijan had never even seen an airport before, never been on a plane. He stowed his suitcase and climbed into the window seat. "The fear was overwhelming as I looked down after takeoff and saw Tehran disappear behind me." I look across the table and see the sixteen-year-old scared boy. It is thirty years later, and Bijan's face is contorted in a grimace. He looks down to wipe away the tears with the back of his hand.

The plane touched down at Kennedy Airport at 8:00 p.m. As he heard the screech of the landing gear, Bijan's fear took over his body and he started to shake. He looked out the window and saw the city stretched out below, "an ocean of light." "I was new to electricity," says Bijan as he remembers the strange sensation of seeing a whole city of twinkling lights that seemed to form the shape of "a fiery dragon." His only thought was that he wanted desperately for the plane to turn around so he could go home. "I wanted to go back to my mom, to bury my head in her bosom . . . to have her hold me again."

Once he was off of the plane, the scene was shocking. "I thought to myself, Everything in New York looks so big! I had never seen people over six feet tall . . . and there were all kinds of people, all sizes, shapes, and colors. They hardly looked human to me." Not only did the people look strange, but New York did not look like the America Bijan had seen on television back in Iran. It was not pretty or spacious or orderly; it was a confusing blur of smells and sensations. "It was as if I had landed on a different planet," Bijan says as he admits to being at a "loss to find the adjectives to describe how foreign the place felt." Even the air seemed unbreathable as he made his way from the international to the domestic terminal where he would board a plane to Washington, D.C. And the water, when he stopped on the way to get a drink at the fountain, tasted terrible, "undrinkable," so different from the fresh well water he was used to having at home.

Bijan Jalili, a handsome and lean light-brown-skinned man, is now the CEO of Purple Rain, a technology company that makes digitally based software for large firms all over the world. The engineers and designers for the company are based in Tehran; Bijan and the design and marketing team have offices in the United States. But the virtual world is really where they all spend most of their time. Storytelling is Bijan's medium, imprinted in his family and his culture, embedded in his passionate personality. He spins his yarns with drama and subtlety, picturing the scene, capturing the sights and sounds, relishing the details, enjoying the rhythm of the words, and loving the surprising punch line. His vivid descriptions help me imagine remote parts of Iran, places I've never even seen in photographs.

He begins with the geography of his childhood. "I grew up in Razan, a small town in the mountainous region in northwest Iran. You don't have that type of smallness in the U.S. . . . There were fewer than a thousand people, and there was no electricity, no running water (we used manual pumps), no utilities. My mother cooked on a small stove top that used kerosene, like the ones you take camping . . . We took a shower in the local bathhouse once a week." Bijan, the second to the oldest, had two brothers and one sister, and they had the special privilege of going to the bathhouse once a week because his father enjoyed a large measure of local status. He was the "equivalent of the school superintendent" for Razan and several of the surrounding tiny villages.

By the time Bijan was seven, the family moved briefly to the ancient city of Hamadān, the site of the old Persian capital, founded twenty-five hundred years ago. When they found that they could not afford to live there on his father's modest salary, they moved again, this time to Shavarin, and they lived in the house where his father had grown up. By the time Bijan was eleven, his father had saved up enough money to move back to Hamadān, where he took out a bank loan and they were able to build a house. "Now we had electricity," says Bijan with excitement. "Gas and oil were hand delivered to the house . . . there was a well for drinking water and an outhouse that was unbearably cold in the winter." Hamadān was located in the shadow of a very high mountain, and the winters were fierce. For several freezing months each year, the town was literally buried in snow. Bijan remembers the snow tunnels he used

to walk through in order to get to school, when the drifts would
pile higher than the roofs of the houses. And he recalls the *koursi*
heater—something resembling a hibachi, fueled by coal—that
would be put under the table and then covered with blankets. All
winter long, while the rest of the house stayed freezing, everyone
would huddle together under the blankets with their feet close to
the stove.

"It was a fanatical religious environment," says Bijan about his
family's deep and unquestioned devotion to Islam. The Muslim
rituals and restrictions were embroidered into their days. Five times
a day they knelt and turned toward Mecca to pray; there was no
alcohol and no hanging around with "the opposite sex." The family fasted for the entire month of Ramadan, and Bijan's father and
brothers went to the mosque for religious gatherings "all the time."
By the time he was fourteen or fifteen, Bijan and his older brother,
Sohrab, had begun to mix religion with radical politics, joining
the political revolution that was beginning to catch fire all over
Iran. "We were teenagers, and there was not much to do in our
town . . . the revolution captured our hearts and our minds. We
were great recruits, revolutionary religious kids, young and impassioned and devout," he recalls.

The brothers joined the Mojahedin, a political party, working
underground in support of Khomeini, where they became part of
the stealth "distribution channel," delivering newsletters and tapes
undercover and hiding them in secret places in the brick walls that
snaked their way through the town. Before they would go off to
school in the morning, Bijan and Sohrab served as the party's
"runners," picking up and distributing political propaganda. In the
evenings they would join the noisy street demonstrations, chant-
ing and cheering radical rants, then gathering to listen to the fiery,
provocative speeches from their party leaders. Their father never
wanted his sons to attend the political rallies and demonstrations.
He did not agree with their "radical ideologies," and every moment

that they were gone, he feared for their lives. "He did not want us to get killed," says Bijan simply.

One night when a prominent and important radical clergyman was coming to speak at the mosque, Bijan's father knew that there was likely to be violence, and he forbade his sons from going. Not heeding their father's threats, Bijan and Sohrab slipped out of the house under cover of night, climbed over the stone walls of the courtyard, and went to the mosque, where a crowd of more than a thousand men—no women—had gathered. As the clergyman delivered his fierce oratory, the guards and police surrounded the mosque, ready to arrest him as soon as it was over, but as he spoke his last words, all the lights went out. In the darkness and chaos that followed, the clergyman escaped and the police opened fire. In the mayhem, bullets were blasting, men were screaming and running; some lay bloodied on the ground.

Bijan managed to dodge the bullets, but he got separated from his brother. "I thought they had got him," says Bijan, trembling. When he arrived home, his clothes torn and spattered with blood, Bijan found his father standing in the courtyard. "He was white as a ghost . . . completely frightened . . . he held his Koran in his hands." Bijan stood silently with his father, hearing the gunshots and screaming in the distance, terrified that his brother would never come home. It was hours before Sohrab appeared, worn, weary, and very scared, but not wounded. No one said a word; their father could not find the energy to punish them. "Having his sons at home was good enough for him," recalls Bijan about the strange, haunting silence that filled the house for several days after. It was on that night, Bijan believes, that his father promised himself that his sons would have to leave the country. There was no way to protect them from the danger and the violence, and no way to blunt their revolutionary fervor.

And then the unthinkable happened. A few months later, Bijan's younger brother, Pedram, was taken from them in a horrible accident in the backyard. Before he can begin the story of his brother's death, Bijan is already weeping.

"Electricity was a new thing in the town, and so there was no regulation, no codes or standards. Our home had electricity, but it was all made up of dangerous, makeshift wiring. It was a steamy day in the summer . . . In the yard of our house we had a wading pool, and my little brother Pedram—he was fourteen years old at the time—decided to cool himself off in the water. The little pool was right next to an electrical pole with a short. As he came out of the pool, he touched the pole . . . and he was fried . . . That afternoon I was at home studying for my exams, and all of a sudden I heard Pedram screaming my father's name. At first I thought he was screaming because my father was punishing him for something. Then I heard my mother's wails . . . so I went outside and saw my father kneeling down with Pedram's head on his lap . . . He was gone."

Soon after the terrible tragedy Bijan's father asked his two older sons to leave the country. "He was afraid of losing another son. He just couldn't stomach it," says Bijan about his father's anguish that his older sons would be taken too, swept away by the revolution. No amount of pleading could convince Sohrab to leave. "He was too deep in the revolution . . . so devoted, committed, passionate. He refused to go," says Bijan. But in the next moment, when his father turned to him, Bijan surprised himself by saying, without so much as a moment of thought, "I'll go." And it was done.

Within a few weeks the papers, documents, passport, and tickets had been arranged, and Bijan had been admitted to a prep school in Washington, D.C., that had to agree to sponsor him before the Iranian government would give him a visa. It was August 1978, and political demonstrations were happening everywhere; violence was erupting in the street and "the shah's regime was falling apart." Fortunately, Bijan's uncle, an official high up in the shah's party, was able to pull strings at the American embassy so that he was able to secure all the documents he needed to travel. "Irony of all ironies"—Bijan smiles—"there I was, having been a young radical with the Mojahedin, the revolutionary party . . . riding with my uncle in the shah's police car through the gates of the American embassy to get permission to leave the country."

When I ask Bijan why he said yes to his father, he looks at me, puzzled, as if he has never bothered—or dared—to ask himself that question. "I had a love affair with English . . . and the English we learned in school was all about grammar, basic and primitive," he says at first. "And I liked the American shows I watched on our neighbor's tiny black-and-white TV . . . *Ironside, Streets of San Francisco, Charlie's Angels* . . . alluring images of America." But Bijan chuckles at the incompleteness of his reasoning, at the way he gave such a huge decision so little thought as a teenager, and at the way, as a mature adult, he seems to have protected himself from having to relive that moment. "Maybe it was my childishness or my stupidity," he concludes, his voice drifting off.

But there is one thing of which he was, and is, certain. As soon as he said that he would go, he began having doubts, fears, and nightmares—all of which he kept to himself as he got swept up in the planning and preparations; as he saw his father selling his land, going to the bank, and counting the dollars Bijan would need to make the journey. And just the announcement of his trip to America changed the way he was treated by everyone in the town. He became Hamadān's newest hero. "As soon as I said I'd go, I became a celebrity. I went from being a child to being a man in their eyes . . . I felt foreign to myself."

It turned out that the prep school in Washington, D.C.— advertised as an elite academy for international students—was a "scam," "a moneymaking machine, where in exchange for getting visas for foreign kids, the American embassy would take kickbacks." The whole school was in a run-down office building, and all the students were rich Iranian and Arab trust fund kids. "There was probably something comforting about finding other Iranian students at the school, but they were rich and I was poor, so there was a large distance between us. They were spending big wads of cash on luxury stuff. Whenever I wanted to buy something, I needed to excuse myself to go to the bathroom so I could unzip the money from my underwear." He shared a shabby dormitory room with another Iranian student, and in order to save money, he ate only breakfast and dinner—no lunch—in the school cafeteria.

By the time Bijan had been there "three months and twelve days" and paid for his dormitory room and fall tuition, his $3,000 was gone. He knew he could not ask his father for any more money, but every few weeks he would call and beg to come home. The phone calls were expensive (three minutes for ten dollars), so Bijan would wait until he could no longer bear not hearing his father's voice, and he would have to put an entire roll of quarters into the pay phone. "I would try to explain to him my condition . . . I feel sick, depressed, and miserable . . . I'm horribly thin and weak . . . everything tastes terrible and smells awful." And although he never told his father, Bijan truly thought that he might even die from loneliness and heartbreak. He could hear the sadness in his father's voice on the other end of the phone; he just could not stand to hear his son suffer. But his father tried hard to be reassuring, comforting him and then staving off his requests by offering him a "deal." If Bijan would stay just three more months and successfully complete the English courses, he would let him come home. At least then he would return to Iran fluent in the language he loved. Never did Bijan have the heart to break it to his father, the top educator in his town, that the school he was attending was just a "moneymaking scam," that even the English training was substandard, that the teachers were not well trained, that grades could be bought.

By the time three months had rolled around, the Iranian revolution was in full swing. Khomeini was in power, the war had broken out with Iraq, the airports were closed, and it was impossible for Bijan to go home. He had run out of all his money and couldn't pay the room and board at school. He managed to rent a small apartment with three of his fellow students in a run-down neighborhood close to the school, and he found a job as a dishwasher in a restaurant, where he worked for $2.75 an hour and was paid under the table because his student visa did not permit him to work. "The apartment was three hundred dollars a month, but there were four of us, so my share was seventy-five. I ate one meal at the restaurant, which had to last me the whole day," he says, remembering every detail of every dollar earned and spent.

After six months, having successfully completed the courses he had promised to his father, Bijan once again begged to return home. But by that time the war with Iraq had escalated, the borders were closed, and military service was mandatory for all young men. This time his father didn't even try to be reassuring. He had no more deals up his sleeve. He told his son, "You will be drafted and sent off to war as soon as you touch down at the airport. You come back, and you will die, for sure . . . I'd rather have you be sick over there than dead over here." Bijan knew his father was right. Even though he was still lonely and miserable and longed to be in the embrace of his family, he couldn't go back. At that moment it hit him that he was in the United States for good, and something in him shifted. Rather than focusing his fantasies on escape from a life that felt unbearable, and rather than hoping his father would somehow save him from it all, Bijan decided to take hold of himself, stay in school, and get a good education. He would somehow find a way to make it on his own.

He spent the next few years finishing school and doing any job—however unsavory or menial—to earn his keep. He throws back his head and laughs. "I've done everything but prostitution and pushing drugs . . . hard labor, working for a moving company, a gas station, a cleaning service, painting houses, dipping ice cream." By the time he was admitted to American University as an engineering student, he was working at a gas station from 7:00 p.m. to 7:00 a.m. and going to his first class of the day at 8:00. He was eating sandwiches of Wonder Bread—which he bought in bulk—smeared with ketchup and mustard, which he took from the condiments counter at Burger King. And he was sharing one small room with two other Iranian guys who were not in school, so they slept in shifts in the one bed that they had on the floor. He shakes his head at how hard his life was then, but he was filled with a fierce determination that seemed to make it all possible.

Despite being chronically tired and hungry during his three years at the university, Bijan made straight A's and graduated with honors. He even made a little money on the side, tutoring other undergraduate students. "But all the time, I'm wanting to go back," he says about the deep yearning to return to Iran that never abated. Sometimes he would call his father to beg anyway; there was some comfort in just hearing his voice, and the exchange between them had by now become a well-rehearsed script. "I knew he would just keep playing with my brain . . . making the old deals which we both knew would never happen."

After college, Bijan got "a big break" when he landed an engineering/technology position at Dell Labs, where he stayed for a year and a half, until they learned that his visa had expired and they fired him. Now he had a visa problem and had to worry about getting deported. Just as he was leaving Dell, the "hostage crisis hit" in Iran, and "overnight, we were the enemy." Bijan remembers the huge painted sign hanging at the entrance to American University—ALL IRANIANS GO HOME—and how his good friends from college suddenly deserted him. He remembers the jeers and racial slurs people hurled at him as he got on the bus or walked by them on the street. For their protection, Iranians closed ranks, hung together, watched each other's backs, and tried to live under the radar.

After several months of looking for work in Washington, Bijan reunited with an old childhood friend he knew from Hamadān, who was now living in Philadelphia. They schemed together, made a business plan, used up all their savings, sold their cars, and opened a restaurant in West Philadelphia. The ingredients for success seemed promising. The food was yummy—they cooked exotic and savory recipes from home—the decor was funky and welcoming, and they worked all the time serving breakfast, lunch, and dinner. They hoped to attract the college crowd and ethnic food lovers from Drexel and the University of Pennsylvania, which were within walking distance. But the restaurant was off the beaten path, so they were never able to attract the necessary foot traffic to make it work and pay the bills. A year after opening, they had to close it down, but the disappointing entrepreneurial venture turned out to have a silver lining. Bijan got $7,000 back on his tax returns that year, and he decided to use it to bring everyone together for a family reunion in Turkey.

It took months of planning and scheming to make it happen, but in the end everybody came. It was the peak of the war in Iran, and their journeys across the borders were taxing and treacherous. Bijan's parents flew from Tehran to Istanbul; his brother and sister and their spouses and children took the long bus ride. There were eleven of them, all "happily stuffed" into a studio apartment Bijan had rented. It was the first time he had seen his family in more than ten years, and he was beside himself with joy. His face lights up as he remembers the scene. "It was an amazing reunion . . . wonderful, passionate, a one-of-a-kind experience. I had such a hunger for them. I coveted every minute of being with them. There was so much to talk about . . . I wanted it to last forever. They listened to all of my stories, and they were overwhelmingly proud of me . . . for surviving, for sticking it out, for doing so well." He laughs. "Of course, they had no idea that I was going home to nothing. I had paid for everyone's trip, and they didn't have a clue that I was completely broke."

There was something about the reunion in Turkey, the loving embrace of the family, the endless conversations, their adoration of him, how safe and secure he felt in their midst that allowed Bijan to finally exit Iran. Nourished by his family's soulful companionship, lifted up by their laughter, he knew then that he would never, ever leave them. He might build a life very far away, he might have friends they would never meet and experiences they could barely imagine, but he knew they would always be inextricably, forever joined.

And as it has turned out, after all those years of painful struggle, decades of dissonance and dislocation, periods of unemployment, and the distaste of absorbing and resisting ethnic slurs and racial profiling, Bijan is now living a life of abundance, doing work that is creative and satisfying, raising two children who are smart and sweet, and running a business that has feet in both his homes, Iran and America. He recognizes the bitterness and cynicism that still rise up in him; he can still sometimes "taste the deprivation" and loneliness of having had to leave his family too early. But all that is mixed with the sweet pleasures and many good memories of his life, an imperfect and exotic brew he has grown to appreciate.

I ask Bijan what in his character or temperament might have contributed to his resilience, his courage and stamina after leaving Iran, and his determination to stay the course. He immediately says, "Loyalty . . . loyalty to my dad. I couldn't dishonor him, and I trusted him to guide me and be there with me even if we were thousands of miles away, living on different planets." He pauses and says quietly, "I knew how much education was valued by my father. And I knew how he suffered after my brother's death . . . My father and mother would never laugh again after we lost him, and I wanted to somehow make up for that loss and live a life of meaning and commitment."

Bijan now brings this same deep loyalty and devotion to his

own family, his wife and his two children, and their close friends. He always wants to be there for them. He knows, however, that he would never ask his son—now a teenager—to leave his family and his country behind, to go and make his way in a strange, foreign place. His final question floats in the air as we both fall silent. "Were my parents stupid or naïve . . . or did they know something about me that I didn't know about myself?"

We hear the myriad meanings of home echoing through Bijan's story. Home as place—the twenty-five-hundred-year-old city, Hamadān, at the base of the towering mountain, where his family huddled together under blankets in the freezing winters, warmed by the tiny coal heater; where Bijan and his brother became young radicals, hiding secret political messages in the ancient brick walls that wound through the city; where the snow got so deep that children carved tunnels underneath to walk to school; where Bijan's little brother came out of the wading pool, touched the electric pole, and "fried" to death.

Home is also the place where we are in touch with the familiar, oblique rhythms of our family; where our communication with one another is often gestural; where words unspoken can carry enormous meaning. As Joan Didion reminds us, home is in the "troublesome" and "oblique" nuances of family intimacies.[5] After telling his sons that they are forbidden to go to the mosque to hear the radical cleric, Bijan's father waits alone in the courtyard, his face creased with fear, the Koran in the tight grip of his hands, praying for his sons' safe return. The gunshots from the mosque ring out in the night air; he can hear the screams of desperate men trying to escape the bloodshed and the mayhem. Bijan comes home first, bloodied but safe, and waits with his father. He knows not to say anything; he knows his father is more frightened than angry. He knows that his father has already made a deal with Allah that he will do anything—including not punish his sons—if he brings them home safely. When hours later Bijan's big brother climbs over the wall, they all go silently to bed. No reprimands, no punishments, no apologies. This is the familiar way they deal with danger and fear and terror in this family; this is the silence and sound of home.

These familiar rhythms and resonances from home stretch across the globe—from Washington, D.C., to Tehran—and across the years, as Bijan pleads with his father over the phone, begging to come back to Iran. He is desperate and miserable, sick, hungry, and lonely. Over and over, father and son cut a deal that they both know will never see the light of day. Over and over, they play the "brain game," knowing the dueling exchanges by heart, shielding each other from the truth. As they rehearse the familiar script, Bijan listens for what Paule Marshall calls the "language and poetry" of home.[6]

The deals and exits last for years and years until Bijan—flush with a new resolve and the surprise bounty from his tax returns—decides to stage his own "homecoming." His parents, sister and brother, their spouses and children—eleven of them in all—crowd into a tiny studio apartment in Turkey, a place that none of them call home. For seven delicious days they experience the thrill and familiarity of one another's company, an orgy of eating, drinking, and most of all talking and telling stories. As Bijan says his farewells and his precious family returns to the country where he was born and raised, the place to which he has been dying to return, the idea of home and belonging are transfigured. He has an epiphany. Home is where the love is, a place that is impossible to leave.

In many ways, Bijan's exit—from the parental home—seems archetypal. It reminds us of the stories played out in fairy tales, myths, legends, and memoirs. The son leaves in due course to start his own family, or he runs away, or he is cast out. All three leave-takings are emotionally searing; all three have their share of turmoil.

Even if the exit in the first scenario is anticipated and planned, even if it fits with what is deemed developmentally and culturally appropriate, it may still be a departure filled with ambivalence, conflict, relief, and liberation. But the drama seems heightened in the exits that deviate from the conventional mold. Those who run away from the parental home and those who are kicked out are exiting an untenable situation. Running away may be a desperate act, but it is an act of will. It is an exit of one's own choosing. Being kicked out is a forced exit, a circumstance that wasn't chosen, but one that must be endured and survived, where the connections to home are harder to repair or brutally severed forever.

Bijan's departure weaves together all three archetypal narratives. He chooses to leave; he surprises himself by saying, "I'll go." But the choice comes on the heels of his older brother's staunch refusal and his younger brother's tragic death. As soon as the words escape his mouth, it does not feel like free choice. It is a choice made out of loyalty, the son protecting his parents from additional, unbearable grief. As soon as he arrives in New York, he wants to run back to his mother's waiting arms and feel the softness and warmth of her bosom. But his leave-taking is also a story of running away—from the seductions of radical politics, from the war, the violence, the bloodshed—and a story of being cast out by a father who does it out of love, not punishment or anger. The father's insistence that he go and stay away are indicative of the tremendous protection and life-giving care he feels for Bijan. Exiting home is a family love story.

DANCING ALL THE WAY HOME

"It always begins with a declaration to yourself."

This next exit narrative—of homecoming—does not have the geographic sweep of Bijan's story; it is not about traveling many time zones away from a parental home or about the clashes in language, politics, and culture that mark the separation between a son and his family of origin. Rather it is a story played out on a smaller scale, where the movements and exits reflect an interior journey, where the borders and barriers are partly defined by public presumptions and societal prejudices, but also by the deeply embedded definitions of manhood and morality that were shaped by growing up in a working-class Irish Catholic family and neighborhood. Andrew Connolly, a fifty-eight-year-old gay man, tells the brave and hopeful story of coming home to himself after a long series of exits from the "closet."

It is impossible for him to talk about exiting from the "closet" without returning to his roots—the home where he was raised; the neighborhood where he played and made friends; the school where he learned, competed, and secured his place in the pecking order; the church he attended; the gods he worshipped. Andrew Connolly begins at the beginning with these pieces of his background. "I grew up in a very Catholic, working-class, ethnically identified Irish family," he says plainly. Andrew's father was a firefighter, his mother a stay-at-home mom until her three children, all sons, finished high school, when she went back to school and became an elementary school teacher. They lived modestly on his father's income in a triple-decker house that they saved for and eventually owned in a neighborhood in Worcester, Massachusetts. Family life—which Andrew remembers as "nurturing and loving"—largely centered on the church. Andrew was a devoted altar boy, donning vestments and participating in services every Sunday morning and a few times a week. Their parish priests and the professors from the nearby College of Holy Cross were frequently honored guests at their dinner table, and Andrew's maternal uncle—a family favorite—was a Jesuit priest, a highly educated, well-traveled, worldly man who was seen as a worthy role model for his three nephews.

Although the family was solidly working class in terms of

income, Andrew remembers home as a "pretty middle-class intellectual environment," with "ideas and politics thrown around at
the dinner table," a huge emphasis on education, and the visiting
professors offering them a larger vision of the world. As a matter of
fact, all three Connolly sons grew up to be highly educated achiev-
ers who earned advanced degrees and enjoyed successful careers.
The oldest is a physician, the youngest a clinical psychologist, and
Andrew—in the middle—is an educator and university professor.

Andrew smiles at the way in which his parents divided up the
world. "They were fighting the Reformation," he says. "It was the
Protestants versus the Catholics . . . the Democrats versus the Re-
publicans." As a matter of fact, all these things were seamlessly
combined into a collective identity. "My parents were Roosevelt,
liberal Democrats . . . Irish/Catholic/Democrats . . . It was all one
word, melded together." It wasn't until Andrew went to college,
when he discovered that there was a tiny but vocal Republican
Club actively trying to recruit student members, that he even knew
there was such a thing as a "Republican Catholic." The "us against
them mentality" extended beyond politics and religion to class di-
visions. Andrew recalls, "My dad was a labor leader. He always saw
the struggle between the workingman and the *man*. I never heard
racist remarks, because blacks were considered allies, part of the
working class . . . on our side.

"The assumption going in was that I would be a priest," says
Andrew about the way in which early on he was identified as the
one who would honor his family in that way. In most of the families he knew, parents hoped and prayed that at least one of their
boys would become a priest. I ask Andrew why he was the one
"chosen" in his family, and the question seems to surprise him a
bit, as if his "being the one" felt so natural and inevitable to everyone. "Well," he says tentatively, "I was deeply religious . . . I liked
church, the liturgy, and all the rituals, and I probably wasn't chas-
ing after girls the way my brothers were." He smiles. "I must have

lacked the same kind of enthusiasm for the opposite sex that my brothers exhibited," he says with understatement.

Andrew's relative "lack of enthusiasm for girls" reaches back to early adolescence, a time when he seemed to be sitting on top of the world. "I was athletic, popular. I loved sports and fishing . . . I liked to do boy things." He contrasts his popularity and his devotion to sports with the characteristics of many gay boys who grow up feeling "alienated from the guys," who are so often marginalized or even bullied by the straight boys who won't let them join the masculine cliques. "You know," says Andrew, underscoring his very different experience, "the story of the last kid chosen for the team . . . I was the one choosing the team. I was the exemplar . . . I very much belonged." The feeling of being one of the boys "with muscles"—one of the very masculine boys—seems to be an important theme in Andrew's exit narrative. In eventually declaring himself gay, he was not leaving a community in which he had been diminished or excluded; he was not responding to being an outcast, derided for being effeminate, a "fag." He was leaving a group of his peers where he was admired and included, where he was considered strong and powerful, a leader. And he was finding his way into a community where he wanted to connect with gays, like him, who had muscles and were winners, whose experience had not been overwhelmed by the feeling of being "other" or "less." Andrew's adolescent experience of being a popular, admired leader in the straight boys' world seems to have provided him with a level of self-confidence that made his exit out of the closet less fraught, less painful. "You see, I was feeling good about myself, comfortable in my skin . . . exiting from a place of strength." he says.

Andrew was thirteen years old when he had his first sexual encounter with a boy who was one of his best friends. At the time—and all through high school—he was openly and "pleasantly" dating girls, but this encounter with his good friend seemed "special and sweet." Andrew chuckles at the memory. "I enjoyed it.

There was nothing negative about it . . . except that it was sinful."
It only happened once, and neither of them ever spoke about it
after that. After high school Andrew decided to attend college at
Holy Cross, where he entered as a day student because his family
did not have the money to pay for room and board. He continued
to date girls, but he remembers "a growing attraction for men at an
emotional and physical level."

Again Andrew recalls one encounter with a straight guy, during his freshman year, where he "acted on his attraction a bit." But
it was more of a flirtation, not the real thing; nothing was ac-
knowledged by either of them. This was 1968, a time when no
one—"not a single guy"—at the all-male Catholic college "would
have called himself gay." From time to time Andrew reminds me of
how "different things were back then," how "gays were invisible
and everything was underground," and "how much guilt, shame,
and secret pleasure were part of the hidden life." Even though no
one at Holy Cross admitted to being gay, there was definitely "gay
sex going on." There were the real effeminate "glee club guys" who
everyone believed were having sex with one another. "But that was
not me," says Andrew about how he never found "those types" attractive. And there was also gay sex going on between a few well-
known professors who were "actively cruising their students." In
fact, Andrew remembers being hit on by two faculty members.
"They came on to me, but I never acted on it," he says casually.

Although Andrew did not identify with the glee club guys, he
did begin to frame a political outlook that redrew the map between gays and straights. "I was beginning to develop an identity
as a progressive thinker," he says about opening his mind and heart
to the gay world. One evening he went with a bunch of his friends
to see *The Boys in the Band*, a play about gay men at a party. Andrew explains, "The playwright had a preliberation perspective . . .
you know, the view that these gay guys are pathetic and we need to
have sympathy for them . . . a view that would today make most

people cringe." Andrew missed all the political and social subtexts. All he remembers is sitting in the audience lusting after the sexy-looking actors on the stage. He is grinning at the memory of his big, surprising response. "I sat there thinking, These are some hot guys who are gay . . . they are not like the guys in the glee club."

After college, Andrew went on to graduate school in Rochester, New York, his first time away from home. But even there—even without "the inhibiting influence of home"—he really didn't do "gay stuff." He shakes his head, remembering a single encounter. "There was sexual stuff with one guy, but we didn't really go far." Occasionally Andrew dated women, but by now it had become "more of a cover." There was some pleasure, but no sexual attraction. His heart was definitely not in it. He remembers one woman that he very much enjoyed being with, so they dated off and on for several months and it "got pretty serious." When she began to talk about the future and hint at marriage, Andrew—for the first time—confronted himself. "I thought to myself, It is wrong to be doing this . . . I'm lying to her and lying to myself. This is not honest, not authentic." And although he didn't yet have the nerve to tell her that he was gay, he broke off the relationship, felt guilty and sad for how he had misled her, and never dated a woman again.

After his year in Rochester, in 1973, Andrew moved to Boston, a city he had known growing up, a city that had a lively gay community and an emerging gay political movement. There was also a tempting nightlife that beckoned to him. He began frequenting a gay bar—the Cabaret—first joined by his friend and roommate, a straight male, and a couple of straight girls who were his "good buddies," then finding his way to the club on his own. "It felt open and cool, and I would go there and dance the night away," he says about his beginning dance steps into gay life. But when he stopped dancing, he realized that the Cabaret was not a place where he really felt comfortable. A lot of the guys there reminded him of the glee club boys from college. "Back then," Andrew recalls, shrugging his shoulders, "it was fashionable to be thin and very effeminate. These were gay guys who called each other by girls' names, and I wasn't comfortable with that . . . I was looking for guys with muscles."

Several months later Andrew heard about another bar—Rizzo—that "catered to guys like" him. "The first time I walked in there," he says dramatically, "I thought I was in heaven . . . and I was!" He reminds me that discovering and finding his way to Rizzo was not easy. This was 1976, and there was, of course, "no Internet and no gay news channel that kept folks in touch with one another or helped direct you to the right gay resources." Finding Rizzo and mixing with the musclemen felt to Andrew as if he had come "home." It was also the moment when he definitively came out to himself, when he said, "I'm not going to fake it anymore. I'm going to pursue relationships with men, and I'm going to call myself gay."

Although he can identify the moment when he declared himself gay—first to himself—he wants me to know that the process of coming out is "long and layered." "It is not binary," he says, "like one day you're in the closet and the next day you're out. It's like peeling an onion . . . slowly removing the layers that cover and mask." And "it always begins with a declaration to yourself" that you are gay, and then announcements along the way to family, friends, acquaintances, and colleagues. It is "tedious and difficult" to carefully spread the news, to not fall back into the old habits of obfuscation, to ride out the ambivalence that sometimes reemerges even if you feel sure of what you are doing.

As he relives those early days, Andrew says that for him the process of coming out may have gone a little more quickly for two reasons. First, by then, he was loving his work as a special education teacher and had become deeply involved in the "disability movement." His advocacy for the fair treatment of disabled students made him think, "If I can do this for them, I can also stand up for myself and other gays." And second, his "progressive politi-

cal orientation" easily mixed and merged into the gay rights movement, which was in its early stages. "All at once, I was having sex
with men, going to Provincetown as a gay person, and joining the
gay rights struggle in the streets. I no longer wanted to live a separate, private life, hiding my gayness, muting my voice."

Even though he was clear that he no longer wanted to be closeted, Andrew did worry about losing his job. At the time, he was
teaching at a vocational high school in a suburb of Boston, where
he definitely would have been fired had they discovered that he
was gay. "There was no job security. We were always having to
watch our backs," he recalls. "This was the terrifying era of Anita
Bryant's 'holy war on homosexuals,' and folks were doing witch
hunts against gays. It was a dangerous time." As a matter of fact,
Bryant's religious crusade—when she unleashed her infamous slo-
gan, "Gays can't reproduce so they have to recruit"—was initially
focused on prohibiting gays from becoming teachers. Andrew felt
somewhat safer when he found an administrative job in the Boston
public schools; he immediately joined a newly formed activist co-
alition called Gay and Lesbian School Workers. "The fact that the
teachers called themselves workers gave a sense of where they were
coming from." He smiles. At first they were suspicious of Andrew's
wish to join; as an administrator, he was seen as "the enemy." All
the other members were lefty teachers—"workers"—who were suspicious of his "establishment credentials." But it didn't take long
before they realized that his heart was in the right place and that
he was a valuable political ally. "Even though Boston was more
open, and even though there were clear signs of political change,
these were still very frightening times," explains Andrew. "We
wanted to make schools safe places for gay teachers. At the time,
we were not even focused on the vulnerability of gay students."
Within a couple of years they had secured job protection for gays
in the Boston school contract.

One of the leaders of the movement—Earl Haywood—became

a close friend and an important and valued mentor. Several years older than Andrew, he was an experienced and savvy activist, an outspoken teacher at a local progressive independent school, and someone who seemed both fearless and strategic. It was at his urging that Andrew and he collaborated in starting the Gay and Lesbian Political Caucus. When Andrew thinks back on his gay identity and his political activism, he often points to the critical role of mentors in his life, Earl being at the top of the list. "I was fortunate to meet guys who really pushed me and guided me." He underscores the ways in which his mentors combined the personal and the political, blending passion and discipline, strategy and courage. As Andrew paved his own path, their influence on him was big and exciting. "Coming out sexually and politically was exhilarating . . . I loved being part of the gay rights movement." He beams. The exhilaration, of course, had its dark and scary side. In the summer of 1979 at Boston's first gay rights parade, many of the marchers wore bags over their heads to hide their identity, and people watching along the parade route threw bottles and rotten tomatoes and shouted ugly homophobic slurs.

The first person Andrew came out to was Greg, his best straight friend and roommate, with whom he "shared political views" and whom he "trusted implicitly." He knew this would be the easiest, least stressful of his coming-out conversations. "Greg was not at all surprised," recalls Andrew. "Within a few weeks we were double-dating." By contrast, another good friend, a working-class Italian kid he had known from his childhood, acted as if Andrew's news were a death sentence. "He said, 'I feel terrible for you. I can't believe what pain you must be experiencing' . . . He was patronizing and sympathetic," says Andrew, shaking his head. "My response was, 'Time out, man . . . being gay is not a tragedy. I see it as a gift.'" He tried to draw an analogy. What if his friend could take a pill that would render him non-Italian, would he do it? Of course not! He was proud of his Italian roots, his heritage, and his culture;

he would never do anything to alter that. So neither would Andrew take a pill to become straight; he loved being gay.

Coming out to his brothers was a "piece of cake; they were completely cool with it." They were right there with him, cheering him on, embroidering him into their straight lives, going out dancing with him at gay clubs. It was mostly the same with the rest of his family, many of whom had not thought of him as gay and expressed some surprise, but then accepted him fully. One Sunday he even hosted a big brunch at his place in the South End for all his cousins, nieces, nephews, and gay friends—bringing his two worlds together—and everyone had a great time.

It was only his mother and father who never fully accepted his being gay. They never wanted to talk about it, and Andrew did not "force the issue." Even though he tried to "have the conversation" several times, they always came back with the same brief, dismissive response. "We love you . . . It's your business. We don't want to talk about it." Andrew's face is resigned but sad. I ask him how he has made sense of his parents' refusal to talk, and he says gently, "They came from a different generation, and sex wasn't anything my parents ever talked about . . . I knew my mother was opposed to birth control because of the church, but nothing else was ever said." He describes the "huge family tragedy" when his older brother got his girlfriend pregnant in college and they had to get married by a justice of the peace because the church refused to allow them to have a wedding. "They were thought to be living in sin," says Andrew as he recalls "where his parents were coming from" and the prohibitions and guilt piled on by the church.

Andrew can somehow manage to understand the generational and religious reasons that his parents could never accept his being gay. What he can't bear, and what still makes him angry and bitter, is the fact that they never recognized his long-term partner, Matthew, "as my spouse." And when he died of AIDS after a decade-long union, they refused to attend his funeral. "It was devastating," says Andrew, his eyes filling with tears. "My uncle, the Jesuit priest—my mother's brother—was completely accepting. He gave Matthew his last rites and did the funeral service, but my parents never came around." Looking back on what now feels like "the ultimate betrayal," Andrew wishes he had at least "forced the issue" with his parents when his spouse was buried. But even now he doesn't seem to have a clue about how he might have confronted them in a way that would have changed their disrespectful behavior.

Andrew had to peel another layer of the onion back at work, in his professional life. Because of his very public role in the gay rights movement around town, most people at work knew and accepted the fact that he was gay. Fairly quickly he rose in the administrative ranks in the school system, and he remembers an incident around his gayness that backfired in unexpected ways. Andrew, the youngest in his department, was about to be promoted to the top position, director of special education for the whole school system. At that time, there were two warring factions in the department—the old guard and the young Turks who had very different philosophical and political takes on the field of special education. Andrew was clearly in the latter camp.

When he was about to be appointed, the old guard decided to voice their opposition directly to the five members of the school board, complaining that a gay person should not be allowed to get the top job. "You see, they used the gay thing because they couldn't get me on my competence," says Andrew about their "pathetic attempts" to be obstructionists. But in each meeting they had with individual board members, their requests were denied, and they were turned away. In fact, in a couple of cases, members of the board actually threw the petitioners out of their offices. The old guard hadn't counted on the fact that Andrew had either exchanged political favors or developed a personal relationship with each and every member of the board, and he already knew the votes were there. And it turned out that the most conservative woman on the board, a middle-aged single mother from Dorchester, was the most sympathetic. She had a son and an administrative assistant who were both gay. The victory was sweet, but the bitterness still lingers. "It was a five–zero vote . . . but for me it was very hurtful."

The evening after the vote, Andrew went to a community gathering, where the man sitting next to him offered congratulations on his new job and asked him for the "backstory." Andrew was forthcoming, telling him about the opposition's efforts to stop his appointment, how they had used his gayness as their rallying cry. The next day, the whole story appeared in the Metro section of *The Boston Globe*. The stranger sitting next to him had never identified himself as a newspaper reporter. Although it was shocking and unsettling to see the article in the paper, after a while Andrew saw the whole thing as positive, even liberating. "As it turned out, being in the newspaper was wonderful. I didn't have to do any more of this coming out . . . it had all been made very public."

From Boston, Andrew moved to Chicago to become associate superintendent of schools, and once again he was forced "to figure out how to be out." Some of his friends said that the Midwest would be a much less friendly place for gays, that he needed to be more cautious. And Andrew didn't want his sexuality to take center stage; he didn't want it to become "the issue" in Chicago. "I was always wanting to be careful that my gay identity wouldn't distort or compromise the work I was doing in the disability movement," he says about a calculation that always seems particularly pointed when he enters a new political environment and must decide whether to peel back another layer of the onion. Before arriving in Chicago, he decided to dismiss his friends' warnings and come out to his boss, who was "cool with it." And soon after he arrived in the Midwest, he met and befriended the mayor and his wife, who had a disabled son, and they became staunch allies in his work on behalf of disabled students and then big supporters of gay rights.

Andrew had arrived just in time to lead the AIDS prevention work in the Chicago schools, developing a sex education curriculum, setting up health clinics, and distributing condoms to students who were sexually active. The culminating event was the walk for AIDS down Michigan Avenue. "That was my very public way of coming out," Andrew recalls of the moment when his political and personal worlds converged and he marched at the front of the line with the mayor.

Andrew's time in Chicago was cut short by the deteriorating health of Matthew, who had stayed behind in Boston. "I gave up my position in Chicago to go take care of my spouse," says Andrew sadly, reliving the traumatic moments when Matthew was hospitalized for six weeks with AIDS and finally died in his arms at home. While he sat nursing Matthew in the hospital, he received a call from President Clinton's people at the White House, offering him the job of director of special education for the United States. He said yes to the new job, told them he would not be able to come immediately, and then notified his new staff that his partner was very ill and on the edge of death. "I came in as a gay widow." He recalls about the openheartedness and positive reception he received from his staff and the huge welcome he got from his new boss, who loved the fact that he was gay. She "saw it as an asset."

It turned out that twenty-four of Clinton's appointees were "out" gays, a record number for the federal bureaucracy. In fact, in order for Clinton to make the openly gay appointments, he had had to rescind a "don't ask, don't tell" order still on the books from the Eisenhower days. The *Washington Blade*, D.C.'s gay newspaper, did a full-page spread listing all the appointees along with their government positions. A big press conference followed, with all of them lined up for the whole country to see. "It was the ultimate coming out!" Andrew shakes his head as he traces the progress. "It had only been twenty years since I was in Boston—so afraid that I would lose my teaching job because I was gay—to that moment when the president of the United States was standing behind us, saying he was really with us and he valued our contribution to the nation . . . and it felt good to feel as if I had been a small part of that change."

Now, at fifty-eight, Andrew sits before me, slender and fit, his muscles bulging under his T-shirt. He is still an athlete, at home in his body. His posture is strong and relaxed; his gaze is intense. His mostly gray hair is cut short and thinning. As he relives his story, his eyes mist over with the emotional shedding of each layer of the onion—"joyful tears" he admits, wiping his eyes. His days as an altar boy in Worcester feel like long ago and far away, even though he has no need to dismiss or disparage his roots or the values he was raised with. "Self-loathing has never been a part of me," he says quietly. "There are no other peels of the onion to make. At this time in my life I don't have to worry . . . I haven't had to worry for a long time."

Andrew's voice rises in a triumphant crescendo. "I love gay people . . . I like being with my people. It is a gift to be part of a counterculture." He bangs his fist on the table, his eyes now filled with mischief. "I live in the South End, and I cruise for men . . . it is spiritual to be around my brothers and sisters. We are different in so many wonderful ways." He is at his most expansive when he stumbles upon another metaphor ("besides peeling the onion") to describe the feeling of being fully out. "It is like being at the dance . . . it is a revelry . . . you're completely free. It is the antithesis of being in the closet. You're on the dance floor, and everyone is smiling and acting foolish." He lifts both arms, spreads them wide, snaps his fingers, and moves his torso to the beat of the dance music that echoes through him.

We are coming to the end of our time together, ending on a high note, an exultant bravado celebrating the long journey. I ask Andrew whether "coming out of the closet" is a good example of an exit story, and he assures me that it is. Not one open-and-shut exit, rather a series of exits that allow you over time to "be fully evolved . . . to be completely yourself." "The closet is damaging," he says pensively. "If you don't get out of it, then you never can be healthy or whole." He flashes to the profiles he sees when he surfs the Internet. "When gay guys use the word 'discreet' online, that is a sign that they are not out." He talks about the pain for those who feel they have to "de-gay" their apartment before their parents arrive for a visit from out of town. He remembers the time, a couple of decades ago, when he was having dinner with some principals in Boston after spending a couple of weeks with his lover in Provincetown, and when they asked him where he had been on his vacation, he told them he had rented a house in Truro. Provincetown would have signaled that he was gay. "The masking and hiding take a toll. We only have one life to live . . . and it goes by very quickly."

There are two more thoughts—about time and place—that Andrew wants to leave me with. He wants me to know that he is aware of the ways in which his coming out of the closet, his gay identity, and his activism were very much shaped by "historical context." He points to a "huge historical marker" that separates generations of gay men. "I am young enough to have experienced the Stonewall riot—Greenwich Village, 1969—that sparked the gay revolution." He muses, "If I were ten years older, I might have been a priest or an alcoholic, or both, not a free gay man . . . I know very few men older than I am who have fully exited."

He also recognizes the "power place has had" in shaping his identity, his sense of belonging and community. Now his voice is almost prayerful. "San Francisco is our spiritual home . . . our Vatican, the place where we can be completely gay." He looks off into the distance, imagining the scene, his arms carving curves in the air. "I remember last year going out there to bury one of my best friends who I had found dead in his place in Provincetown. I was high up on one of the hills, looking down on the Castro Theatre.

The fog was lifting, and the sunlight was hitting the fog . . . there were sprays of sparkling light . . . I sat there and just cried. I was home."

For Andrew, exit is homecoming—not just into the home of self but also into the home of community. His exit makes possible the realization that you can be yourself, and be with people, just the way you are. His homecoming was a hard-won, lengthy process; there were a series of exits. Even though Andrew is able to capture the exact moment when he declared to himself that he was gay— where he was, what he was wearing, how a weight suddenly seemed to lift from his shoulders—he reminds me that being in or out of the closet is not a "binary" experience. Rather, it is ongoing and iterative. It is like slowly, strategically "peeling the onion" as you shed the masks that lie and the personas that deceive, as you begin to reveal who you really are, your "authentic self." For Andrew, there were public exits—the ones that got written about in the paper, celebrated in gay pride parades, and announced at press conferences—and private ones where he revealed himself to friends and family. The coming-out conversation with his parents was by far the most painful, and he still blames himself for not pushing them harder, for "not forcing the issue" with them. Until their death, they "silenced the conversation," deflecting his many attempts to tell them the truth, refusing to come to his spouse's funeral.

Their refusal, of course, reflected their roots and their generation—their Irish immigrant origins, their working-class values, and their unerring devotion to the Catholic Church, all of which saw homosexuality as sinful. As a matter of fact, in order for Andrew to begin his exit story, he tells me he must begin at the "hardest place," where the pulls of gravity and belonging were the strongest—with his "working-class Irish Catholic" family who lived in a triple-decker on a street in Worcester, where everyone believed the same thing, belonged to the same parish, wanted their sons to be priests, and looked to the Vatican as the almighty authority. It is against these powerful forces of home—the close-knit neighborhood where Andrew was raised, where he was loved by his parents, and where he spent a "happy childhood"—that he must begin his exit moves, challenge the deeply ingrained cultural imprints, and calculate his successful advances.

As I listened, I was struck by the ways in which Andrew's exits out of the closet seemed consistently strong and hopeful, filled with self-confidence and clarity. Yes, there were real dangers and fears, ambivalence and retreat along the way, but mostly he seemed to move—even dance—from strength to strength, a self-confidence in part born out of his happy and abundant childhood. Even though his parents would not allow him to tell them the truth, Andrew always knew they loved him, believed in him, and had his back. The self-esteem that allowed him to navigate the gay/straight borders came, I believe, from the security and support that his mother and father provided; from the close-knit Catholic neighborhood where he felt like the "chosen one"; from the embrace of friends and teammates who admired his muscles, his skills, and his leadership; from the professors and priests who sat around the family dinner table and included him in smart, worldly conversations. Ironically, all those early familial, cultural, and religious forces that disapproved of homosexuality and found it sinful were the very same as those that nourished the self-confidence in him that ultimately allowed him to emerge from the closet whole and happy. In the end, Andrew's exit story does not feel unlike the long journey many of us—gay or straight—must take toward self-understanding as we try to make peace with how we differ from the expectations and projections of our parents. In fully accepting ourselves, we pave the way for others to accept us; we both embrace and resist the gravitational pulls of home.

Beyond the shaping influences of family and church, it is important to see Andrew's coming out as part of a larger political and social narrative and to recognize how much "times have changed." Tracing his journey, we see him in the late 1960s at Holy Cross, a Catholic men's college where no one dared admit he was gay, where the glee club boys were rumored to be having sex, and where everyone knew the names of the male professors who cruised their students. Ten years later we see Andrew trying to avoid being fired from his teaching job and growing into his activism while Anita Bryant waged her national crusade against gays, became the national spokesman for orange growers, and was named *Good Housekeeping*'s "most admired woman" of the year. And we hear about Andrew joining the brave marchers in Boston who put paper bags over their heads as they walked in the first gay pride parade and had rotten tomatoes and homophobic slurs hurled at them as they passed by.

Andrew guides us to the most important marker of change—the generational divide, the fault line that put the gay rights movement on the map. The timing of the Stonewall riot was fortuitous, giving inspiration and impetus to Andrew's generation of activists, providing fuel for the movement, and forcing the battle out into the open. Andrew looks at his gay elders, most of whom remain closeted, and recognizes how his exit—his homecoming—might not have happened had he been born a few years earlier. He is a "free gay man," he is "home," he is able to join the jubilation "dance"—not only because he gained strength from his family's enduring love and from being in the struggle with the activist community, not only because he was willing to go the distance and courageous enough to brave the dangers, but also because he was lucky enough to have come of age when he could catch the winds of change.

Two

VOICE

Voice is sound. It is auditory. We listen for its timbre, tone, and texture. We enjoy the suppleness, virtuosity, and range of the mezzo-soprano singing *Carmen*. We immediately recognize the gravelly, deep voice of our son calling long-distance on Sunday afternoon. We recoil from the angry, cynical voice of our teacher catching us—again—in some rule violation. We catch our voice as we talk to ourselves in a moment of frustration or as we scream out when we slip and fall down the stairs. We respond to the timbre and phrasing of the voice as much as—and sometimes more than—the content of the message. We've heard people say "God damn" as if they were sending up a prayer, or "yes, sir" as if they were swearing. In the tonal variations of voice we hear respect, anger, resignation, sadness, confusion, curiosity. We hear the opening and closing of conversations. We sense that it is time to leave.

Social scientists often use "voice" metaphorically to refer to the social, emotional, and political meanings conveyed when people speak up or speak out, claim their space, challenge authority, and become empowered. Political scientists and policy analysts, for example, describing the responsibilities of citizens in a democratic society, see the vote as a way for people to give voice to their views, to make themselves heard, to register approval or complaint. Voice in this context speaks about the individual's responsibility and accountability to the whole community. A democracy cannot function without people lifting up their individual and collective voices. In authoritarian regimes, voices are silenced and dismissed. People are not allowed to stand up for what they believe or give voice to their views.

The feminist psychologist Carol Gilligan stretched the metaphor even further when she wrote *In a Different Voice* (1982), her now classic account contrasting the ways in which women and men define the boundaries of their identities.[1] Men, she argued, tend to see themselves as separate, their identity defined by the lone pursuit, the edges of their autonomy clearly drawn. Women, on the other hand, see themselves in relationships, knowing themselves through their connectedness to each other. It is through relationships that women's development and self-definition is shaped. Here Gilligan uses the notion of the "different voice" of women to challenge the male-centric focus of the developmental studies that not only used men as their primary "subjects" but also viewed male developmental and moral trajectories as normative, even optimal. In lifting up the voices of women, whose life journeys and identities took a different path, Gilligan was not only offering a corrective to the literature—claiming that feminist patterns were different, not deviant—she was also using her own voice, the voice of challenge and critique, to speak to her male academic colleagues. The layering of voices, those of her subjects in duet with her own, offered a powerful counterpoint to the prevailing frameworks that had, until that time, dominated academic studies and discourse.

Economist Albert Hirschman was the first to draw the theoretical links between "voice" and "exit."[2] In 1970 he published a slim volume titled *Exit, Voice, and Loyalty: Responses to Decline in Firms, Organizations, and States*, which forty years later continues to have a huge influence on social scientists' conceptions of why people choose to leave or stay in organizations, communities, or even relationships that are no longer serving their needs. In a book crammed with references to the economic staples of supply and demand, the pricing of products, outcomes, influences, and quality, Hirschman surprises us by quoting some lines from a 1966 satirical play about Adlai Stevenson's inability to resign from government—a bow to how hard it is to leave the familiar, break the bonds of attachment, and become an outsider:

> *To quit the club! Be outside looking in!*
> *This outsideness, this unfamiliar land,*
> *From which few travelers ever get back in . . .*
> *I fear to break . . .* [3]

The beginning of Hirschman's theory is grounded in the inevitable decline or deterioration of organizations. In fact, he holds a deeply pessimistic stance:

> Firms and other organizations are conceived to be permanently and randomly subject to decline and decay, that is to a gradual loss of rationality, efficiency, and surplus-producing energy, no matter how well the institutional framework within which they function is designed.[4]

The situation is this: the firm is not doing what it is supposed to be doing—in terms of product quality, service, or price—for its customers. Management finds out about the firm's failings via two alternative routes or two discrete actions that the customers exercise: exit and voice. When customers stop buying the firm's products or services, or some members leave the firm, they are exercising the exit option. This compels the management to search for ways to correct the firm's faults that have led to the exodus. In the voice option, customers and firm members express their dissatisfaction directly to the management, or to anyone who will listen; this too compels the management to search for ways to cure the firm's failings. As such, exit and voice are generated out of decline and perpetuate the organizational life cycle. Though Hirschman calls his view "radical pessimism," one can discern a more positive outlook within his theory, one that considers decay as the birthplace of new possibilities.

Hirschman paints exit as a neat, terminal, impersonal, discernible, and quantifiable action that is highly efficient. It is the most direct and purest way to express dissatisfaction. Voice, on the other hand, belongs to the realm of politics. Voice is "messy," spanning everything from faint grumbling to violent protest. Moreover, in the political realm, exit has been branded as criminal, labeled as desertion, defection, even treason. Although Hirschman speaks of exit—its clarity and edge—as "uniquely powerful," he claims that "the precise modus operandi of the exit option has not received much attention." A customer resorts to exit rather than voice when he or she no longer attempts to change an objectionable state of affairs, whether through individual or collective petition, appeal to a higher authority, or protest. In situations where there is a lack of opportunity for exit—where there is a pure monopoly, for example—the potential for voice increases. Voice, if effective, can postpone or prevent exit. Voice is both complement and substitute for exit. It is hard to read Hirschman without sensing some bias: "While exit requires nothing but a clear-cut either/or decision, voice is essentially an art constantly evolving in new directions . . . the presence of the exit alternative can therefore tend to atrophy the development of the art of voice."[5]

The seesawing, complementary, yet unequal options of exit and voice are further complicated by Hirschman's addition of "loyalty" to the theoretical mix. Loyalty, the third leg of his conceptual triangle, refers to a special or deep attachment to an organization that helps group members resort to voice when exit is a possible alternative. As a rule, loyalty holds exit at bay and activates voice.[6]

THE ART OF VOICE

"I wanted to become more of a solo voice."

The first narrative in this chapter both echoes and challenges Hirschman's theory, pointing to the complicated tensions, balances, and entanglements between exit and voice. In Theresa Russo's story of leaving the leadership role of a nonprofit that she founded twenty-five years ago, exit is neither clear-cut nor efficient, neither easily discernible nor quantifiable. The "outsideness" that she experiences is messy, ambivalent, and disorienting. Also, in contrast to Hirschman's model, it is in the performance and layers of exit—the public rituals and the private agony—that Theresa begins to discover and to lift up her voice.

Theresa Russo has postponed our interview a few times before she finally arrives on a sunny morning in April. Over the months, we have had numerous e-mails—heartfelt, anxious missives from her about anticipating the interview (will she be able to be coherent and articulate about something that still causes her so much confusion and pain), about her concerns over my methodology (how many interviews, how deeply will I go, will I ask to review any of the documents that she has on file), and about her worry that our time together might add another layer of emotional processing that will further block her movement forward. In my communications back to her, I have tried to be reassuring about the interview process, about my confidence in her ability to express her thinking and feelings with clarity and authenticity, and about my responsibility to create a safe space for us to talk together. I say that others have found the interviews "educative," "illuminating," even "honoring, helpful, and healing." But I am also very careful to offer her—each time—the opportunity to retreat without guilt or embarrassment. It is fine, I say, over and over again, if she chooses not to move forward with the interview.

In retrospect, this dance of approach and avoidance seems right for this time in Theresa's life, when she is so ready to move forward to the next chapter while she still desperately clings to the past; when she has publicly exited the organization with grace, purposefulness, and certainty while she privately feels her decision to leave it was precipitate and ill-timed; when she is mourning a life that used to be incredibly busy, joyful, and productive and—at the same time—trying to forge a positive path forward when the terrain feels barren.

The pain is written all over her face as she sits down across from me, her arms tightly wrapped around her, and begins her soliloquy, which—it turns out—is both coherent and articulate. She has thought deeply about the casualties and opportunities of leave-taking. She has worked hard to find the language for the layers of emotion she navigates every day. And she is openhearted and generous about expressing her anger, her fears, her ambivalence, and her yearnings. Her interview is not in the past tense; it is not a retrospective. She is speaking about the present, about the mixture and mélange of emotions she is currently experiencing that shape her outlook of the future.

Three years ago Theresa began thinking about leaving Red River Expeditions, a nonprofit organization in rural Wisconsin that she founded and directed for twenty-five years. For much of that time, she had combined her work at RRE with teaching in a counseling program at the university, where she also earned her doctorate. The two part-time jobs were really both full-time commitments, filling her days with strenuous, exciting work that she loved, adding up to a very busy life with intellectual and emotional benefits and a "reasonably good paycheck." Theresa enjoyed the balance and counterpoint of teaching and supervising graduate

students and designing and directing outdoor environmental programs for adolescents. Her double commitments required that she
commute in her trusty old Saab three hours each way from the
country to the city, spending half the week in each place.

When Theresa began to think about leaving RRE, she was still
very much involved with and enjoying her teaching duties at the
university, and she was anticipating continuing her work there.
But she began to feel that two "full-time jobs" were too much for
her. She recalls, "I was getting exhausted, realizing that I did not
have the stamina for working twelve-hour days, seven days a week."
But it was more than the weariness of burning the candle at both
ends; although she was confident about fulfilling her duties and
responsibilities at the university, she felt less secure in her capacity
to be at full strength as executive director of a hands-on educational program for adolescents. Her physical stamina was clearly
not what it used to be. The trips she used to organize and lead—
strenuous mountain climbing, weeklong hikes through the back-
woods, camping in the wild, canoe trips, white-water rafting, and
fishing expeditions, all of which she used to relish—now, at fifty-
five, were impossible for her. "Even five one-day trips a year felt
hard," she admits. "Although I was the administrator, I still wanted
some level of contact with the teens, and I hated losing the immediacy and closeness with them."

Theresa was also struggling with significant hearing loss that
made it hard for her to decipher what the teens were saying. "They
talk so quietly. There is so much mumbling . . . so much nuance
and code when they speak, and I began missing what was going
on." She had always prided herself on being an attentive, compassionate listener, listening for what was said and not said by the
teenagers, finding the right question to ask that would unleash
their stuck emotions or support a moment of discovery for them.
Now this kind of close connection was being compromised, even
lost.

At the same time as Theresa was feeling the need to—slowly but surely—leave RRE, she was becoming more engaged at the university and experiencing a new vitality and authority in her work there. When she founded RRE, she primarily thought of her work as "political activism." She saw her role as "making sure the voices of the rural families were heard, and helping youth advocate for themselves." At the university she began to see the possibility of developing her own voice through influencing the work of graduate students, but also through writing her own books and articles. She could begin to reach broader, more diverse audiences. "RRE was always a choir," she says about the collective approach she encouraged. "I realized that at the university I could have this solo voice. I began to feel that in my mid-fifties, if I'm going to have another chapter, I'd better get on with it."

Theresa makes a distinction between the "personal" reasons that motivated her exit from RRE and the "organizational" ones. The tone of her voice shifts—becoming more distant and analytic—as she speaks in general about organizational leadership and change. She begins, "If founding directors stay for more than twenty or twenty-five years, it can become a personality-driven organization." Before starting RRE, Theresa had been a public school teacher who found herself always worrying about the ways in which schools tended to "silence and pacify students," the ways in which the children seemed to lose their curiosity, their authority, and their voices in the process of conforming to the institutional culture. "I always wanted my kids to be assertive . . . to grab hold of themselves," she says passionately. So she invented an organization—outside the walls of school—where she hoped to offer kids a safe place to be themselves, a challenging and supportive educational environment that might help release them from the bondage of caution and inhibition. She wanted to build an adolescent empowerment zone.

Leaving her teaching job, Theresa had a great plan, but no

money. She looks back on those heady and hopeful days. "It was a force of will building this organization. I had no salary, moved in with my sister and her son because I couldn't pay the rent, and worked out of the back of my car." She was driven by passion, by a progressive political agenda, by her determination to "give voice" to young people and their families. And over the years—actually a quarter century—although the organization has grown and matured, the early imprint of her principles and values has survived intact. She reminds me again what happens when founders stay around a long time, maybe too long. "The personality, style, and legacy of the founder get woven into the organization. The habits of work get deeply imprinted on the organization."

Theresa sees an "essential irony" in the way she has developed and led RRE. On the one hand she has always emphasized the collaborative, communitarian nature of her leadership, and on the other hand she is able to recognize her individual mark, her singular imprint. "You know," she says reflectively, "it was always a choir. My manner was one of relationship building . . . but undeniably there was the force of my personality as well that permeated everything." In part it was her recognition of this "essential irony" that helped Theresa know it was time to leave; if she had actually managed to build a sturdy institution, it should be able to go on—even thrive—without her at the helm.

Again Theresa's voice takes on an analytic edge. "For founders who do a credible job, the organization they've loved and nurtured inevitably gets bigger than them. They need to leave so the organization can move from being personality driven to being theory based. It is, after all, a sign of strength and maturity if the organization can survive the founder's leaving." Her voice—so clear and concise about leadership succession and organizational health—barely masks the thunderous emotions that she admits to feeling. Theresa offers an important caveat about the shift from a personality- to a theory-driven organization—a caveat that captures her "principal concern" about the casualties of progress. "Organizations going through this kind of change have to find a way of not living in the past, but they also must not ignore the past!"

Relationship building is the signature of Theresa's leadership style. It also, not surprisingly, reflects her personality and her political stance. She is most comfortable sharing the power, reaching out to diverse constituencies, and being consultative and inclusive. "I gather up as many voices as possible," she says about a process that always hopes to be democratic and distributive but is often slow and inefficient. After twenty-five years leading RRE, she is keenly aware that her collaborative style is deeply rooted in her unwillingness—or inability—to be assertive, in her resistance to being the "solo voice and spokesperson." Her more natural inclination and attitude is one of working behind the scenes, reaching out to others, listening and supporting, leading through developing a consensus. She is gentle, respectful, and gracious by nature, not edgy and aggressive, never personally ambitious.

Yet in the last several years—particularly since she finished her doctoral work in organizational development—she has wanted to become more assertive. Both as a person and as a leader, she has found that it is almost impossible to change in an organization where your "habits of interacting" are so deeply imbedded. "After twenty-five years there is so much in place, so much assumed about who you are and how you operate, that change is hard. Even though I wanted to become more of a solo voice in my last years there, I found that people were resistant to my attempts to be more assertive." The organizational expectations created a kind of inertia that compromised her purposeful efforts to modify her leadership style, and this made Theresa realize that "the personality-based habits needed to change so the organization could be taken into its maturity."

When she reflects on her anguished exit from RRE, she says it feels as if she has been "living two lives"—the public face of transition that has been "cool, calm, and collected" and the private experience that has been "the darkest time" of her life. As she anticipated her leave-taking, she designed and gracefully implemented a rational process of transition, announcing her plans to her board of directors and working through their various concerns about institutional stability—identifying, welcoming, and mentoring the next director; writing an upbeat and heartfelt farewell letter to the various constituencies she has worked with over the years; even enthusiastically participating in a glorious farewell party that featured not only family, community, and friends but also generations of the teens she had worked with over the decades. She was determined, she remembers, not to have RRE go through the kind of "public drama" that ruins so many transitioning institutions—particularly small nonprofits—and leaves bad scars that deface the place for generations to come.

But underneath all her grace and maturity, all her optimism and bright outlook, Theresa was feeling great ambivalence and a growing sense of dread. She was claiming publicly that her departure was the right thing for the organization, perfectly timed to fit the changing institutional narrative, and all the while she was feeling "but this is not the right time for me!" And she has continued to worry daily about the "practicality and rationality" of her decision as she finds herself facing an unreceptive world and an economy in steep decline.

Since officially leaving RRE two years ago (she has continued to serve as mentor, consultant, and senior adviser on various projects, but has relinquished her office space, stayed out of the decision making, and retreated from being the public face of the organization), Theresa has struggled to find work. Part of her original decision to resign three years ago was predicated on the fact that leaving would allow her to focus more time and energy on her university responsibilities. But as fate would have it, her contract at the university was not renewed (her department was being merged with another, and faculty were being let go), and she was given one year to finish up and move on. Even though she understood the "structural" reasons for her dismissal, it felt like a real slap in the face, a painful kick in her gut, an injury to her ego that stung even more than her exit from RRE because it was not something she had chosen. At RRE she was able to publicly write the story of her departure, stage her exit, and plan the ritual events. At least that much was in her control. But at the university she was simply dismissed after doing what she thought was a more than creditable job, and after discovering how much she loved developing her "solo voice."

So when Theresa stepped out into the world in search of new work and a reinvented professional identity, she took in the empty terrain. It felt like a blank slate with few options—options that kept on unraveling right before her eyes. It was a frustrating, difficult, often humiliating time. Her voice is tearful as she recounts the seemingly endless rejections she faced and the doors that closed in front of her. "This is not a world that is receiving me . . . everything was conspiring against me—my gender, my social class, my age, my disability." At first she says that—at fifty-eight—she feels the sting of ageism most deeply. A lean, lithe white woman who dresses in elegant suits of colorful textured wools whose handsome, lined face is framed by thick, curly red hair that is fast turning silver, she is well aware that when people first meet her, they may see her as "old." She is also well aware that in this job market, universities and colleges would rather hire a faculty member in his/her early thirties, with a newly minted Ph.D., than spend their money on an older person with deep experience and a long résumé. Theresa is able to recount dozens of jobs where she has been one of a few finalists, only to discover that the job—sometimes paying as low as $32,000—was given to a person twenty-five or thirty years her junior.

Her age combines with her "disability," a hearing loss that affects both ears and often makes it hard for her to follow discussions or hear the questions being asked of her at interviews. But worse still is the way she starts to grow anxious weeks before the meetings, worrying that she will not be able to hear the questions, that she will respond to what she thinks they might have said and make a fool of herself. She also worries that people will link her hearing difficulties with their perception of her as an old woman who is out of it, who won't be able to function in her job.

Even though Theresa begins with her age as the primary source of discrimination she is facing in her job hunt, she ends up talking about another, more deeply felt discriminatory lens that she believes distorts people's perception of her and undermines her self-confidence. It is her working-class Italian background that catches up to her every time and makes her feel awkward and insecure when she is out there presenting herself to the world. It is her roots that haunt her progress forward and make her feel marginalized.

I see Theresa's face grow gray and mournful. She looks like a wounded child—the young girl she used to be who grew up on the other side of the tracks and struggled mightily, who finally succeeded in gaining access to fancy schools only to be blindsided—four decades later—by the haunts of exclusion and insecurity that marked her childhood. "These are old traces from my family," she says sadly. "I certainly have become savvy about how to posture as a middle-class person who belongs, but I stand up there thinking, Am I using the correct language here? . . . I worry about how I am speaking. Am I being too Pollyannaish, too idealistic, too excited about other people? Am I trying too hard? And then this other voice rises up inside of me that says, You know too much . . . you don't have to temper your voice . . . you don't have to support this male ego who is judging you . . . that's ridiculous!" This conversation—of insecurity and shame pitted against challenge and confidence—rises up in her as she faces her audiences and introduces her work. It is a source of humiliation and insight, insecurity and skepticism. She feels the shame come on at the same time as she feels the righteousness of her journey, the satisfaction of her growing sense of authority and voice.

The formal transition of leadership took place at the annual meeting of the RRE board of directors. Theresa thought hard about how to make the public ceremonial moment "symbolic, meaningful, and ritualized." She was handing off the baton to Michael, a thirty-seven-year-old man whom she knew well, admired, and respected, "a wonderful person with a terrific wife and two beautiful kids," a colleague who had several years earlier done a stint at RRE. Theresa began the meeting telling the board about the smooth process she and Michael had been through, transferring information, wisdom, experience, and files. After saying—"briefly, cheerfully, and coolly"—how she felt about leaving the organization in the capable and creative hands of the new leader (actually, her stomach was churning, her head was hurting, her mind was spinning . . . the last thing she wanted to do at that moment was to hand over the organization to Michael), she gave him three symbolic gifts: a Flair pen, since he would now be in charge of signing all the documents, a box of business cards with EXECUTIVE DIRECTOR written under his name, and a bag of food to eat at his desk, as he would be too busy to leave the office for lunch. Having offered the gifts, Theresa left the meeting, went back to her office, cleared out all her stuff, and loaded it into boxes. "My whole desk area was naked," she says, as if this felt as if she were stripping the clothes off of her body.

The whole time she was packing and hauling the boxes— denuding the space she had inhabited for twenty-five years—she was trying to gird her loins and find a way to be brave in the face of so much sadness and loss. Her eyes fill with tears as she recalls the still-haunting moment. "There I am, all alone, thinking to myself, This is the right thing. You know it, Theresa. You have to be brave and move through it. I was crying and grieving." Then she made the mistake of stopping to look through some of the files, so full of history, so saturated with the blood, sweat, and tears of hard labor. "I couldn't stand it, thinking this is only important to me, no one else cares . . . all that was in those boxes, nobody would know or care about." (Actually Michael has, in the last several months, consulted the files from time to time to see what he can glean from the letters and documents that might help in guiding the organization forward.)

Although the formal transfer of leadership was accomplished at the board meeting, followed by a gracious farewell letter that Theresa wrote to all the folks—parents, kids, teachers, community leaders, and staff—who had worked with her from the beginning, she still did not completely separate herself from RRE. The board hired her on as a consultant, to supervise and train some of the new staff and to work with Michael once a month as he got used to the reins. They even asked her to launch and lead one final major event—her "swan song"—the following summer, a demanding three-month-long project that she completely immersed herself in and then felt a big letdown when it was over. After the dust had settled, she moved to the margins, to her ambiguous status as the former executive who is still around, who still has so much to give but feels in many ways invisible and without voice. "I still have an official role," she says sadly, "but I don't know where I belong or what I can ask for.

"It is Michael's work to lead RRE—my work is to leave," she says, as if she is rehearsing a line she repeats to herself daily. "It was Michael's turn. I knew that intellectually, but I struggled with the level of my emotional need to know. I hated my lack of identity." When she was in the office, she felt invisible. People would walk right by her. A new staff member didn't even know who she was when she arrived to do supervision. "That's pathetic. Somebody should have told her. She knew nothing about the history of the organization or my role in it," she says with hurt in her eyes. "I felt expendable. The door had closed behind me so quickly."

Theresa feels the hurtful sting of being unrecognized and ignored. But what makes her even angrier is the way she has given in
to the hurt, the way she can't seem to let go of her sadness and
neediness. "I'm actually angry with myself for feeling this level of
need. I hate how much I am letting this hurt me," she says, making
a fist. "I'm really angry at not having enough of a life outside of
RRE . . . the feeling of lost identity—no schedule, no purpose . . .
the loss of community . . . all the families, kids, town officials, colleagues who were part of my life." The accumulated losses have
been humiliating. She hasn't even wanted to be seen, for fear she
will look into the face of someone and recognize their pity. Or
worse still, people would stop her on the street and say something
like, "Oh, congratulations. You must feel so relieved," when all she
was feeling was grief and emptiness. "I longed for the kind of big,
fat, juicy problems that I used to solve every day that were now
Michael's problems. I wanted to say, Give them to me, send them
my way . . . and I felt starved for information about what was going
on, completely out of the loop."

One day, she even made a date to have lunch with a few women
friends she had known since high school and hadn't seen for a long
time. Maybe a small reunion with childhood friends would help
her remember herself. Maybe she would feel the warmth and companionship of their shared history and be comforted by the old
memories and stories. But the lunch was anything but comforting.
Even with these old friends, Theresa felt strange and estranged.
"All they talked about were their children and grandchildren and
their work. I found I had nothing to talk about . . . it was a real
mistake for me to have gone. It left me feeling untethered."

Theresa's tears and passion about the excruciating losses and
her reference to the pain of hearing about "other people's children"
make me ask whether leaving RRE felt to her as if she had lost her
baby. She has clearly asked herself this very question many times.
Her voice is strong as she reflects on her complex feelings. "I have

always resisted that analogy, but more and more, part of it is reso-
nating with me. RRE was certainly not my baby in the suckling at
my breast sense, but I do recognize the part where parents have to
let their children go. In order for children to thrive, you have to let
them be on their own, but it is also true that parents are desperate
for children to call . . . and I'm feeling all of those things." Theresa
is trying to convey to me the depth of her grief and her sense of
dislocation, how the anguish and pain have been written on her
body, causing her to actually become physically ill. In the midst of
the leave-taking, she developed Graves' disease, a hyperthyroid
condition that was "the physical representation" of her emotions.
She says wearily, "Physically, I was out of control. Even the name of
the disease—Graves'—is right on for how the pain inhabited my
body and my mind . . . my soul."

I ask Theresa what metaphor comes to mind when she thinks
about how she was feeling during this time, and she first mentions
William Bridges's book—*Transitions*—where he writes about the
difference between a "ghost town" and a "cemetery." In a cemetery,
Theresa reports, "everyone is dead and buried, and people come to
pay homage and lay flowers at their graves, but ghost towns are
places that used to be vibrant communities that suddenly become
vacant. You see signs of life, indications that people were living and
working and loving there . . . but nothing remains . . . it is all gone."
Exiting the place she founded, sustained, and protected, the place
where there was so much good work and life and pleasure, feels like
she has entered a ghost town. There is nothing left for her except
the signs that the place was once alive with people and activities.
Theresa muses, "There is lots of imagery about death and dying . . .
I'm sick of feeling this way. I want it to be about life, not death. I
don't want the exit to be about closed doors. Where is the open
door? Where is the new life?" Her voice trails off in a question.

Quickly she names a second metaphor. "I feel like I've been on
a merry-go-round. My work at RRE was playful and joyful. It was

meaningful, always hectic and busy, maybe too busy . . . Now I've stepped off the carousel and I'm on the ground, still feeling dazed, dizzy, and totally disoriented. I want to be able to focus on something, to gain some sense of perspective, but the world keeps spinning around—and inside of—me." As she sits across from me, Theresa is twirling her arms in circles, literally looking as if she is struggling to find some balance, some stability. After ghost towns and carousels, she moves on to her third and last metaphor for the life she is now experiencing as dizzy and deathlike. "I see myself leaving the shore, setting out to sea . . . but I'm not sure what I'm taking with me. I find myself out in the water, and I can no longer see the shore. I've lost all sense of direction, no reference points. There is no sense of place in my work, my relationships, or my family."

Hearing her talk about being unmoored from her family and friends, I ask Theresa to whom she goes to for support, for nourishment, for counsel. She immediately mentions her closest sister (she is the eldest of five children). "Rosa is my anchor," she says gratefully. "I tell her everything. She is my sole consistent source of support." Rosa was the sibling Theresa moved in with when she left her teaching job to start—on a wing and a prayer—RRE twenty-five years ago, and she is the one Theresa has depended on during these hard days, weeks, and months of farewell. Sometimes she feels as if Rosa knows her better than she knows herself. She is definitely less judgmental and more forgiving than Theresa is likely to be of herself.

Theresa admits, however, that she has not gone to her friends for support and counsel. Part of her reluctance comes from the dense web of relationships between her friends and her colleagues. They are almost interchangeable, and she does not want her disillusionment or her insecurities to become part of the unruly grapevine that includes both professional and personal relationships. But a bigger part of her reticence in approaching friends is that they are used to coming to *her* for help and reassurance; they have always brought their worries to her, and she has always been the listener, the counselor. As we talk, she seems to discover a new insight. "It could be," she says tentatively, "that I need to find new friends who know me in a different way. When I'm sitting at the table with my old friends these days, I always end up feeling excluded. My friends know me as a listener, not a speaker. All of this is about needing to change habits."

In fact, changing habits is at the core of moving forward. She knows she will have to shift the way she enters relationships. "I'm entering a part of my life that will require that I let go of the old baggage, the old inhibitions and constraints," she says. And one of the biggest pieces of "letting go" is "worrying less about someone else's ego and concentrating more on developing the authenticity and authority of my own voice."

She offers a small example, one "tiny step" in that direction. Recently she was working with a group of high school teachers—mostly male and middle-aged—in a public school where she is currently serving as a consultant. Several of the men were resisting the idea of teachers being required to lead student advisory groups, an innovation Theresa had suggested as a way to build a stronger educational culture and more caring relationships in school and as a way to give students a more welcoming home base. In the past—actually the recent past—Theresa might have let the men's voices dominate. Or she might have tried to carefully, gently nudge them toward her point of view. She might even have retreated from what she knew was the right thing to do. Instead, this time, she said forcefully to them—as she spoke, she could even hear the strength in her own voice—that "if they were not prepared to develop real relationships with their students, they would be missing the boat." Surprisingly, the teachers did not balk; they did not dismiss her. Rather, Theresa "experienced respect" from them. They seemed to like the fact that she was "claiming her authority position." "I am,"

she says hopefully, "testing the waters of being assertive and discovering that when I am, the sky does not fall."

In Theresa's arduous and poignant story of exit she uses the metaphor of voice to try to capture her quest for autonomy and authority, to describe her journey toward strength and self-definition. All
her professional life, she has counseled, supported, and listened to
others. In fact, she founded her nonprofit because she wanted to
empower teens who had been caught up in a school bureaucracy
that rendered them passive and "voiceless." She wanted to help
them discover what they believed and express what they needed;
she wanted them to take responsibility and stand up for themselves. "I wanted to help them discover the power of their voices,"
she says over and over again. In taking on the leadership role of
RRE, Theresa was also seeking to nourish the expression of voices
in her staff. She worked to develop an organizational structure that
would be collaborative and inclusive, a place where everyone would
have a say and be able to participate in decision making. Over time
and with intentionality, she created a "choir" by casting a wide net,
"gathering up all the voices." Her singular and dominant voice—as
distinguished from or more important than theirs—was rarely
heard. The choir sang out the institutional culture and mission,
creating a sound at once harmonious and dissonant.

After a quarter of a century at the helm of RRE, Theresa recognized the organization's need for new leadership. The place had
become "personality driven," too enmeshed with her style and
character. There were many voices in the choir, but they had all
gotten stuck in the same groove—a groove that echoed Theresa's.
This "essential irony" helped her see the path toward the exit. But
she also felt the need to leave RRE for her own reasons. In her
other job, at the university, she had—through her teaching and

writings—gotten a taste of speaking in her own "solo voice," and she had begun to like the sound of what she heard. Besides, she was feeling the developmental imperative. At fifty-eight, she wasn't getting any younger. If there was to be a new and bold chapter, she had better get on with it.

It was one thing, however, to be convinced that it was time to leave RRE—for personal and institutional reasons—and quite another thing to do it. The public departure was nowhere near as difficult as her private journey. With grace and gratitude, with parties and accolades, Theresa was "cool, calm, and collected" as she invented goodbye rituals. But privately she was bereft, tormented, rudderless. The losses seemed overwhelming—the loss of community and relationships, of a structure and purpose, of being at the center of the mix, of being needed as the go-to person. In the midst of the chaos and suffering, grieving and weeping as she packed up the boxes in her office that contained her life's work, Theresa began to glimpse the light at the end of her "dark tunnel of despair." She began to recognize that the "authority and authenticity" of her "solo voice" would require that she exit RRE. The separation would mark the beginning of liberating her voice. As long as she remained tethered to the choir, she would never be able to see her full reflection in the mirror, never be able to even know herself fully.

When Theresa finally takes that small leap of faith and expresses her views at the meeting with high school teachers, she can actually hear the literal change in her voice. It sounds more confident to her, more clear and powerful; and it seems to strike her listeners in a way she never expected. They stop their whining and listen to her respectfully.

Theresa's path to exit is different from the one suggested by Hirschman's theoretical triangle. His framework argues that when organizations are in decline, members must choose between exit ("a clear-cut either/or decision") or voice (a "messy" engagement,

more like an "art form").[7] Those who choose the latter work hard
from within to support the institutional changes that will help the
organization become more efficient, more rational, and more
forward-looking. However, for Theresa her exit is not at all clear-
cut (in fact, she is still in the midst of it); neither does it stand in
contrast to the expression of her voice. Voice and exit are not divergent paths. Rather, she discovers their necessary convergence.
In order to "discover and nurture" her "solo voice," she finds that
she must exit the organization. And unlike Gilligan's notion of
women knowing themselves through their relationships and connections with others, Theresa discovers that she can develop her
authoritative, critical, singular perspective only if she draws boundaries around herself. The emergence of her voice requires that she
begin to practice the messy and creative, hard and imperfect "art"
of separation, exiting from her former way of being in the world.

VOICES IN CONVERSATION

"I was entrusted with people's most intimate stories."

When I think about the roots of my interest in examining the motives and meanings of *exit*, I am often drawn back to my fumbling
experiences as a young researcher, making it up as I went along, trying to figure out how to comfortably and gracefully leave the "field"
after I had spent months or even years living among the people I
was studying. The methodology texts I read as a graduate student
offered me little guidance, no road map, no useful protocols, no
suggested rituals for exiting. Instead, they focused on beginnings,
suggested strategies for the best ways to *enter* the field—in the
trade we call this "gaining access"—which included recommenda-
tions for mapping the research terrain, identifying good informants, and developing trust and rapport with them.[8] Novice
researchers were instructed in developing the casual and attentive

stance of "hanging out"; trained to wait, witness, and listen before questioning; and warned about navigating the balance between being a participant and an observer. The textbook guidance that I read and heeded attended to both empirical and moral consider-ations, focusing on good science and ethical behavior. Of course, success in gaining access allows the researcher to begin her work, collect the data, and get the goods. Being turned away and prohib-ited entry can cancel out months, even years of anticipation and planning.

If the folks we hope to study do not trust our motives, if our presence feels too intrusive, if our asking seems disrespectful and our tone entitled, then people are likely to deny us entry into their lives. We will be turned away. The research will not proceed; the whole thing will unravel. No wonder researchers—mostly out of self-interest—have traditionally focused on the treacherous and nervous moments when we do not have the upper hand, when we are suddenly thrown into the role of supplicant asking for some-thing we desperately need: the consent and participation of those people we want to study. And if researchers are not careful, their supplications can turn into begging, overpromising, pushing too hard—and everyone's dignity will be at stake. Not surprisingly, then, we have invented and codified a set of strategies for gaining entry, methodological protocols that will help us open doors, mask our nervousness, and let us get on with our work.

Once we have gained the consent of our subjects, developed trusting relationships with them, shared their stories, mined their insights, observed their lives, gathered our data, and gotten the goods, we leave. We exit. Sometimes we just disappear, avoiding the farewells that may feel awkward or too painful. We may even convince ourselves that it is kinder for "them" if we just slip away unnoticed, better if we don't make such a big deal about it. For the most part, researchers make it up as we go along. As we exit, we are given very little guidance or direction, no rules or rituals, no clear

codes of ethical conduct for saying our farewells. Anyway, this lack
of clear methodological direction and moral vagaries are what I
experienced as a new researcher, searching for guidance and wanting to say a responsible goodbye to those whose life narratives I
had harvested. I wanted to exit in such a way that people would
not feel abandoned or ripped off. I wanted to thank them, let them
know how much I cared and how much they meant to me. I
wanted to rebalance the scales of give-and-take.[9]

Over the last three decades I have come to understand that
researchers' exits from the field are at least as important as our en-
tries and even harder to accomplish with dignity and grace. We
must never just disappear. I feel strongly that we must anticipate
our departures, announce our plans, express our heartfelt gratitude, and always leave the door open for reconnection. But it is
still true—three decades later—that methodology texts and those
of us teaching research methods courses to our students tend to
focus on the empirical, ethical, and social dilemmas of "gaining
access," and we continue to neglect the equally complex and
treacherous processes of leave-taking.

The exit stories of social scientists engaged in doing fieldwork
also raise the question of voice. How is the informant's voice being
heard, interpreted, and represented by the researcher? Whose story
is this anyway? Who is the creator? Who gets the credit? In exiting
the field, are we stealing people's stories, rifling through their draw-
ers and making off with their valuables, their precious life experiences? Anthropologist Shin Wang wrestles with these ethical and
empirical conundrums of voice and discovers the complex relationship between exiting and good storytelling.

From the time she was very young, Shin Wang wanted to be a teacher,
like her father. She always loved school and excelled in it; she loved
reading and writing and thinking; she loved the competition and

public praise. When school let out in the afternoon, she even loved playing pretend school with her friends. So after she graduated from college, becoming a teacher seemed the only natural path forward, a career choice that she knew would fit her like a glove. She chose to teach in the inner city, at a charter school for brown, black, and poor kids, because she felt most at home working with the kids who needed her the most. And because she had always believed in the inextricable link between education and opportunity in our society, she saw schools as the engines of equality and social justice. Shin Wang had come to this country with her parents from South Korea when she was two years old, and she knew firsthand how important schools were as sites of access, assimilation, and achievement for newcomers.

In the five years that she taught at the charter school, Shin began to recognize the ways in which her students' learning outside the classroom—in their families and communities, on the streets and among their peers, through music and digital media—were often seen as in conflict with or as a distraction from their in-school instruction. And she began to see the ways in which their families were systematically excluded from or at least not welcomed into their children's classrooms. The parents had no idea of what their children were being taught or how to navigate the school bureaucracy; they felt marginalized and powerless in making the school work better for their children. In her efforts to connect with her students and make their education seem real and relevant, Shin became interested in figuring out how to build more productive relationships with their parents, not in a superficial or symbolic way, but in a way that showed her respect for what they knew and might bring to the education of their children. But soon she began to realize her limits as a teacher trying to chart this new ground with families, limits that she believed were both conceptual and pragmatic. She realized that she needed to know more about the broader ecology of education, more about institutional change and relationship building, more about the power dynamics and politics of educational reform.

Shin decided to return to graduate school and enter a doctoral program in the anthropology of education, focusing on the ways in which urban schools in poor neighborhoods can partner with families and communities in an effort to better support the development and achievement of students. Her doctoral dissertation and subsequent research as an assistant professor have given theoretical heft and empirical definition to her study of the ways in which community organizers working with parents—particularly first- and second-generation immigrant parents—can begin to participate in school improvement efforts, the ways in which parents can become engaged and informed actors who can help make schools better places for their children. For the past four years Shin Wang has taken her anthropological research to Via Victoria, a densely populated, mostly poor and working-class Mexican American neighborhood in Denver. She has recently made her "exit from the field," a process of farewells and retreats that has raised many relational and ethical challenges for her.

When I ask Shin how she navigated her exit from Via Victoria, she considers my question for a long time and says tentatively, "You know, I was consciously concerned about entry . . . about whether they would like me, about learning Spanish well enough to communicate with them, about gaining their trust, but I did not put a whole lot of thought into how I would leave." She remembers being nervous about the part of her personality that is "introverted," shy about connecting with lots of people, and the part of her that is "extroverted" and enjoys knowing a few folks deeply and well. In gaining access, she realized that she would have to pass the first difficult hurdle of greeting many—circulating, networking, glad-handing—before she could get to the second, the place of knowing, trust, and intimacy with a few people. Shin's preference—and her gift—she realizes, is building and sustaining relationships, getting to know a few people deeply, learning what is most important and precious to them, all the while doing it "carefully, appreciatively, and respectfully."

I listen to Shin drawing the contrasts between her extroverted and introverted sides, and I feel surprised by the two-sidedness she sees in herself. One of the first—and lasting—impressions I have of her is her wholeness, her completeness, the way she always seems balanced and centered. Part of her balance definitely resides in her body. In her mid-thirties, she has a lean, strong, and graceful body, revealing her three decades of dance training. But her balance also seems to reflect an essential quality of all good researchers. She is a listener—attentive, receptive, nonjudgmental. I look into her face, lovely in its unadorned beauty, and imagine that the quality of her listening and the earnestness of her curiosity must make people feel that they can trust her, that she will keep their stories safe, that she will not leave them without saying goodbye.

From the moment she set foot in Via Victoria, there was some "heaviness" tugging at Shin. "I felt the ominous presence of leaving from my very first trip. As I entered, I struggled with my worries about leaving." Shin never felt the burden of worry with the folks she interviewed just once or twice, the people with whom she never established a deep emotional connection. But she felt very differently about those who shared their "anxieties, fears, frustrations, and stories" with her, who often told her things they had never revealed to anyone else. It was these "close people" whom she worried about leaving from the moment she met them. "A lot of people, the closer I got to them, the more I felt that I did not want to lead them on." Shin can't think of any other way to say it, even though she recognizes that "leading them on" feels like language that belongs with romantic entanglements. "I was entrusted with people's most intimate stories. They were baring their souls to me, and I felt a huge responsibility."

Shin wants to make sure that I recognize that this "heaviness" she carried around right from the beginning was "not guilt." "I was not fooling them. Everyone knew I was not moving to Denver, that I lived in New York, and that my family was there." As a matter of fact, over the four years that she moved in and out of Denver, her exit was designed to be slow, staged, and anticipated. For the first two years, she spent a week of every month at Via Victoria, hanging out in the schools, interviewing and observing the mothers—mostly Mexican immigrants who were being trained as teachers' aides and community liaisons—as well as documenting the work of the community organizers, the leaders and trainers from the local nonprofit. By the third year, Shin was visiting less frequently, narrowing her focus to deeper conversations with fewer people, and by the fourth year everyone knew that she was beginning her retreat.

Shin remembers trying to do "something different and special" in her last conversations with the Via Victoria mothers. She saw their final encounters as "conversations," not interviews, much more informal. The tape recorder was not running; she did not take notes. "I planned them as special events," she recalls, her voice tinged with the sadness she must have felt then. She took them out for coffee or lunch and brought with her an excerpt from one of the hundreds of memos she had written about her observations of them. "I wanted them to know that they had been seen and documented. After all, they had no idea how their individual stories would figure into the narrative that I wrote." I imagine, too, that the experience of being "documented" must have held special meaning for these new arrivals from Mexico—a marker of their presence, their visibility, their significance in this still-foreign place that was becoming their home.

As well as wanting this moment of farewell to mark their documented identity as community workers and advocates for their children, Shin saw it as a moment to "shift the balance a bit." She did not want to leave without sharing more about herself. So for the first time in four years she talked more than they did. "I not only wanted to acknowledge and appreciate them . . . I also wanted to tell them how much I learned from them about being a good person, about becoming a good mother, about becoming a better researcher."

In retrospect, Shin is very glad that she made "such a special deal in these last ritualized, appreciative conversations." Something in her must have suspected that it would be hard to track them down once she left, hard to stay in touch. Her voice is tinged with regret. "I wonder if I had some sense that it might be difficult to stay connected with the mothers after I left. Maybe I realized that they would probably not be there when I returned." These were families in transition, she explains, vulnerable and fragile, who struggle mightily to hold it all together. As it turned out, Shin's premonitions held true. When she said goodbye to them, for most it was a final separation. They did disappear. Some moved out of the neighborhood; their phones were disconnected; there were no forwarding addresses that she could find to track them down. Not being able to "follow up with them" felt like a huge loss; it made her feel as if she'd let them down in some way. Her mind lingers over the question: Should she have looked harder for them?

The same was not true, however, for the staff of community organizers and trainers who remained in place and continued to be in touch with Shin after she left—often telephoning, e-mailing, and texting her several times a week; catching her up on what was happening in the "hood"; alerting her about the important events, the births, deaths, and arrests; and occasionally seeking her counsel and guidance on matters personal and professional. When she finished writing up her research, she remembers feeling both thrilled and deeply anxious as she shared the first draft with Blanca, the lead organizer, and waited for her response. "Opening up my manuscript to her was like offering her the chance to look inside of me," says Shin about the surprisingly intimate feeling of "really being known" and the lovely sensation of trusting that Blanca would never take advantage of "this shift in roles from observer to being observed." But even more striking than the new closeness Shin felt for Blanca was the recognition that the work was not hers alone. She may have been the chronicler, she may have written the manuscript, but the recorded lives and voices represented a collective, communal effort. Shin almost whispers this discovery. "In that moment, I realized that this was not purely my project; this was her story too. I really grew to understand that she cared as much about this work as I did . . . and I understood this only after I had exited the scene."

As Shin recalls the final conversations with the Mexican mothers and the continuing relationships with the community organizers, she realizes that the exits in each case were navigated very differently. "I now recognize that there were two treatments of exit. With the families whose lives were so full of transition and upheaval, they were lost to me and I to them after I left," she says, still seeming to struggle with the "forever loss." "With the organizers, there is no sense of wrapping it all up. When I go to Denver the next time, I know exactly where to find Patricia or Maria or Sophia, and I know I will walk in the door and they will greet me with huge hugs!" With both "exit treatments," however, Shin sees the strength and intimacy of the bond defining the exit. It surprises her that the exits—in both cases—"felt so personal, so wrapped up in connection." "I now," she muses out loud, "think of exit as relationship."

When Shin anticipated making her entry into Via Victoria, she worried not only about the part of her that feels "introverted" and finds it difficult to meet and greet scores of people, but also about the distance between her life and theirs. "Here I am," she says, "a middle-class Asian American academic and researcher, flying in from New York, very worried about my proficiency in Spanish . . . and there they are, poor Mexican mothers, new to this country, many speaking only Spanish, skeptical, I'm sure, about what re-searchers do, and having no real reason to trust me." As it turned out, they did share something very important; she and they were mothers. But they did wonder about her. If Shin was such a good mother, why in the world would she leave her one-and-a-half-year-old daughter behind in New York and come to Denver to be with them? It seemed a curious choice.

Even though "on the face of it," Shin was "very different from them in so many ways," she probably worried most about her "cobbled-together Spanish"—a literal barrier to communication and the perfect metaphor for all the potential problems they might have bridging the cultural chasm and understanding each other. As it turned out, Shin's stumbling Spanish seemed to invite empa-thy from the mothers, who were very patient and solicitous, reach-ing out to help her with her fractured sentences. "By virtue of me trying so hard, my effort and vulnerability provided a point of connection with them."

And although Shin left her young daughter at home, she was able to tell them that her baby was being very well cared for by her husband and her mother, who traveled to New York from her home in Pittsburgh and moved into their apartment every time Shin traveled to Denver. In fact, the grandmother's "taking over the child raising" seemed familiar and comfortable to the Mexican mothers; they experienced the same kind of closeness and devo-tion with their own mothers. As a mother and as a daughter of her child's grandmother, Shin soon forged deep bonds with them; they began sharing their stories and confidences with her, revealing their failures and successes, and, each time she traveled back to New York, sending kisses home to plant on her baby's cheek.

But the place where the connections seemed the deepest and most natural was in their shared history as immigrants. Shin re-calls how hard it was for her family—she was two, and her brother was born soon after they arrived—when they immigrated to the

United States. Her memories of her first days in kindergarten are the most vivid. "I remember my first painful experiences of public school in Pittsburgh," Shin says, drawing the connections with the Denver mothers. "I remember my parents struggling to speak English, and the ways in which my teachers did not understand, appreciate, or respect them. My parents also had a hard time making ends meet. They struggled to put food on our table. My father had been a politician in South Korea, and when he came here, he had to sweep the floors at restaurants and clean the pots in the kitchen to make a living." Her eyes are moist with the memory of how hard it was and how painful it was to see her parents—well educated and dignified—reduced by the disrespect of the people who were so unwelcoming. "The Mexicans in Via Victoria tell similar stories . . . of being teachers and professionals in Mexico and having to work in some plastic factory in Denver."

But with all the connections Shin had with the Mexican mothers, and all the ways Via Victoria began to feel welcoming and familiar, for the four years that Shin was there, she always felt that she "was leaving somebody." "Even though I was a mother and an immigrant," says Shin, "I came there to go to work, and then I would leave. All along, my identity was shaped by the expectation that I'd be going back to my home, to my city, to my family. I think my anxiety about exiting was much more pronounced in me than it was in them . . . and of course, leaving my family behind was very hard for me." She sums up the chronic heaviness about which she was rarely aware until we began talking about it together. "Most of my research journey turned into leaving relationships, and it all had a very personal and emotional dimension about it."

The "feeling undercurrent" reminds her of the ways in which we "as a culture don't tend to acknowledge the deep connections we have, nor do we honor the difficulties of leaving." She shakes her head, thinking about the rushed tempo of her life, her friends in their thirties and forties whom she rarely gets to see because they are all so programmed and busy—young, ambitious professionals still very much on the make, "wrapped up in the logistical details that keep us running." From her point of view, the ambition, the busyness, the striving keep them from offering support to one another, developing nourishing relationships, and building a sense of community. "We are people," she says passionately, "who need and thrive on connection." Even in a culture that does not appreciate "deep connections," and even living among friends and colleagues who rush through their overscheduled lives, Shin has tried to hold fast to her belief in the power of human connection. "I am," she says softly, "careful and intentional about the relationships in my life."

The "intentionality of connection" reminds Shin of her husband, Willard, an oncologist, who studies and treats patients with cancers (including sarcoma and chordoma) that originate from bone and connective tissues in the body and helps his very sick patients plan for how they will live out their final weeks. Many of them, says Shin, have an eerie sense of the end. "They've aggressively tried to treat the disease, it has gone into remission for a while, and they have a last chance at life. Then the disease slips back . . . and there is a quiet acceptance that the end is near." Tears well up in Shin's eyes as she talks about witnessing the "beauty and passion" in Willard's connections to his patients and how he helps them prepare for their final exit. "I live with a husband who deals with death regularly. As a physician, he has a healthy, honest view of dying. For a lot of oncologists, death is not something they want to deal with. At the end, they focus on giving the most aggressive treatments, hanging on, engaged in a frenzy to prolong life. Willard believes that there should be a certain intentionality and care about how you leave this life. He helps patients grapple with the closing chapter. They've got to do it on their own terms."

Now Shin is weeping, letting the tears roll down her face. Her husband's ability to travel the final road with his patients, always following their lead, is rooted in his "deep connection" to his patients. When he first started treating cancer patients seven years ago, Shin assumed that he would be able to sustain himself and serve his patients only if he kept some "professional distance" from them, some clearly drawn boundaries, a practiced objectivity. But now she realizes that she was wrong. In fact, Willard is able to do the work because he "is emotionally connected to his patients." His close connection to them nourishes him. And he is not afraid to stick with them and stand by their side until the very end. "He considers the end full of meaning and choice and willfulness . . . respect and dignity, and he is in there with his patients, watching their backs, listening to their yearnings, advocating for them."

Just last week Shin heard Willard screaming into the kitchen telephone late into the night ("The only time he gets furious is when he feels a patient is not getting good care. Then he's a man on fire!"), trying to convince Delta Air Lines to let one of his patients fly home to Puerto Rico so she could die in the arms of her family. This was where she wanted to spend the last moments of her life. "During her long, painful treatment in New York, she had lost a couple of limbs, her body was badly disfigured . . . and Willard is on the phone with the airlines, spending a ridiculous amount of time, first reasoning with them, then begging them, then screaming as if his life depended on it. Please let her fly . . . we will send a doctor and nurse with her." He finally was successful in convincing them, a small victory in a long day packed with sadness and grief. The woman died the day after she arrived home, surrounded by her family.

The intentionality of Willard's helping his patients design the closing chapter of their lives contrasts sharply with Shin's memory of her father's death a year ago, when "one fine day, he suddenly collapsed" while he was teaching, and he was pronounced dead after being rushed by ambulance to the hospital. He had left home that morning looking fit and healthy. Shin and Willard just happened to be visiting their folks in Pittsburgh because her grandmother was very sick and in the hospital, and they had driven down to say their last goodbyes. Shin had even packed a black dress just in case she had to attend her grandmother's funeral. When the call came from Shin's aunt—saying that her father had fallen down at work—they rushed over to the hospital. Her tears return as Shin relives the terrifying moment. "This is the kind of exit you can't prepare for. It is so sudden. The day before, he was healthy and doing well."

But even in the case of a sudden and unexpected death, says Shin, "the moment of exit is profoundly shaped by what happens before it." She is able to tolerate the loss—although she misses him every day—because theirs was a relationship that was loving and deeply satisfying. "My father leaving this earth is very much about my relationship to him. If I had lost him and our relationship had been unresolved, difficult, and painful, I would still be consumed by regrets and anguish. But as my life has unfolded, it is very much the life my father wanted for me. Perhaps he wasn't thrilled when I decided to become a teacher, because he worried about the low status of teachers in this country. But then he saw me teaching, saw how good I was at it, and his mind was completely changed. He admired, adored, and approved of me."

Even though the goodness and completeness of Shin's relationship with her father has allowed her to mourn and move on, still feeling the support of his uncomplicated adoration, she rails at the idea of exits ever being clear and simple. Whether we are talking about leaving "the field" after finishing the data collection on a research project; whether we are witnessing the compassionate and intentional work of an oncologist helping his patients choose how they will live their last hours; or whether we are faced with the loss of a loved one who has suddenly dropped dead—from Shin's point of view the exits are "messy" and complex. Her voice is as passionate as I have heard it as she challenges the "black-and-white" version of exits. "I have trouble with the traditional ways we characterize *exit* in this culture. It makes it seem so concrete, so tangible, so open-and-shut. But exits are actually very messy. There is no instruction manual. It is not like an exit sign on the highway, where it assumes that you have a clear idea of where you are going, are looking at a map, have a route you are following, and can see the right exit and get off the road. And it is not like an exit above the door of a building, where you neatly file out under the neon sign. It is so much more complicated in reality, so much more messy because it involves people's life stories. In this culture we are always so tempted to see things simply . . . but they are not simple." Shin seems surprised by the passion that has risen in her voice. She sums up her feelings in a joyful flourish. "I'm mesmerized by the complexity."

Exits on highways and exit signs above the doors of buildings are not useful ways of describing a process that is often fumbling and awkward, uncertain and ambiguous. Shin muses about a metaphor that might more accurately reflect her views and her temperament, and she says finally, wistfully, "I think of exit as a new beginning." "Instead of the idea that you are closing a chapter . . . instead of the idea that you live life facing backward, looking behind you to see what you are leaving—I do not think of exits as the end. As human beings, we are creatures of the moment and tomorrow. Our life is always changing and evolving. We are moving forward, focused on the future." She admits to being a "planner," someone whose style is not to be preoccupied with the past, but rather to gain energy and momentum by anticipating and designing a future.

Yet it is more than her temperamental inclination to face toward the future that makes her see exits as new beginnings. Since exits are "about relationships," and since relationships can live on in you even if someone departs or dies, then exits can certainly usher in new beginnings. Shin seems to be surrounded by the good ghosts of her father as she offers a closing reminiscence—a final prayer—about how he lives on in her. "Today, I see my father in

my son. I see him when I look in the mirror and see him in the
way I am growing older, the lines and contours on my face . . .
There are so many ways he is still alive in me. He stays with me
always and helps me chart the new beginnings."

Shin Wang, like Theresa Russo, sees exits as "messy." The metaphor of exit signs on highways—where you follow the map and
know where you are going—does not adequately reflect "human
exits," which are so much more complicated because they "involve
people's life stories." But unlike Theresa, Shin does not find the
messiness of exits painful or unmooring. Rather, she embraces,
even relishes the surprises, the ambiguities, the fuzzy boundaries.
The messiness, she believes, reflects the embeddedness of exits in
every relationship. At one point she says sharply, "Exit is relationship." And she vividly remembers the "heaviness" she felt when
she first met the Mexican mothers in Via Victoria, the "ominous
presence of leaving" that consumed her from the moment she arrived there. From the very beginning she felt the responsibility of
exiting in a way that was honoring and respectful of the people
whose stories she was gathering. More than anything, she did not
want to "lead them on."

As she reflects on the best way of navigating through the
messy terrain of exit in her work as an anthropologist, Shin sees
inspiration and guidance in the way her husband, Willard, cares
for his patients in their dying days. He believes that "there should
be a certain intentionality and care about how you leave this life."
As his patients make their final exits, he lets them lead; he finds
out what they need and want; he begs the airlines to let them fly
home to die surrounded by their families. It is this "intentionality
and care" Shin wants to mimic as she designs special occasions
and rituals in her farewell conversations with the mothers in Via
Victoria. She also notices that Willard seems to draw clarity and

strength from the deep bonds he develops with his patients, who he knows, from the moment he meets them, will likely die in his care. He is able to sustain his energy and devotion as a doctor not by erecting professional barriers between himself and his patients, not by objectifying and distancing them, but by entering into "authentic relationships" with them. He too welcomes the messiness of intimacy. For him, "doing no harm" means exiting with care.

Finally, there is another part of leaving honorably that Shin discovers as she tells me about the rituals that shaped her exit from Via Victoria. The special occasions she designed at the end gave her the chance to let folks know how much she admired and respected them and how much she valued their contribution to the work. But even more important was her realization that she needed to shift the balance of give-and-take between herself and her "subjects." In her final conversations with them, she was not just the listener, hiding behind the mask of receptivity, soaking up their stories. This became the moment to let them hear her voice. She became the storyteller, revealing more about her own life, letting them know how much living in the midst of them had changed so much in her.

Months later, when she let one of her key informants review what she had written, she was amazed at how "opening up the manuscript to her was like offering her the chance to look inside of me." She had—for the first time—the surprising and welcome feeling of really being known. At the moment of exit, the tables were turned; the observer became the observed. But even more striking was Shin Wang's realization that the manuscript was not hers alone. It belonged to both of them. This was their shared story, a duet of voices and care.

Three

FREEDOM

Jean-Paul Sartre's *No Exit*[1] was first performed in a theater in Paris in 1944. It is a one-act play with four characters and is forty-seven pages in length. It presents a version of hell—a place from which it is impossible to exit, a place that is surprisingly banal, and a place of interminable suffering through the torture of self-reflection and the toxic relations among human beings.

When I first read *No Exit* in a college philosophy course forty years ago, I found it beautiful and terrifying, searing, haunting. I couldn't stop imagining the agony of people forever imprisoned, ravaged by their dark histories, their malevolent deeds, their guilt and shame, their inaction. In my most recent reading of the play, I see even more clearly how Sartre captures the hellish opposite of freedom. We are free when we are able to exit from those forces and circumstances—the people, relationships, institutions, countries, ideologies, religions, ourselves—that hold us down or back, that hurt and oppress us, that limit and lie to us. Sartre helps us understand the powerful and productive forces that propel leave-taking—the lifesaving and life-giving meanings of exit.

For those of you who have not read—or recently reread—this short and towering play, let me draw the scene and briefly summarize the plot, a prelude to this chapter's narrative of a young boy who was mercilessly bullied and tortured by his peers in school. After years of numbing abuse, humiliation, and heartbreak, he found the door out of the hellish place where he and his family had been held as prisoners. He discovered the exit that would set him free.

The three condemned souls in Sartre's play are a man named Garcin and two women, Inez and Estelle. The fourth character, the valet, appears at the beginning of the play. The action takes place in a room furnished in the Second Empire style. The valet ushers in three characters, Garcin first. Through Garcin's questions to the valet, we learn several interesting features of this hell. The room contains no mirrors, no reflective surfaces at all. There are no instruments of torture. There is no sleep, no dreams, and no blinking. Garcin comes to understand the horror:

> Your eyelids. We move ours up and down. Blinking, we call it. It's like a small shutter that clicks down and makes a break. Everything goes black; one's eyes are moistened. You can't imagine how restful, how refreshing it is. Four thousand little rests per hour. So that's the idea. I'm to live without eyelids. No eyelids, no sleep; it follows, doesn't it? I shall never sleep again. But then—how shall I endure my own company?[2]

Also, you cannot turn off the lights in the room, there are no windows, and there is a bell that rings but is not guaranteed to bring the valet. A penknife, a heavy bronze ornament, and three couches complete the description of the room.

Inez and Estelle are next to be brought into the room/hell, and the play's momentum and action are carried by the conversation among the three characters. They first share their manner of death—Estelle by pneumonia, Inez by a gas stove, and Garcin by twelve bullets in his chest. As they begin to wonder why they were placed in this room together, it is Inez who puts forth the idea that they themselves will carry out the torture that is their punishment:

> We'll stay in this room together, the three of us, for ever and ever . . . and no one else will come here. In short, there's someone absent here, the official torturer. It is obvious what they are after—an economy of man-power, or devil power, if you prefer. The same idea as in the cafeteria, where customers serve themselves. Each of us will act as the torturer of the other two.[3]

They make a pact to "look into themselves, to never raise their heads"[4] and thereby avoid harming one another. However, it is not long before they are drawn back to each other. Estelle wants to apply her lipstick and needs a mirror. Inez offers to be her mirror and expresses her attraction to Estelle. When Estelle rebuffs her, Inez points to an ugly spot on her face. Estelle seeks refuge from Inez with Garcin, who is busily ignoring the two of them, seeing their drama and incessant bickering as part of his punishment. In despair, he acknowledges that the three of them were less than honest, that they did not disclose the reasons they were deserving of hell.

By turns, we learn of the sins of their lives. Garcin was a deserter, refusing to fight with the army by claiming to be a pacifist. When he tried to escape to Mexico, he was captured and executed. Estelle, married to a rich and much older man, had an affair that produced a child. She drowned her baby and returned to her wealthy husband; her lover shot himself in the face. Inez drove her husband to despair by having an affair with his female cousin.

Garcin then proposes that they help each other. But that fails too. He asks Inez for pity and sympathy, which she refuses to give him. Estelle asks Garcin for attention and affection; he in turn rebuffs her. With the voices of the living clamoring in his head, proclaiming him a coward, he asks Estelle for her trust in exchange for his love. Estelle is not capable of faith and trust; neither is she capable of receiving Inez's attention without disgust. Garcin exclaims, "There's no need for red-hot pokers. Hell is other people."

As the reality of their situation becomes more and more horrible, Garcin flings himself upon a locked door, which suddenly flies open. As they peer into the dark hallway and argue about who should go, none of the three leave the room. They shut the door themselves. Rage mixes with sorrow as Garcin says that he died too soon, that he wasn't allowed time to finish his life's deeds. Inez cuts that line of thinking short: "One always dies too soon—or too late. And yet, one's whole life is complete at that moment, with a line drawn neatly under it, ready for the summing up. You are—your life, and nothing else."[5]

Spare, ironic, and thought provoking, Sartre's play presents hell as a place or condition from which exit is impossible. It pointedly suggests that just as we take living for granted, we take the ability to exit for granted. We live knowing full well that we could leave, change, be different, do something else, start anew. But having this potential does not mean that we use it; in fact, many of us do not. Like Garcin, who cries that he died too soon, we live in the comfort of being able to change without making the change. Exit, in this scenario, symbolizes potentiality, possibility, movement, freedom, life itself.

For Ehsan Kermanian, going to school and facing his tormentors every day is like being sent to Sartre's room without mirrors or dreams. For several years, there seems to be no exit from the hell of abuse and humiliation he is subjected to, no light in the scary darkness, no path to freedom. The assaults from his bully classmates begin to define him; he becomes imprisoned in their view of him; he blames himself for his own victimization; he absorbs their blows to his body and spirit. The story of Ehsan's entrapment and his fight for freedom are told by his mother, Neda, who, in her fierce protectiveness and advocacy for her son, struggles—courageously and desperately—to do the right thing, the loving thing.

A FRAGILE FREEDOM

"I've used up all I've got. There is no more."

It started right away, the bullying and harassment. Neda begins the story by asking the question that has haunted her for the last seven years, the question that always causes her so much pain and guilt. "Why didn't I see the signs?" she asks, her eyes misting over. "Why did we hang in for as long as we did?" Actually, Neda can't remember a time when school was safe for Ehsan, not one day that was peaceful and joyful. She remembers him coming home with a sad face the day he started kindergarten. She remembers his stories about how the kids were teasing him and making him do things he didn't want to do. He told her that the scary kids would make him be "a soldier" and order him to hit or kick another child. At first Neda asked him in disbelief why he would do such things. This was not the sweet and reticent boy she knew; she had never seen him do anything the slightest bit hurtful or cruel to anyone. He was not a fighter; he didn't have it in him. But he told her that the kids threatened him if he didn't do what they ordered him to do, that he was afraid.

The Kermanians had moved to Waverly when Neda was pregnant with Ehsan. For months they had looked for a house they could afford in a suburban community with a reputation for good schools and high-achieving students. In fact, they had almost closed on a house they loved in Brookhaven when the Realtor—seeing their brown skin and suspecting that they were Iranian—refused to accept their larger-than-usual down payment. He claimed that the certified check must have come from suspicious origins. How could people who looked like they did have that kind of money? And if they did, the Kermanians certainly could not have gotten it lawfully. Neda explains that Iranians often save up for large down payments on their homes—it's "a cultural thing"—wanting to be assured that they will be able to afford the mortgage payments later on.

Neda and her husband, Toraj, knew that the Brookhaven Realtor's response to them was racist and that they might well have been able to sue him for housing discrimination. But frankly, they did not want to spend the time or money to bring him down (even though he had been stupid enough to record his "suspicions" in a letter to them), and besides, they did not want to live in a lily-white neighborhood where they were unwelcome. So Waverly was actually their second choice, another largely white, well-educated, middle- to upper-middle-class Connecticut community also known for its fine schools and its record of getting students into elite colleges and universities. Five years later, when Ehsan was entering kindergarten—in the place they had chosen because they wanted their children to have an excellent education, where they hoped to live out the American Dream—everything seemed to turn sour. Their son, Ehsan, who could barely wait to be old enough to go to "real school"—so enamored was he with books and learning—was returning home each day with terror in his eyes, afraid to speak of his torture.

A few weeks after the opening of school, when Neda could no longer bear to hear Ehsan's scary stories or see his bruised spirits, she made her first trip to the school and spoke to the principal about what was happening to her son. She told him that the five-and six-year-old bullies in his class called themselves "a team" (she always thought of them as "gangs"; they were horrible "little punks"), and they had leaders and soldiers, special handshakes, rules and routines, and tactics of torture and exclusion. The "team" seemed highly organized and very scary. The principal, dubious that these young children were even capable of such mean offenses, nevertheless gave her a hearing, asked a few guarded questions, and, before she departed, came up with what he saw as a "solution."

The next morning, he made a big announcement at an all-school assembly that there would—henceforth—be no more "teams." Neda, of course, knew immediately that the principal's facile prohibition wouldn't solve anything. The "problem was not the word 'team'"; the problem was that there were some violent little kids in her son's class who picked on the weaker ones. The problem was that the adults in the school were not adequately supervising the children; they were not intervening to protect the vulnerable ones; they were doing nothing to stop the threats and the bullying. The worst place, of course, was the playground, where there was no teacher supervision. The teacher aides were supposed to be in charge, but they stood up against the wall, talking to one another, ignoring the kids. No one was watching or taking any responsibility. And when Neda inquired about who was in charge during recess, "everyone just passed the buck."

As everyone at the school kept dismissing their concerns and complaints, at home, Neda and Toraj had long conversations with their son, trying to offer him support and reassurance. They would cheer him on. "We are your team. We are with you, Ehsan." Almost every morning before he marched off to school, Neda would whisper in his ear, "Just look behind you, and I'll always be there." To which he began to respond, more desperately each day, "I look back, but you're not there." Their counsel and love were not nearly enough to protect him; there was no shielding him from the "bad kids."

Neda shakes her head, as if she is trying to chase away the memories of the ways her precious son was selected as the victim, "partly because of his personality and partly because he is brown and Iranian." It is harder for her to name the individual qualities of Ehsan that might have "brought on the bullying" than it is for her to identify the currents of racism and xenophobia that surely had a part in his victimization. Her voice is sad and tentative. She is searching for a way to give an honest appraisal of "how Ehsan might appear to his peers," but she does not want to be disloyal to him. "Ehsan is a follower, very fragile and not assertive. Anyone who would see him would guess that he is studious, bookish, very earnest. He's not a boy's boy who is strong and athletic, not tough and aggressive. Maybe there is something in the way he moves through the world that announces his openness, his vulnerability . . . He broke his leg in the first grade, and he still walks with a bit of a limp. After he broke his leg, I didn't take him to physical therapy, so he never walked quite right again. That's a source of huge guilt for me." Her face is stained with tears as she looks back on a moment when she might have helped him make a stronger comeback—a mother's guilt and self-incrimination seared into her memory.

But even though she is able to admit Ehsan's fragility and the ways he might have made himself an easy target for the bullies, Neda is confident that "a big piece" of the abuse was rooted in racism, prejudices passed down from parents to their children, and the harsh echoes from the post-9/11 fears that swept through the community. Neda's voice is hard and angry as she recalls the "virulent brand of racism" they have suffered as a family living in "lily-white Waverly" and the ways in which Ehsan has absorbed the worst blows. "Some of the racism here comes out of sheer ignorance and lack of sophistication. When we moved into Waverly, the woman across the street said to me 'Oh, it's so exciting you are here . . . we love ethnic food, so long as it's clean.' Mr. Howard, a few doors down, came up to my husband as he was watering the lawn and said, 'What are you, Indian or Pakistani?' Toraj told him we were Iranian, and he actually jumped back with a kind of panicked look on his face, as if terrorists might have moved onto the block. Things have settled down some, and some of these folks have become good neighbors, but there are still undercurrents of fear. At school, Ehsan got the brunt of it. You know, I think that if there were black kids who were getting treated like this at school, no one would have put up with it, but there is tolerance for assuming Iranians might be terrorists—a tolerance for their making my son into a violent soldier so that he will fit their stereotype of him. It's horrible!"

Neda's whole body is shaking and her fists are clenched as she recalls "the awful coming together" of Ehsan's personal qualities—"how he moves through the world"—and the "virulent racism" in the town. She hates that those same qualities she loves so much in him—his studiousness, his earnestness, his empathy, even his softness—are the very ones that seem to invite the bullies' torture. And she hates the fact that it is so hard to identify the roots of abuse, so hard to actually figure out why a child—any child—might become the chosen target. It is complicated and painful to unravel the sources of victimization.

She thinks, for example, of a boy in Ehsan's class who is from Sri Lanka, whose skin is much darker than Ehsan's, and who turns out to be "one of the top bullies." "He knew," says Neda bitterly, "that in this all-white class (actually there is one Asian girl), if he didn't join in the bullying, he would be next." And closer to home, Neda notices the contrasting experiences of her two children, both brown and Iranian. Sadaf, Ehsan's younger sister, has always "fit in and thrived" in school; the "world is her oyster." In fact, ever since she entered school, Sadaf has enjoyed popularity among her peers, who seem to respond to "her exuberance, her fairness, and her strength." Whatever the complex causes of abuse are, whoever initiates it, however it happens and gets sustained, Neda knows one thing: it is bad and wrong, and no one deserves to be bullied.

By the time Ehsan reached the second grade, he had learned that "you don't snitch." The awful stories of being terrorized seemed to disappear, and "everything went subterranean." Although in retrospect it is clear that his sullen silence was hiding the ongoing abuse, Neda and Toraj hoped desperately that things had changed at school. They greeted his silence as good news, or at least as evidence of his toughening up, his developing survival skills. Without the everyday evidence of torture, second grade seemed relatively uneventful—except for some troublesome reports from his teacher, who complained that Ehsan was "getting stuck on stuff," that he was unable to complete his assignments in class and move on to the next thing. He would "analyze things to death." But even the teacher's worries did not upset Neda that much; she admits she also is a bit "obsessive," also someone who "analyzes things to death." Maybe these were qualities in Ehsan that he simply inherited from her.

But by the third grade, Ehsan's teacher was suggesting that he was not merely getting "stuck"; she claimed that he was "falling further and further behind cognitively." This description of Ehsan—as cognitively impaired—did not at all square with his parents' view of him. "How could that be?" they asked his teacher. "At home he speaks and reads Farsi as well as English fluently. He devours his science books, asks great questions. He plays the piano and practices diligently . . . He seems to have a really good mind." But the teacher persisted, offering enough "evidence" to prove her point and raise doubts in the minds of Neda and Toraj. She insisted on signing him up for a battery of special education assessments before sending him on to fourth grade.

When Neda consulted with family, friends, and colleagues who had known Ehsan over the years, they all—each and every one of them—expressed suspicion at the way he was being seen, labeled, and pigeonholed by his teacher. They urged Neda to resist and refuse to follow the teacher's wrongheaded prescriptions. They begged her not to let her child endure what they were sure were racist insinuations. But her desire to prove the teacher wrong got tangled up with her own real worries about her son's struggles and caused Neda to agree to the teacher's plan for an evaluation.

Fortunately, the results of the special education assessment, scheduled for the beginning of the next school year, arrived at the same time as Ehsan's scores on the fourth-grade Connecticut state exams, on which he received a "remarkably high score" that put him well beyond most of his peers in academic preparedness. And when Neda and Toraj met with the school counselor, social worker, psychologist, and neurologist—the diagnostic team that had tested Ehsan as part of the special education assessment—each of them talked about his intelligence and thoughtfulness, his eagerness to please, and his capacity to engage in relational conversations. They could see no evidence of a cognitive deficit.

They did report, however, that he was being compromised by a hostile educational environment, by his fears for his own safety, by his isolation and ostracism in school. Ehsan's fourth-grade teacher, who liked and admired Ehsan from the start and could see that he was both very bright and very vulnerable, designated herself as his "big protector," an assignment that she took seriously. Neda remembers her fondly. "Mrs. Rhodes was a large, plump woman, a protective figure who took him under her wing," she says appreciatively. When the other children went out for recess, Mrs. Rhodes would have Ehsan stay inside with her to help with classroom chores. She was careful not to assign him a seat close to one of the known bullies. She had eyes in the back of her head, always alert to the subtle, covert signs of threat and harassment in her classroom.

As Neda tells the long, painful saga, there are moments that stand out as pointed and powerful, moments when she felt as if someone were kicking her in the stomach. One such moment happened right before returning to the United States after spending the summer in Iran, just before Ehsan's fourth-grade year. Every summer, the Kermanians visited Iran, the place where Ehsan always seemed happiest, where he loved hanging out with his cousins, who treated him like some kind of "rock star" because he lived in America, the country they thought of as the promised land. As they were packing their bags to come home, Neda remembers Ehsan saying out of the blue, "I don't have any friends." His face—which had been animated and smiling the whole time they were in Iran—turned sad and sullen. She asked, "Who do you play with at recess?" "No one," he responded. "How about lunchtime?" "Ricky won't let anyone sit with me at lunch." Ricky was the ringleader who had bullied Ehsan since kindergarten, a big, scary figure who ruled all the other kids, whose threats had for four years defined and limited Ehsan's life at school.

Ricky was the boss of everyone, even Jessica, a popular Chinese American girl who often did his bidding and was the first to confront Ehsan when he returned from Iran. One day at recess she got up in his face and said provocatively, "China is the best country in the world." To which Ehsan responded with as much strength as he could muster, "No, Iran is the best country in the world." "Iran," said Jessica, "is where all the terrorists come from!" Ehsan slunk back from her, but when he got home, he told Neda that he wanted her to "take action." This felt like such a deep insult to him, so stupid and mean and untrue.

The next day, Neda took herself to school and found Jessica and her mother standing just outside the front door. Seeing Neda striding toward them, Jessica's mother (one of the "in moms" in town) urged her daughter to go inside. "Go along, my darling," she said gently, pushing her daughter toward the door. But Neda insisted that Jessica stay; she wanted to talk to both of them. She made the little girl repeat what she had said to Ehsan about Iran being the place where all the terrorists lived. And when Jessica's mother asked her daughter why in the world she would say such a thing, the girl responded immediately, "Because that's what you tell us at home." There was nothing her mother could say; she had been "outed" by her daughter.

After hearing the story, Mrs. Rhodes sat down and talked with both children and afterward made Jessica write an essay on Iran, a seven-page paper on the country's rich and long history. "For Ehsan," remembers Neda, "it didn't take away the hurt, but it felt like some small redemption." But the exchange caused Mrs. Rhodes to worry. Maybe the bullying might be avoided if Ehsan would stop wearing his cultural identity on his sleeve; maybe he was being the provocateur. If he would just stop boasting about Iran to his classmates, they might stop teasing him. "She was trying to be helpful," says Neda. "But in this post-9/11 environment, where everyone saw us as the dangerous enemy, there was no way Ehsan could avoid their prejudice . . . and besides, he is very proud of his country!"

Soon after the Jessica incident—just when Neda was beginning to hope that things were settling down at school—she was drying Ehsan's head with a towel after he had taken his evening shower, and she discovered several bumps and lesions. "Ricky pushed me on the playground," he responded when she pressed him about what had happened. "But I don't want any trouble. He's done it many times before," Ehsan mumbled. Neda stayed quiet, but she was shaking, and her stomach was in knots. "That was the biggest mistake I've ever made," she confesses about her silence and inaction at that moment. Because the brutality didn't stop as Ricky and his "team" continued to beat up on her son.

One day, when she couldn't hold her tongue any longer, Neda approached Ricky at school and tried to find a tone that was both casual and threatening. "Hey, Ricky, cool it on the playground. Ehsan's coming home with bruises." That night, just as they were sitting down for dinner, the phone rang, and when she answered it, Neda heard Ricky's mother raging at her. "Don't you ever speak to my child like that again!" she screamed. Ricky's mother, a big-time lawyer, refused to believe that her son was bullying; and she wanted Neda to back off and leave him alone. There was no apology, no effort to understand or empathize. No remorse. "After that," says Neda, weeping, "the thing began to crescendo, and I began to realize the huge role that the mothers were playing in this harassment.

It was the mothers who were promoting this at home." Just as their children were ostracizing her son, so too were those mothers beating up on Neda. Her voice is almost shrieking at the double injustice. "I am not one of those kiss-ass moms. They resented me. When I would approach them, they would stop talking and just stare at me, as if they were hiding something."

I look across the table at Neda—a beautiful, graceful woman, with ringlets of cascading black hair framing her face and fine features that reveal every emotion—and wonder why the "kiss-ass" mothers hate her so much. Is it her brown skin, her mother country, her steely strength, or even her effortless grace that gets stuck in their craw? Or is it their fierce protection of their children, who have inherited their parents' prejudices, whose guilt they are determined to hide? Whatever their motivations, Neda has the clear sense that the bullying begins—and is condoned—at home. And these mothers are power brokers in Waverly, not only in the way they band together and protect their children but also in the way they influence and control the teachers and principal at school, who do not want to get on their wrong side.

By the time Ehsan reached fifth grade, it was obvious to everyone that he was suffering; the abuse had turned inward. In class he would often be seen staring vacantly into the distance, rocking back and forth in his chair, or holding his pencil in his tight fist until it splintered under the pressure. He was anxious all the time and developed lots of nervous tics that became the focus of further teasing. At home he engaged in obsessive rituals around food and eating, washing up, and cleaning his room. Neda and Toraj found a child psychiatrist for him to see, and Ehsan had regular appointments with the school counselor. They went into crisis mode, seeking support, searching for answers, plotting interventions. Their efforts to help sometimes brought out conflicts among them as they tried to figure out the most protective strategies of defense for Ehsan. The psychiatrist, school counselor, and to some extent Toraj thought that Ehsan needed to develop a thicker skin, a tougher stance; he needed to learn how to fight back. They suggested karate lessons; they used role-playing to help him learn quick, automatic responses to the attacks. Neda, on the other hand, hated the thought of violence, even if it was for the purpose of scaring the bullies away. And she believed that training Ehsan to be more aggressive would certainly backfire. He didn't have a fighting bone in his body, and his abusers would surely see through his brittle armor.

As they all searched for some way to "fix" the situation and watched Ehsan spiral into despair, Neda felt more and more helpless—a helplessness that soon turned into rage, which finally got unleashed. She speaks in the present tense, as if she is still in the midst of the pitched battle. "Now I am really angry. In America, if you show passion, they call you a crazy woman. All along, I had been trying to hold it in, appear calm and collected, stay focused . . . but now I was ranting and screaming." When Ehsan's class was preparing to take a weekend nature expedition at a camping site a couple of hours away from Waverly, Neda put "everyone on alert." She insisted that the teachers and parents, who were accompanying the children, let her know what their plan was for constant and vigilant supervision. Her voice was threatening. Her "teeth were bared" in her fierce lioness protection of her boy. The whole time they were away, she worried, tossed and turned in her sleep, and woke up screaming from her horrible nightmares.

Another unforgettable moment sticks in Neda's mind as a "turning point." Soon after the class returned from the camping trip, she went up to the school to pick up both of her children. The kids were outside in the back field, and as she turned the corner around the school, she could see far across the field—Ehsan in the center of a circle of taunting children, swinging his backpack, trying to protect himself from their threatening advances. She could hear the nasty singsong in their voices: "Ehsan where's your gun? Don't you terrorists have guns? Shoot us if you want to . . . Kill,

kill, kill." Then she saw her daughter running toward the school, screaming as she tried to get some teachers to come out and help. Neda tore across the field, yelling at the top of her lungs. The bullies scattered when they saw her coming.

But this time she could clearly see the "escalation of things"; this time she knew it was "the beginning of the end." "I saw this as the beginning of physical violence against both of my kids," she says, her voice hard and angry. "This time Sadaf was being pulled in as she tried to protect her brother. It was as if the whole thing was rotting away, with worms coming out of it." Returning to the car, with both of her children sobbing, Neda decided that school had become much too dangerous and that life—for all of them— had grown toxic and "rotten." There were only a couple of weeks left to the school year, but she was determined that her son would not enroll in the sixth grade in September. He would not advance to one of the two middle schools in Waverly.

It turned out that Ehsan was not ready to give up. After all, he had been raised by his parents to believe that "giving up meant failure." If he threw in the towel, he would always be seen as weak and unworthy. For as long as he could remember, his mother and father had told him what their parents had always told them: "The Kermanians never give up." It had been the family litany, their immigrant survival chant, passed down through generations, spoken with bravado and pride. Those four determined words—"Kermanians never give up"—had covered over their fears, stoked their courage, and made them feel as if they had the upper hand even when they were being threatened and ostracized.

Besides, Ehsan thought that he had a chance in middle school, where there would be some new kids from two of the other elementary schools in town; maybe this would offer him a new opportunity to change the way other kids treated him. He knew that William, one of his neighborhood buddies who lived right down the street and had always been nice to him, would never turn against him.

A year older than Ehsan and well liked in school, he might even become a kind of protector. Ehsan pleaded with his parents. "William will watch out for me . . . I'll be okay . . . let me try it." Reluctantly Neda and Toraj gave in to their son's pleadings. They worried a lot, but they admired his courage, his determination to stick it out. And once they gave him their consent, they stopped their doubting and offered words of encouragement and support. "We're with you . . . always with you."

Neda and her children had just come in from buying school supplies at Staples when they discovered the bullying messages on Ehsan's computer. "You are a disgusting creep." "You fucking asshole." "There we were, the night before school opened," recalls Neda sadly, "with all of these new, shiny things—backpacks, notebooks, pencils—allowing ourselves to feel so hopeful, and then this crap comes over cyberspace. We were feeling so violated." She searched to find the address of the offenders and discovered that the messages came from a housing project across town—Atrium Homes—one of a handful of places in Waverly built for low-income residents. Toraj was out of town on business. Neda's mother rage could not be contained. She told her children to lock the door behind her, and she jumped into her car and raced across town, determined to track down her prey. Even though she found the apartment complex, she had no idea where the cyber-bullies actually lived. She stalked around in the darkness for a while, checked the mailboxes downstairs in the entry, watched a few residents come and go, and finally realized that "this was crazy." Her rage had taken her to a dangerous place. "If I had been able to figure out where they lived," she says without bravado, "I would be in jail now."

It turned out not to be the bright opening day they had all hoped for, filled with new energy and resolve. Neda headed up to the middle school without her son and announced to the principal that she was pulling him out. The principal heard her story of the night before, promised to follow up immediately and punish the offenders. Then he begged Neda to let Ehsan return to school, claiming that he would take "personal responsibility" for seeing that the boy was safe. Neda was wary of the parade of promises, weary of hearing all the principals (by now she had dealt with four of them) express concern and offer solutions that never worked, but there was still something in her, some shred of hope, some shadow of belief in her son's ability to survive. Maybe this time the principal's words would be followed by protective actions that would keep Ehsan out of harm's way. So she gave in. And Ehsan—with fear and hope in his heart—arrived at middle school the following morning.

"The principal did try to provide him with a safe space," Neda recalls with resignation and rage creasing her face. "He talked to the teachers and asked them to keep a special eye out for Ehsan. He had him come to "quiet lunch," a small room set aside for the children who felt intimidated in the big cafeteria. He allowed him to stay in from recess whenever he chose to." But it was only days before Ehsan was coming home with bruises from being thrown up against the lockers by the bullies from his old school, with stories of their dumping his science notebooks in the garbage, with tales of being cornered and roughed up in the boys' bathroom. If anything, the bullying was more brutal and treacherous than what he had suffered in elementary school.

When Neda—once again—begged the principal to contact the parents of the children she knew to be the culprits, he was reluctant, then dismissive. "You should have seen how fast he retreated when he realized how thick all of this was . . . and which parents were involved. They were the blue bloods, and he was not going to approach them." Her voice oozes cynicism. "Very quickly that principal made the political choice not to confront them.

"It was a Thursday afternoon, on a very cold, blustering day in January," Neda begins, shuddering with memories of the frigid weather and the horror that was on the horizon. "I drove up to the middle school to pick up Ehsan and waited for a long time out front, after all the buses and cars had left. When he didn't come out, I decided to drive quickly over to get Sadaf at her school and then circle back. Sadaf and I drove back to the school. It was now more than an hour after dismissal. Finally I went into the school and found only the janitors sweeping up the floors. Everyone had gone home. We looked around outside. He was nowhere. I decided to call the police to tell them he was missing. Everything in me was trembling with fear. As we're driving back toward home, I spot a figure moving through the woods along the side of the road. It's Ehsan. He's all scratched up, looking terrified. At the end of the day, those punk kids had ambushed him inside the school building. They wouldn't let him leave. He laid low, and finally, after they had grown tired of taunting him and left the building, he escaped and made his way through the woods so they wouldn't spot him."

A couple of weeks later, as he was getting his books out of his locker between classes, Ricky and his guys pushed Ehsan so hard against the locker that he came home with blood running down his face. Neda remembers the scene as if it were yesterday. "When I picked him up from school, he was wearing his big winter boots, and he kicked the side of the car so hard . . . I can remember the sound of his boots hitting the car, and I remember thinking, This is the sound of a wake-up call." Ehsan was angrier than Neda had ever seen him, dark with fury. He walked into the house, shoved his sister out of the way, stomped up the stairs, crawled into bed, pulled the covers up over his head, and refused to move or talk to anyone. It was at that "dark and miserable moment" that Neda knew they were at the end. "I can't take this anymore," she recalls saying out loud to herself. "This is tearing my family apart. I'm done. We're not going back!"

Neda and Toraj had no idea what they would do after pulling

their son out of school. They had no Plan B. They were propelled completely by their "sense of desperation, exhaustion, helplessness, and hopelessness" and their determination that they would no longer allow Ehsan to be brutalized. For several days they flirted with the idea of sending him to live with Toraj's brother in Iran. On their annual summer visits there, he had developed a close relationship with his uncle, and Iran was the place where Ehsan always felt strong and safe, embraced and adored by his extended family. But the thought of sending him so far away, even to trusted relatives, felt unbearable to his parents. Private schools were well beyond their means, and they reasoned that those elite places might also be sites of abuse for Ehsan. They "thrashed around," hoping to find a viable option. Every day, it seemed, Neda spent "hours and hours" making calls and sending e-mails; reaching out for guidance and advice from friends, colleagues, and associates.

In one such conversation, with a former professor and trusted mentor, she wept her way through the long and terrifying saga of the bullying, and she received a surprising response. "Why," said her mentor, "don't you homeschool him?" A wave of relief washed over Neda as she listened to the "sage advice" of someone whose judgment she trusted. At that moment a door seemed to open for them, an option they had never considered, and Neda and Toraj grabbed on to it for dear life. "It was as if something very heavy and ominous lifted from around us . . . we could finally let go and breathe!"

Monday, February 23, 2009—the date is etched in Neda's mind—was Ehsan's first day of homeschooling, and at the end of that week they marked the occasion with a family celebration. Toraj made special Iranian treats for dinner; they decorated the table with their fanciest silverware and dinner plates, warmed themselves around the woodstove in the kitchen, and raised their crystal glasses to make toasts. It was a beautiful moment. Neda looked over at her son and for the first time in years saw the sparkle in his eyes and heard the magical sound of laughter come out of his mouth. "In five days," she recalls, "he was giggling . . . he had returned to us. From that moment on, we never looked back."

Now Neda is smiling, a radiant mother-lion smile. But almost immediately her tone turns somber again as she asks herself the question that began our interview. "Why, oh why, did I wait so long to rescue my boy?" This time she turns toward the past, revisiting images and feelings from her own childhood. When she thinks about the abuse of Ehsan and the way in which the terror almost destroyed their family, she sees herself as a young girl of eight watching the sadness that was eating away at her father when he moved his family from Brooklyn to Matunuck, Rhode Island, hoping to escape the dangers and dirtiness of the city, hoping to find some measure of safety and peace. Instead they found themselves in a place where they were even more isolated and ostracized, a place that felt foreign and strange and inhospitable to them. Her father had moved his family to this small fishing village—"we are from the desert," says Neda with exasperation—where everyone in the town was white except for one African American family.

"My father was so depressed," Neda recalls tearfully. "I would go into that tiny room where he was sitting all alone, all bent over, the air thick with his anguish." But even in the midst of his deep sadness and disappointment, her father "loved America and everything American," and he believed that the hardships and prejudice they faced had to be endured, that they could not give up; they needed to push on. When Neda and Toraj were "self-destructing as a family," when they were enduring "battle after battle, trying to push Ehsan when he was in so much danger," she must have been hearing the echoes of her father's admonitions. Never, ever give up. Be grateful that you have the opportunity to become a part of this great country. Count your blessings. "As a matter of fact," Neda muses, as if she is discovering this for the first time, "I'm now realizing that Toraj and I probably bought this house in this neighborhood so that my father would approve of us . . . approve of our very American choice."

When Neda's family arrived in America and moved to a tenement in Brooklyn, it was the middle of the school year, and she spoke not a word of English. Her older brother, who knew some English, walked to school with her on the first day and registered her in the first grade. The second day, he also accompanied her on the mile-and-a-half trek to school. But on the third day she was on her own, with a note pinned to her that said, "My name is Neda. I am lost. This is my phone number." "It was very scary, and I was desperately lonely," she says, reliving the moment and connecting it to her own deep survival instincts, her own capacity to endure the pain and keep going, and her own reluctance, as her son's mother, to give up on his behalf forty years later.

When her family moved to Matunuck a few years later, she, like Ehsan, had no friends. She, like Ehsan, endured lots of teasing, although no physical bullying. And she was torn apart by her desire to fit in, her pride in being Iranian, and her devotion to the place her family still called "home." Now she is able to see and name what was going on. "These are the struggles of an immigrant," she says evenly, "the contradictions and tensions of assimilation and acculturation . . . the casualties and choices we are faced with." But being able to offer an analysis of the "contradictions" is not the same as witnessing your son being beaten up and feeling—in your stomach—the burn and fury of a very personal unfairness. She feels the mother rage in her body. "When I think back to that day in January when Ehsan was so furious and out of control that he kicked our car, I still can feel it in my gut. It is still in my body . . . the fear, the rage, the anger . . . and the feeling that I've used up all I've got. There is no more." Now she is raising her fist and beating the air at the memory of the moment when the decision to exit was made. "This is not quitting. We're done."

When Neda says "in my body," she starts to weep. Several

months ago she was diagnosed with breast cancer, and she is
certain—beyond a shadow of a doubt—that the malignancy is a
result of the stress and grief that consumed her life and settled in
her organs. "My cancer is a response to all the toxic nights of no
sleep, all the pain and anguish running through my body," she says
definitively. Lean and strong, Neda has been a marathon runner
and vegetarian for most of her adult life; she has never been seriously ill or hospitalized for even a day. The evening that the oncologist called with the diagnosis, Neda knew the bad news before
he even said the words.

   She had been standing outside on the deck of their new country house, looking out across the lake. The house had been in
foreclosure, and they had "bought it for a steal." After all the stress
over the last several years, they had wanted a place to go on week-
ends for peace and healing, where they could go with friends to
"create laughter in the house," where the family "could compose a
new set of memories." "After so much suffering," says Neda softly,
"we wanted a place to change the energy, to detox as a family."
Their first night there, with hope shining through the moon's rays,
listening for the laughter of her children, Neda heard the news of
her illness, and all she could say—softly to herself—was "of course."
"I knew something like this was going to happen . . . it was inevitable. The cancer was the embodiment of all of those years of
anguish."

   It turned out that not having to return to school not only
brought laughter back into the house, it also meant that Ehsan was
able to pursue learning in a way that was more in keeping with the
way his mind—and heart—works. Without the regimen of schedules and classes and tests, without the constraints of teacher-
directed learning, without having to worry about what his classmates
might think of his earnestness, his seriousness, and his probing
questions, Ehsan was free to follow his curiosities, learn at his own
pace, pursue subjects and fields deeply, and work late into the eve-

ning. His path could be self-directed and organic, completely individualized to his appetites and ambitions. Very early on, Neda and Toraj knew that they would not become his teachers. They each had full-time work—Toraj is a financial analyst, Neda a graphic designer—and they knew the costs and casualties of trying to combine teaching and parenting. They saw themselves as "resources" for Ehsan—perusing Listservs for homeschoolers, collecting names of people, curricula, and programs, and networking with a new community of parents and children who were also making it up as they went along. And they were able to find a fairly well-developed set of resources—a myriad of classes, experiences, and settings that could be quilted together to create a rich and rigorous curriculum for Ehsan.

The town of Waverly required them to submit a plan that spelled out the principles and pieces of his educational program—an "odyssey of the mind" workshop at the Museum of Science, a research apprenticeship in a university chemistry lab, a comparative religion class for children and their parents in the next town, tutoring in math, karate, piano lessons, and of course self-study on topics of his choice at home. "I'm not doing any of the teaching," Neda reminds me "I check out the resources, and I do have to drive him from place to place." She and Toraj also decided that there would be no testing, no assessment of his work. "Let the town ask whenever they want to have him tested," she says dismissively. "Let them knock themselves out!" Then, more gently, she reflects on their philosophy of "constructivist learning" that "fits Ehsan like a glove." "There is no homework. Ehsan just keeps on working until he stops . . . sometimes until nine-thirty or ten at night. He moves forward at his own pace and in his own way. I've stopped worrying whether he will learn specific content . . . I've begun to think that now that he has a clearer and freer mind, he will absorb it all."

Neda offers me an example of how Ehsan follows his own

learning path, how his fascinations lead to questions, study, data
gathering, and projects. A few months ago he went to the bat mitzvah of one of his friends who lives across the street, and he became
fascinated with Judaism. His curiosity led to questioning and reading. They got the DVD of *Fiddler on the Roof,* which they watched
on one of their ritual family pizza nights, which led to a "unit" that
Ehsan designed for himself on World War II . . . which led to his
reading *Maus: A Survivor's Tale* and *Anne Frank: The Diary of a
Young Girl.* Then Ehsan became interested in knowing more about
the Japanese side of the war, so they watched Clint Eastwood's
movie *Letters from Iwo Jima.* Soon after, when Toraj had to go to
Hawaii on a business trip, he took Ehsan along so that they could
visit Pearl Harbor. When Ehsan returned from Hawaii, Neda
tracked down the class in comparative religion for homeschooled
children and their parents, extending and expanding his original
interest in the Jewish ritual of bar mitzvah—a learning journey
that had taken some amazing twists and turns.

Ehsan is focused and disciplined about finishing the work that
he sets out for himself. Occasionally he will take a break and go to
Home Depot with his mother to buy plants for the garden, or he
will play some computer games, or he will practice the piano or get
on his bike and take a ride around the neighborhood. But the self-
directedness and autonomy he relishes come with a haunting loneliness, a lingering sense of failure, shadows of self-doubt. He still
wishes he could have survived the bullying and found a way to feel
comfortable—even make some friends—in school. Although he
feels himself learning so much more at home than he ever did in
school, he still longs to be a "regular kid like the other kids" who
hang out and have fun together. And Ehsan is still afraid. He will
not ride his bike into the town center after three in the afternoon,
because he is still panicked that he might run into the bullies
when they are getting out of school and heading home. He can
still hear their harassing threats; he can still feel the pain of being

hit hard and physically hassled. Neda encourages him to take small steps out into the scary territories, but Ehsan's movements continue to be circumscribed by fear—a fear, however, counterbalanced by a freedom he has never known, the freedom to learn, to be himself, to push the limits of his intelligence.

The other day, when Neda was buying vegetables at the Orchards, she spotted the mother of the big bully Ricky standing by the tomatoes, and she offered her a broad smile. Ricky's mother looked back quizzically and then forced a stiff smile in her direction, trying to figure out why Neda seemed to be greeting her so kindly. "I smiled at her in thanks," says Neda genuinely. "I wanted to say to her, You pushed us over the edge until we could not bear it any longer . . . and now we are free!"

In Sartre's play, the condition of no exit—hell—is one that has no mirrors, no sleep, and no dreams. This represents total entrapment. Without a mirror, you cannot see yourself with your own eyes; you must rely on other people to tell you what they see. This inability to regard yourself is compounded by the fact that others will never see you the way you see yourself. Without sleep, there is no rest, no respite, no suspension of reality. And without dreams, you cannot conceive of nor make a different reality. The ability to exit, then, is the ability to see yourself, to give yourself a break, to make yourself a new life.

Ehsan faces the horrors and evils of hell each day as he walks into school. He is bullied and beaten, taunted and terrorized by the gang of kids who—on the first day of kindergarten—decide that he will be their victim. The bullies force this gentle, reticent boy, this lover of books, to become a street fighter, always watching his back, raising his fists to his face to deflect their blows. They call him their "soldier" and force him to do their dirty deeds. They egg him on: "Kill! Kill! Kill!" They enjoy watching him try to turn into someone that he isn't. He gets so beaten up that he becomes unrecognizable to himself. Like Sartre's hell, there are no "mirrors" for Ehsan to see his own reflection; there is no chance to "sleep," to rest up for the next onslaught; there is no safe place "to dream" of a different reality. Like the three protagonists in *No Exit*, he turns the torture back on himself; he absorbs the abuse; it becomes who he is and how he feels about himself. Over time, the way out becomes less and less clear. Even when he is given the chance to leave, to escape from the hell in which he is entrapped, he resists. As we listen to his mother tell this tale of torture, the suffering of this child becomes unbearable, even for us. We want to scream, "Get out! Get out!"

Through it all, Ehsan's mother is by his side, fighting for his protection, bolstering his spirits, cheering him on, weeping as she cleans his wounds, suffering with him every day. She suffers as well, not knowing what advice to give her son. Should she—as the child psychiatrist suggests—prod him to learn the moves of a fighter, help him learn to fake his fierceness? Or should she—as his fourth-grade teacher, Mrs. Rhodes, warns—tell him to stop wearing his Iranian heritage on his sleeve? Or should she try to help Ehsan find within himself a sturdy self-confidence, a nonviolent self-defense that might eventually erode the motivations of the thrill-seeking torturers?

The daily grind of humiliation and abuse are punctuated by unforgettable moments that rock their world. Neda discovers the lacerations on her child's head as she dries him after his shower; she tries to track down the cyberspace bullies when they sully Ehsan's e-mail with dirty name-calling; she chases away a crowd of kids who are circling him in the field behind the school, hurling racist jeers at him. Each time Ehsan gets hit, Neda feels it in her gut; his scars are seared into her body. With each mounting transgression she struggles with herself; she weighs the toll of suffering, the costs of staying. And she looks for the exit sign.

Finally the day arrives; it is crystal clear in her memory. That day, when she goes to pick him up after school, Neda can hear the sound of Ehsan's deep pain, his desperation, his big winter boot kicking the side of her car—"the sound of the wake-up call." At that moment she knows in her bones it is over, all over. There is no turning back. Unlike Sartre's three prisoners who are so far gone, so damaged and ruined that they refuse to leave hell even when they are given the chance, Neda and Ehsan see the exit sign over the door, and they walk through.

We listen to this tortured tale and wonder why they stayed so long, why they remained so stuck in their misery, why they were willing to absorb so much abuse. As she tells the story of her son, Neda discovers echoes from her own childhood. She remembers the lonely, scary walk on her first day of school after her family arrived in Brooklyn, and the sign her parents pinned to her jacket just in case she got lost, since she did not speak a word of English. Rehearsing Ehsan's story has made her recall the ways in which she too was bullied and ostracized by the white kids in Matunuck who hated her because she was brown and foreign. (Wasn't it punishment enough that this desert girl was forced to live by the sea?) She suffered and survived. She absorbed the blows (although hers were not physical) and kept moving. Perhaps it took Neda so long to save her son because the terrain—of terror—felt so recognizable; it was ugly, but painfully familiar. She has the scars to prove it.

But beyond her childhood memories of abuse at the hands of her schoolmates, Neda can still hear her father's voice singing his love for America, claiming it as the land of opportunity, urging his children to be grateful for their blessings, admonishing them to face and endure any hardships, any barriers that might stand in their path. "Kermanians never give up" was the family chant that Neda absorbed and then passed on to her son. It is an immigrant story—a story of sacrifice and endurance, of punishment and survival, of selling your soul if that is the price of admission, the bargain you make for reluctant acceptance. The "American choice" sliced in with grief. When Ehsan faces the bullies in school and suffers their humiliations, he is carrying on the proud and painful generational legacy. He is not just trying to stand up for himself; he is suffering in the name of those who came before him. His battle scars are signs of his gratefulness. Over and over, he battles and suffers and is grateful, until he can do it no longer. When the torture finally becomes too excruciating for this noble and beaten "soldier" to bear, he wins by walking away.

But the freedom is fragile and the wounds are deep. It is a costly win. For the first time in years, Ehsan's parents see the light return to his eyes; they hear his giggles of laughter. He is set free to learn, to be curious, to be as smart as he dares. But the wounds are still raw; he is wary and afraid; he is still watching his back and staying under the radar just in case the bullies might ambush him in town when he passes by on his bike. His mother protector also suffers the "exit wounds" from their fight for freedom. They are seared into her body; they have taken over her organs and given her cancer, an "embodiment of all those years of anguish." But even their wounds and their grieving do not stop her from feeling gratitude toward those who "pushed them over the edge," because if it weren't for them, Neda and her son would never have seen the exit.

Four

WOUNDS

The costs and casualties of Ehsan's and Neda's escape to freedom remind us of the wounds we may carry with us long after we have walked through the exit to freedom. The wounds are physical and emotional, visible and invisible, conscious and unconscious, layers of injury that cause damage and leave scars. Ehsan's bloody face after he is thrown against the locker, the lesions on his head after Ricky has pounded him on the playground are the physical signs of battle, but they may not be as brutalizing as the injuries he suffered to his soul and spirit. Likewise, Neda's cancer appears to be a physical expression of all the years of grief and anguish she absorbed trying to protect her child.

Their years of suffering at the hands of the bullies (and their "kiss-ass" mothers) also remind us that wounds are both inflicted by others and self-inflicted. The entrapment of Sartre's protagonists is a result of the unspeakable deeds that landed them in hell but also a result of their own self-hatred and shame, the tortured ways they caused themselves misery. Likewise, after years of abuse at the hands of his schoolmates, Ehsan begins to punish himself, banging his head against the wall, obsessing over his food, cutting himself on the shards of pencils he has gripped too tightly. His self-destructive acts are as toxic and deeply felt as the bullies' taunts.[1]

The wounding also travels across generations. The loneliness and pain from Neda's childhood echoes in her heart, messes with her mind, and distorts her judgment as she struggles to protect her son. She can visualize her own father bent over in a dark room after he has moved his family to the town by the sea, his face creased in despair even as he chants the blessings of his American life. This sadness gets passed down from generation to generation,[2] coursing through the bloodstream, making the grandson more susceptible to melancholy, more accepting of the loneliness that his parents and grandparents endured. Freedom is the opposite of entrapment. It is also the balm for the physical, emotional, and spiritual wounds passed down through the generations.

Sometimes the visible and invisible scars left over from our injuries are disabling; they hold us back, distort our self-image, compromise our strength, and make us feel ugly. We try to hide them, repress them, camouflage the pain that they represent. But scars can also signify the opposite. They can be badges of courage, signs of survival and resilience, beautiful adornments of our hard-won victory. They can remind us of our strength and our fight, and the wisdom we have earned from having endured.

The stories in this chapter are of those who seek to heal the invisible and visible wounds. Linda Gould, a psychologist and clinical psychotherapist, and Anthony Brown, an intensive care unit attending physician, minister to patients who have been deeply scarred by emotional and physical trauma. And both of them keep their eyes focused on the exits. Much of Linda's therapeutic work, in fact, is designed to help her patients exit from the histories, relationships, and self-perceptions that have made them anxious and depressed, compromised their happiness and productivity, and prevented them from realizing their full potential. She listens to their anguished stories of addiction—to alcohol, drugs, food, pornography—their tales of infidelity and abuse, their everyday neuroses, and she tries to help them discover the roots of their pain and a way out of their misery. She helps them trace the wounds that echo across the generations, from their grandparents to their parents to them. Many patients come to her in their determined effort to stop the emotional toxins that seem to flow across the generations. They do not want to pass the psychic wounds on to their children. As she helps her patients identify the path out of their misery, she also prepares them for their exit from the therapeutic relationship that they have forged together—for the day when she and they decide it is time to move on, even though their work is rarely done.

HONORING THE WORK AND THE WOUNDS

*"Farewells are often bittersweet ... fruitful
and sad ... just as life is."*

We meet in her home office, a simple, sun-filled space containing a large oak desk and swivel chair where the therapist sits, a cozy couch where her patients perch, lots of books lining the walls, and fresh flowers in a handblown glass vase. Linda Gould, a clinically trained psychotherapist, has for thirty years had a private practice working with adolescents and adults in individual, couples, and family therapy. At seventy, she swims half a mile every morning, takes vigorous daily walks, and happily loses track of long hours as she tills and trims her "wild" city garden. Her short and chic silver hair frames a lined face, a cragginess she has begun to appreciate and call "handsome." She moves her strong and lean body with a sexy swagger, wears lovely amber and turquoise jewelry, and decorates herself in designer clothes, most of them carefully chosen from thrift shops. She loves a good bargain. As she talks, she digs deep for emotional insights, and she punctuates her intensity and seriousness with raucous laughter.

As she talks to me, Linda avoids the therapist's chair and sits with me on the couch—a signal that she is prepared to change roles from listener to talker, from guiding to receiving the questions. Piled around her on the couch are patient folders filled with the notes she writes after every session, documenting their time together. In anticipation of our interview and wanting to protect the privacy of her patients, she has temporarily taped over their names and written pseudonyms that she refers to from time to time as she tells their stories, masking, as well, some of the details of their histories and backgrounds. Occasionally Linda glazes over the specific data that might be identifying, or she deftly refuses my inquiries for more information, all in the name of shielding her patients and doing no harm.

I have come to talk to Linda about how she guides her patients through their exits—the word therapists use is "termination." I want to hear her stories of farewell—what principles she applies, rituals she designs, protocols she practices—and I want to know how she feels saying goodbye, how she herself is affected by their leave-takings, whether she experiences relief, abandonment, or sadness. Before our meeting, she has done her "homework," gathering documents, letters, and articles from professional journals and displaying the "genograms"—her specialty—multicolored drawings on a poster-size pad that visually record the "intergenerational maps" of her patients, their family, medical, and psychological histories. From her very first meeting with her patients Linda uses the huge pad to chart the roots and branches of their stories, filling in the information as it unfolds over the months and years, and ultimately producing a summary document of intimate discoveries, often painful revelations, and surprising epiphanies.

"I start by asking new clients if they have any questions for me, before I begin to ask them my many questions," she explains. "Then I tell them how I work, which is by taking notes on this pad so that they may see the patterns. I quickly flip through the genograms of former clients and point to colors that represent major life events and experiences . . . saying, 'The black lines and circles represent alcoholism; blue is drug abuse; red refers to sexual issues; green is for prison.' I want to make certain that as the sheets flip by, they see that this is a safe place to talk about these often hidden and humiliating issues. This is a place where we can speak about anguish, shame, and guilt. I draw a horizontal line on the page, indicating whether they are only children or whether they have siblings . . . and we begin. It is often sputtering and halting at first; it takes a while to get going, but soon the information begins to flow, and they can begin to see themselves on the page." This beginning drawing, filled in over time, is the very first step on the path leading to the exit.

Linda's "generic" comments about termination quickly move to specific stories. In fact, it turns out that all the farewell rituals are highly specific, shaped by the individual and idiosyncratic relationships she forges with each of her patients. Painting with a broad brush, she begins, "Generally, in my mind, I make sure that the endings are formal. It is very important to honor the client, honor our relationship, and most of all honor the work. It is also important to help them know what work still needs to be done. We are all works of art . . . there is always more to do." Optimally, it takes two or three sessions to say goodbye productively and meaningfully, to feel that there is closure or to make a successful transition to the next therapist.

Even though Linda says that primarily she is talking about the endings of long-term therapeutic relationships, often lasting several years, she starts with her most recent example, fresh in her mind, of a patient who terminated after only two very intense months of therapy. At age twenty-four, Allison had come to Linda in early April, just before graduating from law school and just before her anticipated move to her first job in a fancy Washington law firm in late May. They knew going in that this would be a short-term therapy. From an affluent white Protestant family in Dallas, Allison had gone to an elite prep school, done her undergraduate work at Mount Holyoke College, and graduated near the top of her law school class at Georgetown University. Beautiful and graceful, she carried herself with a smoothness and dignity that belied the turmoil and terror she was feeling.

The "crisis" that brought her to therapy had to do with sexual addiction. Linda recalls, "I named it in our first session together, surprising myself by asking her whether she looked at porn . . . and that opened the door for her to talk about the trauma and shame of contracting herpes with Andrew, the man she had been seeing for three months. She came in saying that she wanted to maintain the relationship because she had herpes, even though she knew their relationship was destructive—that Andrew was emotionally distant and dismissive of her—and she lamented the fact that her herpes would keep her from having the one-night stands that had become routine for her." During their sessions Allison did a lot of crying, and "she remained addicted." Sex with Andrew, she reported, was extraordinary, "like a drug," "a monkey on her back" that would not let her go even though the pain of his disrespect and deceit was a constant and she did not trust him. The therapeutic work was primarily focused on doing what she had to do to end the relationship. They role-played together how Allison would break up with him, a termination that—ironically—paralleled the anticipated termination of their therapeutic relationship. "This was crisis management," says Linda, reflecting on the focus and rapidity of their work and the need to get it done in the two months they had together before Allison's move to Washington. Allison did manage to end her relationship with Andrew, although not in the way she and Linda had planned. The first—and easiest— place she was able to let him go was on Facebook, where she deleted his name. But she refused to change her telephone number and found it almost impossible not to respond to his text messages.

Linda was able to refer Allison to a therapist in Washington, hoping she would be able to do the "deep work" that was impossible for them to accomplish. Even though their time together was brief, Linda felt as if they had done some "good work" together; it was a start, and it was promising. At their penultimate session, Linda asked the two questions that usually frame the termination ritual with her patients. First, "What was useful in this therapy?" And second, "What do you wish that we might have covered—but didn't get a chance to—in our time together?" Allison's answers came with tears of sadness and appreciation: "This was a validation," she reflected bravely, "that I am not crazy . . . that I am not deluded. I was able to explain myself in an ordered way to someone who is not bending in my direction, someone who is wise and impartial, someone who has seen it all before."

Allison paused, looking down into her lap, trying to regain her composure, and Linda let the silence linger. Even though Allison had named the progress she had made in therapy, she knew she was far from "cured." "I could not have done what I did without therapy. But I know I need more fortification, more strengthening so I can move on and get better." Allison's awareness of the value and edification of her short-term therapy and her cognizance of those things left undone were instructive to her therapist. "I learned a lot from her," says Linda gratefully. "When someone is really focused, is as smart as hell and as motivated as she is—and has a good support system like she has with her mother and her best friend—then you can make some progress, even if they are the first baby steps, in a very little time."

The endings seem clearer and more definitive when the therapy is intentionally short-lived, when both therapist and patient are anticipating termination from the very first meeting. Exits from long-term therapies of several years are more layered and complex, with fits and starts, ambivalence and uncertainties. "In these cases," says Linda, "termination is a flow, not an end point . . . or perhaps there are a series of end points." She thinks of Mandy, now forty-two, in therapy for seven years, who came to Linda when she was twenty and a first-year law student. Linda pulls out a bright yellow folder and shows me the more than twenty years of correspondence between them, mostly holiday cards and greetings (always signed "Be well, Love, Mandy and family") and short responses by Linda, that she has xeroxed before mailing, offering appreciation and support, cheering her on (always signed "Warm wishes, Linda").

Mandy was one of seven siblings from a "dysfunctional family" where she "got very little parenting." Her mother, who suffered from psychosis, was verbally and physically abusive, unleashing most of her rage on Mandy, who, as the oldest child, was primarily responsible for parenting her younger siblings. Over their seven years together, Linda saw Mandy through several suicidal episodes, through the discovery that she was not gay, through her studying for, failing, and then passing the bar exam, through the struggles of her love relationship with John and their marriage, through the birth of her first child, through discovering that she could manage to continue being a lawyer if she took a relatively undemanding job where she would not be working to make partner in the firm. When she moved with her family to Cleveland, Linda found her another therapist but continued to be in touch from time to time. Now that Mandy is the age of Linda's own daughters, Linda reflects on the "comfortable and easy" relationship that has survived their years of separation. "For those patients who are about the age of my children, I always feel as if I'm raising them . . . in a detached parental way." Now Linda is laughing. "Maybe I'm raising my patients in the way that I would like to be with my own kids as a parent, somewhat less involved and intrusive, somewhat less judgmental."

The kind of detached raising of Mandy, where distance and time have shaped a caring but remote relationship, is in sharp contrast with Linda's "almost boundaryless" connection to Nadine. "Nadine is in my life," Linda says unapologetically. Now thirty-one, Nadine started treatment with Linda when she was twelve, and there "has been no formal termination." Very bright, but suffering from a mild form of autism, Nadine has showed slow and steady improvement in her ability to connect with the social world around her; she has successfully completed high school and college, become certified in information technology, and is now volunteering at a hospital and working to find gainful employment. Over the years, Linda and Nadine's mother, Rachel, have seen themselves as "co-parents," "working as a team." (Nadine's father, who is divorced from her mother, lives on the other side of the country, a distant but benign presence.) The collaboration does not confuse their different roles. Linda is quick to say, "I tell Rachel that she is the mother. I'm in Nadine's life a few hours a week, but the work has to continue when I am not there." And she points out that Rachel is a very "competent, sensitive, and artistic" woman whose vulnerabilities and challenges mothering Nadine are related to her own abuse suffered at the hands of an alcoholic mother.

When Nadine enrolled at the University of Miami, it was Linda—who happened to be vacationing in southern Florida—who helped her through registration and settled her into her dormitory room. Even though it has been ten years since they have met for formal therapy sessions in Linda's office, they will sometimes meet for conversation at a local coffee shop ("At least I've stopped paying for her lattes." Linda smiles. "Now I tell her, 'When you can afford it, you can have it.'"); or they will sit outside on a bench and strategize about how Nadine might more successfully deal with the "horrible bureaucratic maze of state mental health rehab," where she is seeking additional resources and support. "I take notes as we talk," says Linda, "and then give her the notes so that she can follow up. Our work together is very focused and practical."

As the longest of Linda's ongoing clients, Nadine is special, in a category of her own. Their connection to each other is deep and heartfelt; there is no end in sight to their long relationship, even though its tone and texture have changed over the years. Linda is parent and therapist, cheerleader and strategist, mentor and guide; and she combines these roles with alacrity, without hesitation. When I ask her how she thinks about the traditionally drawn "boundaries" that mark most therapists' relationships with their patients, Linda claims, again, that the boundary drawing is "very individualistic," defined by the nature, depth, and duration of the connection. As an experienced clinician whose work has become almost intuitive and whose moves are not constrained by orthodoxy—the traditional rules or protocols of therapy—she claims that she doesn't "worry or obsess" about boundaries. But that does not mean she doesn't "think about being more restrained and contained" or occasionally feel that she has transgressed in territories where she does not belong. Occasionally there are missteps and mistakes in judgment that haunt Linda for days afterward. During these moments of confusion and disorientation she will often consult with a trusted colleague for feedback and guidance.

When I ask her about the boundaries she draws with Nadine, she searches for some defining markers and comes up with only two. "Nadine has never met my husband. Steven is trained to wander away when my patients approach me. And Nadine has never been in any other room in my house, only in my office." And there are the other boundaries that all her patients, including Nadine, experience—the white noise machine outside her office door that creates a sound barrier, the message on her telephone that directs patients to emergency services when she is out of town or unavailable, and of course the HIPAA forms she tells patients about when they first arrive, alerting them to the fact that she is legally bound to report evidence of child abuse and inform the authorities when she believes her patients might hurt themselves or others. As we talk, I hear the connections between boundaries and endings, between defining the contours of the therapeutic relationship and being able to leave it, move beyond it. It somehow doesn't surprise me that with the minimal boundaries that have been in place for twenty years between Nadine and Linda, termination would be neither desired nor necessary for either of them.

With almost every termination—however formal and ritualized—Linda offers a last salvo. "The door is always open," she says to those who are departing, whose faces are often creased with sadness and wet with tears. The emotional weight of these goodbyes reminds Linda of another reason that "good terminations" are so valuable. "They serve as a corrective emotional experience," she muses. "They help people understand that farewells are often bittersweet . . . fruitful and sad . . . just as life is." The bittersweetness reminds her of saying goodbye to Cecelia, a Czechoslovakian doctor who had been in treatment for two and a half years. When Cecelia arrived, she was having a "major depressive episode," and her life was unraveling around her. Because of her depression, her professional life had deteriorated and she had recently been relieved of her clinical duties at the hospital. Linda's voice is angry and protective as she describes a major reason for Cecelia's cycling down. "There is only one word I can think of for her mother—a word I don't think I've ever used before in my practice. She was *evil*. I was trying to help Cecelia end the endless attempt to get anything from her mother . . . her ceaseless attempts to get kindness, empathy, attention, even civility from her mother. She was spending all her emotional energy in pursuit of something she would never get." At one point Cecelia's father, an engineer who was still living in Czechoslovakia and spoke no English, came with her to her therapy session. Even with Cecelia's expert translation, the emotional connections were hard and brittle, so distant was he from his daughter's life, so out of touch with her emotional needs.

At one point in her therapy Cecelia decided to "take a break." Without any fanfare she announced that she was leaving and would return when she was ready. But she offered her therapist no explanation, no opportunity for conversation or negotiation about her decision. Linda recalls how hard this was for her, how bad she felt. "I immediately thought I had made a mistake, maybe a mistake in the billing that might have upset her . . . then I was feeling very sad, as if I might have done something that violated her trust." Within three months Cecelia had returned, resuming the relationship "as if nothing had happened . . . as if nothing was wrong." Perhaps she just needed the space, thought Linda, because she returned ready to work harder and go deeper. The next months were very productive. "She did such great work," recalls Linda admiringly.

As they approached the end of her therapy and together anticipated its termination, things began to fall into place in Cecelia's life. "She presented her research at a professional conference and this time took full credit for it (in the past she had always taken a backseat and been overly deferential to her colleagues); she managed to get the job she really wanted; she learned to express her thoughts and feelings more forcefully and feel less marginalized at work." Her answers to Linda's two ritual questions at termination were fulsome and self-reflective. She recognized how far she had traveled, how hard she had worked, and how much she had done. She saw the connections between the insights and courage she had gathered in her therapy and the progress she was making in "real life." And she understood that there was so much more to do and conquer, so many ways she still retreated into herself, so many times she still cycled into sadness and despair, so many ways she was still involved in trying to gain her mother's love.

On the day of their last session together Cecelia arrived dressed in pink from head to toe. She was wearing a plaid pink jacket, pink high heels, and a pink band in her hair, and she was carrying a pink patent leather pocketbook. "She looked like a bowl of strawberry sherbet," says Linda with tears in her eyes. This was a moment that needed memorializing. Linda asked her whether she wanted to have her picture taken, and with an enthusiasm that seemed to indicate that this had been her plan all along, Cecelia said she would. She helped Linda figure out how to work the lens on her digital camera, and Linda took six pictures, both of them checking after each one to admire the pretty shot. As Cecelia walked out the door that afternoon, Linda said gently, "I hope to hear from you." To which Cecelia responded without hesitation, "You are family." "I teared up in that moment," says Linda, remembering how surprised she was by her own deep emotions. "I was so profoundly moved." As she relives the satisfaction of work well done by her patient, the staged ending, the emotional leave-taking, and the symbolism of the pink photos recording Cecelia's sense of herself as put together and pretty, Linda discovers the value of the termination ritual for the therapist. She discovers how she needs to review the work and say goodbye perhaps as much as her patients do.

I am interested in how Linda works with patients who come to her wanting help with an exit in their own lives. How, for example, does she guide a couple through a separation, a divorce? She immediately thinks of Riko, a thirty-seven-year-old Japanese woman who recently returned to therapy after a hiatus of seven years because of trouble in her marital relationship. She and her husband, a white American with a very high-paying job, had not had sexual intimacy for four years, although Riko claimed he was the love of her life, the man of her dreams. And although he claimed that he loved her deeply and she was his best friend, he said he had no interest in having sex with her except for when they both decided that they wanted to make another baby. Linda saw them each separately a few times and then several times together, uncovering the story of Riko's nightly practice of sleeping with her three-year-old child, not with her husband, and his nightly viewing of porn on the Internet. Their sessions together gave them a forum for learning how to communicate in a way that eluded them in their

daily lives and offered them a place to unleash the disappointment
and rage they each felt. Within the first few weeks of therapy Riko
decided that she and her husband were too far apart in what they
each wanted from the marriage, and she said she had no interest in
trying to salvage it. Her voice shrieked as she spoke her horrible
feelings. "I'm not going to be married to a turkey baster . . . and let
him insert his penis into me only when I'm fertile." Riko wanted to
file for divorce and be done with it.

Linda's response was purposefully "instructive, almost didactic," urging her to give the process some time—at least six months.
"Riko tends to be very moody and erratic, with large swings of
emotion from one extreme to the other," says Linda, enumerating
one of the reasons she cautioned Riko about being too hasty. But
Linda admits that in general, her attitude is one of wanting to help
her patients try as hard as they might to save their marriages. "I
definitely have a point of view," she admits. "In fact, I used to be far
more opinionated and rigid about it." Now she at least tries to get
couples to slow down. She suggests a longer time frame before a final decision is made, or she might recommend a trial separation,
where they agree not to have sexual intimacies with other partners
while they continue their couples therapy. And she hopes that if
they ultimately decide to split, they will choose to use a mediator
rather than lawyers, that they will find a way to preserve the dignity of both parties, and that they will work out a way to peace-
fully co-parent their children. If all these goals are met, Linda
believes that they have done the groundwork for a successful exit.

Some of Linda's wish to preserve the marriages of her patients,
or at least to insist that they "try their best and work their hardest"
before declaring them over, may be related to the suffering she experienced when her own parents decided—after almost forty years
of marriage—to divorce. Even though her parents' marriage had
been troubled by extramarital affairs for as long as Linda can remember, and even though she was a grown woman with children

of her own when they divorced, she was surprised by their decision and consumed by a sadness that lingered for years. I ask Linda whether she believes that her own painful history of her parents' divorce frames the way she approaches her patients' experiences, whether she offers her patients the counsel and guidance that she wishes her parents might have followed. My question seems "obvious" to her, but she gives a "counterintuitive" response. "One of the things I believe about myself as a clinician," she says with great certainty, "is that after all these decades, I continue to be riveted on the content of what my patients are saying. I'm focused on what they need. I feel myself being fully present with them. I do not think of myself except to the extent that I'm obviously formed by my own history. My story does not override theirs."

The question of her own emotional history distorting or interfering with the way she is able to "hear the content" of her patients' narratives brings up for Linda the ways in which her work as a therapist allows her to be her best, offering her the chance to use her plentiful gifts and insights. For a moment the tables turn, and I feel myself drawn into the role of therapist, listening to Linda's ancient haunts. She tells me of a dream she had the night before our interview. She was preparing to take an exam for a graduate course in which she was enrolled, and she couldn't focus on the material or remember any of the facts that were sure to be on the test the next day. She woke up in a panic, disoriented and drenched in sweat, and realized almost immediately that her dream was about the "huge anxiety and dread" she was feeling in anticipation of our interview. "I was so fraught and so worried," she says, reliving the moment and recalling the way she used to throw up every day before going to elementary school because she was so "school phobic." "I was never enough in school. I went to a private high school on the Upper East Side of New York, and I never felt as if I was enough intellectually or financially," she recalls sadly before snapping her fingers and bursting into laughter. "In high school I developed the persona of Sexy Linda to avoid feeling that I wasn't enough . . . a creative and provocative teenage solution to escape feeling all that pain."

As Linda prepared for our interview—gathering folders, journal articles, and correspondence, trying to anticipate the questions I might ask, role-playing with herself the smart and impressive answers she might give—she realized that she was rehearsing the awful experience of preparing for an exam that would reveal, once again, that she was "not enough." Now there are tears in her eyes as she says to me, "This is so unbelievably sad that—at seventy—I still struggle with these old feelings."

But when Linda sits listening to her patients, her mind "riveted," her "heart open," she knows she's good. She's more than enough. Now she's smiling broadly. "I feel plentiful and abundant as a therapist. I do not doubt my competence." As she practices therapy, attentive to her patients' journeys, living fully in the present with them and honoring their work, she is released from the old school phobias that made her feel incompetent and anxious. She finds freedom and plenty in her work, a freedom that allows her to engage fully with her patients and, when it is time, to let them leave . . . an exit that is dignified, a "termination" that admits there is still much work to be done.

I am struck by how much of Linda's work is focused on helping her patients figure out a way to leave those relationships, marriages, families, institutions, and communities that are compromising their lives, undermining their self-confidence, and making them feel anxious and depressed. Whether she is helping Cecelia, the Czechoslovakian doctor, relinquish her desperate quest for her mother's attention and love, even when she knows that her mother does not have the interest or the capacity, or whether she is supporting Allison, the young lawyer, in breaking up with her boyfriend, who is dismissive of her, whose attraction to him seems to be tangled up with his abuse of her, the path to healing is defined by exits. Exits are the markers of recovery and development, of becoming.

Linda's long years of experience free her from the conventions and orthodoxies practiced by therapists who rigidly mark the boundaries of their professionalism. As she helps her patients navigate their exits, she plays many roles. She is their critic and advocate, their guide and mentor, their companion and confidante. She listens for the sound and the silences in her patients' revelations, their masking of pain, and their detours away from the truth. She is attentive to the places where they fear to tread, the spaces where they continue to get stuck. She is nonjudgmental and fearless— she has heard it all before—but clear about what she believes, confident about her knowledge of the human psyche, its capacities and frailties. Several times, in fact, Linda calls her approach to therapy "didactic." She sees herself as a teacher—attentive, probing, challenging, and directive. She wants to teach her patients a new way of seeing, an alternative view, the "art of reframing" their experiences so that they might be released from the unproductive perspectives that have haunted their progress. Looking through a different lens, they might be able to identify the blind spots that have inhibited their progress; they might be able to rewrite the ancient narratives and see the path toward healing.

But Linda is also a pragmatist; her work is not purely retrospective—delving into the dark history of her patients and helping them see the light. It is prospective; it searches for what they might actually do today and tomorrow to make themselves feel better and happier. She gives them "homework," exercises they must do between sessions that will help move their work from talk to action, from the asylum of the therapist's office to the rough-and-tumble of the real world. In addition to the reframing and the pragmatism that are part of her pedagogy, Linda hopes to teach her patients courage—the courage to speak the truth about what they are feeling. Exiting the wounding afflictions of their lives, then, requires that they refocus their lenses, learn and practice new habits of interaction, and find the courage to tell the truth.

When the therapist and her patients have gone as far as they can go—the work is always unfinished, always imperfect—they make plans to "terminate," a ritual exit that "honors the patient, honors their relationship, and honors the work" they have done together, a ritual that is both generic and idiosyncratic, anticipatable and improvisational, formal and spontaneous. Optimally, all of Linda's patients use their last three sessions to wrap up, review their time together, and say their farewells. As they stand poised at the threshold of their therapeutic exit, Linda asks everyone the same two questions: "What was useful in this therapy? And what do you wish we might have covered—but didn't get a chance to—in our time together?" But even though the ritual is framed by these "generic" practices,[3] each goodbye is different, individually shaped by the doctor and her patient, by the depth and length of their relationship, the chemistry of their personalities, and the complex excavation of the emotional layers they have uncovered together.

The Czechoslovakian doctor comes to her last session all dressed in pink, looking like a bowl of strawberry sherbet, her bright prettiness and femininity an expression of her hard-won self-confidence and a sign of her emerging visibility and voice at work. She stands tall, clutching her pink patent leather purse, and her therapist takes a series of photos, capturing her courage, documenting her healing, marking the exit. By contrast, Nadine—who is now thirty-one and has been in a therapeutic relationship with Linda since she was twelve—never fully exits. There is no formal end point with pictures and declarations to mark the occasion. Rather, the relationship evolves and changes over time as she grows from a child to an adolescent to a young adult, as the mother and therapist become "co-parents." The boundaries between Linda and

Nadine shift; the therapy moves from the office to the coffee shop. Says Linda unapologetically, "In these cases, termination is a flow, not an end point . . . or perhaps there are a series of end points."

As I listen to Linda rehearse the exit stories of her patients, I am fascinated by the language—of "termination"—that she and her colleagues use to describe these moments. It is a word that sounds both inadequate and misleading to me, seeming to connote a finite moment in time when things are over and done and people move on. For me, the word even seems to have a dismissive quality, as when an employer speaks about having to terminate his employee. Similar to the leave-takings described in the previous chapters, the exits from therapy are, in fact, not open-and-shut, not black or white; they are not "binary." Rather they are layered, messy, and iterative, and they are embedded in relationships. The boundaries and bonds that get forged in therapy shape and light the path to the exit.

In addition, the finality carried in the language of "termination" does not reflect the fact that when people emerge from therapy, they are never "done"; they are never "finished" with their work. The ritual of exit, in fact, is in part about "honoring the work that is still to be done." "We are all works of art," says Linda, pointing out the ways in which we must—after the intervention of therapy—continue to revise the shapes and designs that we paint on our life canvases. Armed with the skills, insights, perspectives, and courage that have been forged in therapy, Linda hopes that her patients' paths toward healing will be more productive and rewarding, but she knows that their wounds will not disappear.

As a matter of fact, Linda Gould's last story, which concludes our interview, speaks to the subterranean presence and the surprising reappearance of our wounds when we least expect them—even when we have not felt the injuries for many years, even when we have developed successful strategies to compensate for them, even when we, like Linda, have been through therapy, more than once.

As Linda prepares for our interview, she grows more and more anxious. She has a horrifying nightmare whose interpretation is so transparent that we don't even need the help of Dr. Freud.[4] She dreams that she is in graduate school studying for a big exam, that she is sure to fail no matter how hard she tries, no matter how much she cares, because school was always the place where she was "never enough." Now, fifty years later, Linda worries that she will not be enough for me. She will not know enough, not be smart enough, not be articulate or wise enough, and I will be disappointed. And she worries about these things even though she knows that she is very good at her work, even though she "feels plentiful and abundant" as a therapist, even though she doesn't "doubt her competence" for a moment.

The frustration and sadness gather like a storm on Linda's face. She does not welcome the dark undertow of grief that has momentarily overtaken her. But she does recognize how the unmasking of her own primal wounds is a perfect coda for our conversation. The therapist—who, despite her worries about not being enough, has spoken most eloquently and wisely about the healing power of exits—is able to confirm that in revisiting our haunts, in analyzing our hurts, in discovering the way forward, in terminating from therapy, we will never fully escape our wounds. Rather, the exit will take us to that imperfect place where—if we are lucky—our scars will turn into badges of courage.

EXTREME WOUNDS

"What is the core problem here?"

Dr. Anthony Brown's patients have wounds that are physical, multiple, and critical; their diseases require dramatic and lifesaving interventions. As the director and chief attending physician in the intensive care unit (ICU) of University Hospital, he works with his residents to care for the sickest patients, those who are plagued by serious illnesses, who require the most extreme measures to keep them alive. He teaches the young doctors in his charge how to read the daily cataloging of scientific data, how to synthesize the various consultations from the myriad medical specialists, how to talk with the patients' families about life-and-death decisions, how to read the clinical signs that may trump the scientific evidence, how to act swiftly and with courage. As he guides his team of nurses, technicians, and physicians, they are all pointed toward the two exits out of the ICU. The patients who get better in their care are wheeled through the exit that takes them to the "floor" of the hospital, where they will stay for a while before heading home. For those whose lives cannot be saved, there is the final exit of death.

Dr. Brown meets me in the downstairs lobby of University Hospital, and after a warm greeting he guides me through a labyrinth of back corridors and elevators up to the ICU. Along the way, he gives me a snapshot description of Mr. Arthur, the patient his team is now visiting on their morning rounds, an eighty-five-year-old man who is "so sick in so many directions" and will probably die before leaving the ICU. When we arrive, the team—three residents, three interns, and the nurse taking care of Mr. Arthur—are emerging from behind the curtains covering the entrance to his hospital room. They automatically head toward the sanitizer dispenser outside the patient's room to clean their hands, take off their yellow plastic protective smocks, and then crowd around the computers and desks at the center of the unit. I know it is my age, but the young doctors look to me like adolescents dressed up in blue hospital gear. Silvia, an intern, sports a nose ring and orange hair, and Paula, a first-year resident, has old-fashioned black Converse All Star sneakers on her feet with Day-Glo socks peeking out. A few are chewing gum; all have stethoscopes dangling around their necks. But as soon as they open their mouths, to report on the patients' current status, they are all business, very focused, and completely adult in their demeanor.

They talk quickly, spitting out lots of numbers and acronyms and speaking the foreign language of procedures, therapies, consults, and medicines that sounds like gibberish to my ears. Dr. Brown—whom everyone calls Tony—takes a central place standing behind a large computer, consulting the charts, graphs, medicines, and data on each of the patients; listening intently to the residents' reports; occasionally asking a question, providing a clarification, or offering a historical perspective; and sometimes giving a brief monologue on some facet of their diagnosis, a rare didactic moment. The residents listen to his every word, look into his eyes for confirmation, or respond to his nod of affirmation and approval. Although he is doing many things at once—listening, searching the data, asking and answering questions, offering alternative perspectives, keeping track of the dynamics among his team—Anthony seems to be the still center of the storm surrounding him: soft-spoken, calm, unflappable. When his beeper goes off, he looks at it briefly, returns it to his pocket, or hands it off to his chief resident, never stopping the flow of conversation. When the respiratory therapist—a large, dark-skinned black man—steps behind him to whisper something about a patient's ventilator, he takes it in without skipping a beat.

Dr. Brown is the opposite of my caricature of the autocratic attending physician who screams at his residents, barking orders and bullying them into submission. If I did not know that he is forty years old, it would be difficult to guess his age. He is about six feet tall, with handsome features and a medium build; his head is balding and shaved close; his face is ageless, with the unlined, open, and somewhat innocent look of a very young man and the calm, wise, knowing gaze of someone much older. He wears brown khakis, suede loafers, and a light blue shirt with a burgundy-patterned tie. The stethoscope dangling around his neck offers the only signal that he is a doctor. Three white doctor coats hang on the back of his office door, looking barely worn. He moves quickly but with an economy and grace that doesn't ruffle the environment around him.

Anthony's authority is unquestioned, but he never seems to use or flaunt his position or status. He models curiosity, expertise, rigor, and professionalism—showing, not telling; questioning, not demanding. As I watch him in action, I suspect that his quiet, absolute authority reflects his gentle personality and empathic style as well as his intentional philosophy of education. He seems to believe that people learn best in an environment of openness and fairness, where everyone feels free to ask questions and no one spends time worrying about getting clobbered for mistakes. Later on, he tells me that "yelling and screaming just produces in learners a conditioned response, but it doesn't help the residents learn to think through a question or reason toward a diagnosis."

When he prods one of his interns about what medicine she would suggest for the diagnosis she has made, she blushes for a moment, then says, "I don't know, one of those weird endocrine things." In the midst of the laughter that follows, the chief resident helps her out with the exact name of the medicine. "I did not know that," she says gratefully, but without apparent embarrassment. There is an atmosphere of collegiality and support, a culture of teamwork. Anthony is a rigorous, focused taskmaster, intent on getting the work done—the pace is breathtakingly fast—but always aware of creating space for the questions and uncertainties that are part of the science and the art of clinical medicine.

There is a rhythm, pace, and routine to rounds. The intern begins the presentation of data: the patient's blood pressure, heart rate, respiratory rate, significant lab results, medicines, therapies; the consults with neurologists, radiologists, surgeons, orthopedics, etc. I am fascinated by the length and complexity of these reports,

signaling the multiple, layered, interactive illnesses of their very
sick and fragile patients. Then the nurse responsible for the patient
reads from her chart—a close-up descriptive view of what she has
experienced on the ward, a detailed clinical appraisal that sometimes raises questions about or challenges the course of action
presented by the resident. Anthony is the disciplined arbiter, naming the disparities, seeking to understand and resolve the contradictions, searching for patterns, themes, and meanings in the data
presented. He asks one of the residents to consider alternative
perspectives or strategies. "Any other things you worry about with
this kind of guy? It's a little like a fishing expedition." He asks the
nurse for her clinical view of the patient's mental state during the
night. "What are your observations, Sue?" "Well," she says, looking frustrated and exhausted, "he is awake and agitated, or he's
asleep . . . nothing in between. It is one extreme or the other . . .
very difficult."

When they have gathered all the pieces of information together, they put on the yellow plastic coats, sterilize their hands,
and visit the patient. Anthony raises his voice as he enters the
room, the only time he ever speaks loudly. "Hello, Mr. Shulman.
This is Dr. Brown and the ICU team. Can you open your eyes, sir?
I'm just going to listen to your heart." He spends a couple of minutes at the bedside, checks the monitors and ventilators, asks the
nurse about the patient's comfort and stability, and makes a quick
exit back to the computers. His movements are swift and practiced
as he braids his observations of the patient in with the data they
have before them. "I'm concerned that he is not moving his arms
more," he says simply, the one sentence whose language I understand completely. "Last night he had a wildly elevated PTT," offers
a second-year resident. "Not sure what to make of that."

At the end of the reports and bedside visits, Paula, the first-year
resident, is in charge of summarizing each case and articulating the
plan of action moving forward. She makes sure they have covered

all the essential areas—an automatic inventory that one of the interns on this rotation has named "the Big Six" (more traditionally called the "core clinical measures"). Anthony smiles as he explains to me later what the Big Six stands for: nutrition, pain control, vascular devices, code status, prophylactic care, and referrals.

Occasionally during rounds, someone mentions the patients' families who come to visit, who are frustrated and fearful, who hope for a miracle, who have a voice and point of view about how far the doctors should go in extending the life of their loved ones. The last patient they review, Mrs. Washington, has been in the ICU for forty-eight days, longer than any other patient. At fifty-two, she is mildly retarded and has multiple serious illnesses, including renal failure, anemia, heightened fever induced by the drugs she is taking, and gastrointestinal bleeding. She has had several blood transfusions, is attached to ventilators and multiple monitors, cannot speak, and is in great discomfort. "If anything," says Anthony, emerging from her room, "in the last two weeks she has looked worse." As they reconvene at the computers, the resident says that she has had an ongoing discussion with the family about a possible tracheotomy, but they seem unsure. "They keep waffling." Anthony's voice signals a crucial fork in the road, marking a moment when they all need to "step back" and take stock. "This is the time," he says in summary, "when we have to have a big-picture discussion with the family." The nurse nods in agreement and says that the family—the patient's sister, brother, and daughter—are coming in at 5:30 to meet with them, to have the "big-picture" conversation, to consider whether they have all gone far enough in trying to keep Mrs. Washington alive.

Later, as we talk in his small, unadorned office, Anthony tells me that of the eight patients they have seen in morning rounds, two will die. "Death," he says evenly, "is inevitable for many of our patients." On average, about 20 percent of the patients in the ICU die there, and Mrs. Washington will be one of them. There are two kinds of deaths, explains Anthony. The first he calls "letting go." "Mrs. Washington and Mr. Arthur would die very quickly—within minutes—if they were not in the ICU. With this kind of patient, you have to start by setting limits, being clear about how far we will go. In these two cases, and in consultation with the families, for example, we won't use chest compressions, shocks, or do further surgery. Every day they will get weaker . . . there is an inevitable decline where we de-escalate care and choose the therapies around comfort." The "letting go" Anthony refers to obviously includes the doctors and nurses as well as the patients and their families. It is always a hard and painful call; and a big part of Anthony's job is distinguishing between "fixable versus non-fixable" problems.

When he speaks to Mrs. Washington's family this afternoon—one of a series of ongoing conversations with them—Anthony will review all the things they have done to try to save her life and all the things that have not worked. "I will begin by sharing with them my sense of where she is clinically—what I see as the options now—and present the information in as objective a way as possible," he says solemnly. Together they will talk about some of the more "invasive procedures" that might allow them to sustain her for a little while longer. Anthony will ask whether this is what the family wants. At some point they will consider whether it is time to take the breathing tube out. These conversations are never perfunctory or brief. The doctor proceeds with caution and empathy, careful about his tone and pace, committed to hearing the voices of everyone, respectful of the complex, often tangled relationships within families.

This afternoon he will probably repeat a line he often uses when he is consulting with families about the end. "We can do a lot to her, but we cannot do a lot for her"—a line that usually follows the family's request that Anthony finally "say what he really thinks." When there is nothing more to be done, when everyone agrees it is time to let go, the efforts shift, away from "aggressive interventions" toward therapies that offer comfort and reduce pain. "Most patients facing death," says Anthony, "want to be comfortable. They don't want to suffer. They don't want to have pain. In the end, most people do not say they don't want to die."

Anthony estimates that 90 percent of the deaths in the ICU are of the "letting go" kind. The other 10 percent are the rapidly progressive extreme illnesses that you "can't keep up with because they are moving too quickly." Those are the ones that look like scenes from the television program *ER*, where someone is in cardiac arrest and everyone is in the room fighting to save the patient's life, using chest compression, inserting breathing tubes, using electricity to start the heart, offering acute life supports. Even though this scene—of disaster and heroism—is the one we imagine, Anthony says that these kinds of deaths are actually very rare in the ICU. "My job," he reports, "is actually to anticipate these problems so that we can avoid these crises."

Death in the ICU is the final exit that the team must anticipate, prepare for, and navigate, always considering the objective evidence, calculating the limitations of medicine, listening for the voices and views of the patient and his family, and occasionally consulting with other medical professionals who have treated the patient before he entered the ICU. The "letting go" is an "iterative process"—with conversations started, stopped, and returned to; weariness and frustration mounting; relief and sadness coming together with the final realization that it must be over. The other— more dramatic and much rarer—kind of death hits all of a sudden, requires immediate action, and offers no time for deliberation or conversation. It is a no-holds-barred fight for life. The ICU team is left defeated and exhausted, having done everything they could, but not able to do enough. These ways of dying in the ICU—one slow and iterative, the other fast and dramatic—are both anticipatable, though not welcome, exits from the ICU.

The other kind of exit that everyone refers to is the one that crosses the boundary between the ICU and the rest of the hospital—"the floor." For at least 80 percent of the patients, the single goal is to get them well enough to send them on to a bed in the regular hospital; very few patients leave the ICU and head home. As a matter of fact, Anthony underscores the boundary lines and amplifies the exit when he frequently tells his residents, "There are two kinds of people in the world: ICU patients and everyone else." As he draws the clear distinction for his residents, he encourages them to focus on those "fixable" illnesses that have brought their patients to "the most controlled environment" in the hospital. Why are they ICU patients? What makes them different from everyone else in the world? Anthony wants his residents to "identify the problem" that must be fixed so the patients will be "okay enough to go to the other part of the hospital."

As I listened to the morning rounds, this exit—to the floor—seemed to be the primary focus, the one that required deliberation by the team and preparation of the patient, the one that brought out the us-versus-them dichotomy between the ICU team and the regular hospital staff. As attending physician, Anthony keeps this boundary line and goal of exit in mind. He is aware of the myriad roles he plays and balances, and the ways in which they overlap and occasionally conflict with one another.

First, he is the doctor who, above all, seeks to "offer rational, safe, and reasonable care" for his patients. Being a good doctor, engaged in excellent patient care, is always his first priority. Second, he is mentor and teacher, guiding his interns and residents to a deeper understanding of clinical practice in the ICU; helping them identify the problems, offer diagnoses, and develop an organized way of presenting the relevant information; modeling for them a calm professionalism, "a gravitas," an approach to the work. "These are complex and confusing patients with an unusual and difficult array of diseases," he says, "and there is a lot to learn to decipher, a disciplined approach to moving forward, and a daily review of the data followed by a plan of action." Anthony tries to help his residents see the patterns that can be traced through the data. The young doctors tend to be sharp at identifying the discrete pieces, but they are less likely to see the shape of the whole, the inconsistencies and surprises or the disruptions to the patterns in the data.

Anthony admits that the teaching part of his role is not the most straightforward way of getting the work done. "There are much more efficient ways to do the rounds," he says. "If I did them alone, I could do them much more quickly and productively. I would not always be thinking about what the skills are that will help the interns and residents do my job. I would just be—based on my long experience, knowledge, and clinical judgment—doing it myself." But this is not a private practice where he works on his own; it is a large teaching hospital connected to one of the country's top medical schools. And Anthony believes that despite the obvious inefficiencies, he always learns from the residents' observations and questions. When he teaches, he becomes more articulate about what he knows, and how he knows it.

The third role that Anthony plays as he keeps his eye on the exit door to the hospital "floor" is as team leader, communicator, and coordinator. He is very conscious of building a "team" with a "horizontal" authority structure, where everyone has an important role, a legitimate perspective, and a valued voice; where he is always being intentionally inclusive. The culture he is creating in this professional community is purposefully different from the traditional hierarchies in most hospitals, with the attending physician at the top and the nurses close to the bottom. Anthony turns the traditional structure on its head, recognizing, for example, that the nurses have the best clinical intelligence on the team. They are the ones closest to the action, the ones creating relationships and establishing rapport with the patients, the ones with the most subtle and complex "granular view." The nurses' voices and views are particularly important in the ICU, where the patients are so sick, where the interaction of medicines and therapies can so easily go wrong, where data need to be fed back to the team in a timely, immediate way. "The nurses," says Anthony, "are the experts in this environment. They know so much more than the residents do about the patients, the illnesses, the therapies . . . and their impact on individual patients. We listen to them very carefully. We respect their point of view."

As a matter of fact, as a convener of the team, Anthony believes that his authority as an attending comes not from some show of dominance or power, or even from his knowing the answers to all the questions. Although I suspect this is one of the many places where Anthony is being overly modest (several doctors and nurses tell me, without my soliciting their views, that Anthony is the best doctor they have ever worked with, the most brilliant and the most compassionate), he sees his authority and reputation growing out of the way he "deals with an average busy day." It is the small, everyday stuff that deserves vigilant attention. It is his ability to remain "unflappable" in the face of all the chaos and complexity that comes at him every day—that is what gives him his authority (he does not use the word "power") as a teacher, mentor, and doctor.

A critical part of handling the "everyday stuff" rests on his getting to know the individual qualities of his interns and residents, their strengths and weaknesses, their ambivalence and fears, their learning styles, their personalities and character. Luke, the chief resident, does not have the social skills or the "gravitas" you would expect from someone in his position. In fact, Anthony admits with a smile that he is "a bit weird" and turns people off with what strikes many as immaturity and a lack of professionalism. But, says Anthony, "he is very bright and has trained himself to do other things very well. He is interested in organizational issues—how to create safer, more efficient medicine in the ICU—and has developed operating systems that increase the cohesion and communication among the team." By contrast, Roger, a second-year resident, is "thoughtful, conscientious, capable, and very smart . . . a natural leader, a talented clinician whom everyone likes." During the morning rounds I observe Roger's ease and geniality as he mixes with the nurses, technicians, and interns, his blend of confidence and humility, his curiosity and attentiveness in listening to his colleagues. Even though he has been there all night, his attention does not flag. And there is Paula, the first-year resident, who just a couple of weeks ago made the transition from being an intern and has found the move to her new status—and the responsibilities that go with it—unsettling. Anthony tells me that she is bright and learns quickly, but she expresses a lot of "fear and uncertainty."

The mention of Paula's fears reminds Anthony of one of the things he stresses and talks about openly with his residents. "Even if you have fears," he tells them, "you must act courageously. Courage is not the absence of fear. Courage is what you can do in spite of your fears. And courage is something you have to practice." In the ICU, the stakes are high and the fears mount—fear of patients dying, fear of making a mistake, fear of missing a crucial diagnosis. Anthony tells me about a former resident who was so uncertain and afraid that he was reluctant to "own the care of his patients." His fear not only put his patients at risk, it also alienated and angered the nurses. When the resident came to Anthony wondering why the nurses seemed to "hate" him so much, Anthony explained that they did not hate him; they just "smelled the fear" on him. They wanted him, above all, to do his job, and his job was to make a decision. They wanted—and needed—more from him.

Sometimes the fear and stress of doing this high stakes work is relieved by humor. As I watch the rounds, there are some moments of quiet laughter, when everyone seems to ease up a little bit, a brief rest from the speedy staccato of voices reporting measures

and diagnoses. I ask Anthony about those rare moments of re-
prieve, and he tells me that humor in the ICU is a "double-edged
sword." In such a high-anxiety environment, it is important to be
able to laugh, to lighten up from time to time. But it is critical that
the laughter never degenerate into "adopting a gallows humor,
which tends to be a pretty typical defense mechanism for doctors,"
and it is critical that it never devolve into making fun of patients.
As I observe the rounds, there are, in fact, a couple of times when
I hear laughter erupting in response to an intern's slightly off-color
remark about a patient, a response that I suspect is mostly a reflection of his own frustrations and uncertainty. At these moments
Anthony's face, I notice, remains impassive, clearly but quietly
projecting his sense that such remarks are inappropriate. One way
to avoid the "dehumanizing" echoes of gallows humor is to be
slightly self-deprecatory. "Self-effacing humor helps." Anthony
smiles. "I'll often tell my residents about silly mistakes I've made
that have led to unlikely outcomes. But even those kinds of remarks I do in moderation."

Our time together is drawing to a close, so I ask Anthony a
question that has been on my mind since I entered the strange and
extreme environment of the ICU several hours ago and noticed
immediately how much at home he was—and is—there. I ask him
what draws him to this work that he so clearly relishes, and he re-
ceives the question as if he has been given a gift. This is not the
first time he has considered these sources of commitment and attraction to his work, and his answers are immediate and revealing.
He comes up with a list of seven dimensions that still—after ten
years of directing the ICU—continue to excite and engage him,
continue to turn him on.

First, he points to the spreadsheet of numbers and graphs on
his big-screen computer and says, not surprisingly, "I like the data.
I like to make sense of the data." As I see him in action in the ICU,
it is impossible not to notice his command of and appreciation of

the numbers, his curiosity and skepticism about what the numbers and patterns seem to be saying, and his experienced understanding of the ways in which the numbers blend with, and sometimes contradict, his clinical insights. Second, he likes the fact that in the ICU "the stakes are so high," allowing him to feel "viscerally connected to the work." Third, he mentions how much the work gives him a chance to build relationships with patients and their families, the kinds of deep and trusting bonds that are forged especially when life and death are in the balance. Fourth, he talks about how much he likes the "procedural aspects" of clinical practice, the experience of actually placing the tubes in the patient's arm, hooking up the ventilators, doing the emergency heart compressions. Fifth, he loves the pace: fast, focused, and efficient. Things change very quickly, and you have to be prepared to stay out ahead of crises. Sixth on the list, he says tentatively, is "control . . . something about control." I wonder whether he means his own need to be in control. His explanation, however, offers a somewhat different perspective. "The ICU is the most highly controlled environment in the hospital, and in that way it is the safest. On a very small scale, for example, I can look on the screen here and see how much urine Ms. Johnson made between eight p.m. and nine p.m."

And finally, Dr. Brown mentions his love of teaching—all the ways he hopes to convey knowledge and compassion; standards, rigor, and courage; and clinical insight to the young doctors in his charge. "When I was a new attending, I used to be much more didactic, telling them all about the most recent randomized trials. I used to cite the newest journal articles. Although I still know all that stuff and stay current with it, when I teach my residents now, I'm likely to ask, Is this patient sick or not sick? What is the core problem here?" These questions—simple and stark—require that his residents do something very complex and difficult. In order to respond, they must synthesize the data, trace the patterns of disease and therapies across time, use their clinical judgment, think on their feet, actually see the whole person who is their patient, take "ownership" of their diagnosis, and finally draw on their practiced courage to make a decision. These are the hard-core questions that—when answered thoughtfully and rigorously and acted upon quickly and gracefully—lead the way to the exit.

Exits are absolutely necessary for the existence of some places. In fact, they may define a place. The boundary between there and here is marked by the exits. The ICU is such a place, set apart from the rest of the hospital, the rest of the world. In fact, Anthony Brown frequently marks the clear boundaries, and the unique space within, when he claims that the ICU is the "the most controlled environment in the hospital" and when he tells his residents that "there are two kinds of people in the world: ICU patients and everyone else." With patients who are "sick in so many directions," with extreme wounds that are hard to diagnose and fix, Anthony urges the young doctors to see the ICU as a place unlike any other—a protective, respectful, safe place; a dangerous, daunting, high-risk place—where exit is the goal.

This controlled—brilliantly lit, highly sanitized, densely staffed, intensely monitored—environment is the opposite of Sartre's dark and banal hell. People are not left alone to prey on one another, to indulge in self-mutilation, to remain in the inferno even when the exit door beckons them toward freedom. Rather they are carefully watched and fiercely protected. They are allowed to sleep and dream, ask for help, and decide when the pain has become unbearable. In this benign, extreme environment, Anthony urges the young doctors to focus on the "fixable" illnesses, the "core problem" that will—when solved—lead to the exit. He is the guide, master of "the way to the exit," modeling what it takes to accomplish exit—courage and authority; rigor, precision, and decisiveness; attentiveness and respect.

As he leads the way, Anthony wants his residents to embrace the contradictions and appreciate the art and science of clinical practice.[5] He urges them to pay attention to the details as well as the whole, to work fast as well as deliberately, to dig into the data and transcend the numbers, to identify the many layers and pieces as well as synthesize the whole and notice the patterns, to consider a multitude of options and possibilities as well as make a clear diagnosis, a definitive decision. This balancing act, this mix of paradoxes is what is needed to bring the ICU patient to the other side—"the floor" or death—successfully.

The exits can be classified into specific types based on the answers to simple—yet immensely complex and subtle—questions. Exit can be a letting go, inevitable but deeply considered and decided upon, an "iterative" process that depends on a series of difficult conversations with the patient's family. Exit can be unstoppable, too fast to catch, running ahead of the dramatic interventions, out of control. Exit can be a move out of the extreme environment of the ICU to a more stable condition on the floor, executed with calculated interventions and treatments. Exit can be shepherded by a master and teacher. The art and science of leading the way to the exit can be taught.

Just like Linda Gould, who sees teaching as a critical dimension of her therapeutic work with patients, Anthony Brown thinks about himself primarily as a teacher. He is teaching his residents how to blend the clinical and empirical aspects, the relational, aesthetic, and moral dimensions of their practice. He is aware of modeling calm, seriousness, and "gravitas," respect and empathy for patients. He recognizes the "inefficiencies" that would not be there if he did the work by himself, but he is also aware of the ways in which his students raise questions, search for explanations, and challenge presumptions that bring insight to his own learning. His teaching has changed over time. In the beginning it felt more like performance—citing the newest findings and insights from journal articles, displaying his deep and vast knowledge to his young charges. Now he teaches through inquiry, asking the fundamental questions that get to the "core problem."

He is guided by a well-developed "philosophy of education" that includes building a nonauthoritarian, inclusive culture where there is space for everyone to reason and question, to try alternative interpretations, to fail and recover; where the traditional hierarchies of medicine are upturned.[6] The nurses—who are close to the action, have a "granular view," and spend the most face-to-face time with the patients—have the most comprehensive and pragmatic take on things. The young doctors begin to appreciate the nurses' perspectives, learning to be especially attentive to those aspects of the work that cannot be reduced to quantitative measurement or scientific data, those understandings and actions that grow out of long experience, those insights that come from closely connecting with patients.

In the extreme environment of the ICU, courage is essential, and Anthony—like Linda Gould—believes that it can be taught, practiced, and learned. Courage, he says, is not the absence of fear; it is "what you do in spite of your fears." The fears and terrors are always hovering in the ICU, and there are lots of opportunities to do the wrong thing, with life-threatening consequences. The stakes are very high. Anthony keeps a steady hand, anticipating crises, distinguishing between what is "fixable" and what is not, guiding his residents toward the "big-picture" conversation with families whose loved ones are facing the final exit. But even as he holds it all together—the calm in the middle of the storm—he insists that his residents begin to "practice courage," reduce their awkwardness and uncertainty, and start to "own the care" of their patients. He wants the residents to develop a fearlessness and courage that will help them know when to keep fighting for survival, for life, and when it is time to let people let go.

Five

YEARNING

As I listened to people tell stories about the events, experiences, and motivations that precipitated their exits, I often heard a quality in their voices—a sound of longing, struggle, and desire—that I began to call "yearning." As they described their fears and ambivalence, their reluctance and caution, even their anticipation and excitement about leaving the old and entering the new, their reflections resonated with melancholy and tenderness, as if in facing the challenges of change and new choices, they felt a certain sympathy for themselves, a recognized vulnerability for wanting something so much, a hunger for what remained out of reach. Sometimes the yearning was for something concrete; they could visualize the place, the lifestyle, the new identity they wanted to get to, and the exit that would take them there. They could see the path forward, and they yearned for the courage, the energy, the resources, and the imagination that would allow them to get moving. Other times the yearning was for something inchoate and ephemeral, something unclear and elusive, something they could not name—perhaps an earnest and heartfelt thirst for experiencing something more meaningful and worthy. I am intrigued by both kinds of yearning—for the known and unknown, the named and unnamed—and by the ways in which exiting, at least voluntary exiting, always seems to begin with a disappointment and melancholy about what is and a burning desire, a yearning, to make a change.

In a language far more theoretical than the exit stories I listened to, the sociologist Helen Rose Fuchs Ebaugh begins to uncover some of the texture and dynamic of the yearnings I heard in the voices of my interviewees. In her book *Becoming an Ex* (1988),[1] Ebaugh offers a dense and comprehensive analysis of the processes of leave-taking experienced by people exiting from roles that they defined as central to their lives. Her huge and diverse sample included more than one hundred people who had experienced career changes (ex-cops, ex-doctors, ex-teachers, ex-athletes, ex-military, ex-professors), people who underwent major changes in familial roles (divorced people, widows, parents who lost custody of their children), and people who exited highly stigmatized roles (ex-convicts, ex-prostitutes, ex-alcoholics). Her interviewees even included ten transsexuals who were going through sex change surgery. Even though a quarter of a century has passed since the publication of her book, her study remains the only serious inquiry into the reasons that people, as Ebaugh puts it, "learn and unlearn, engage and disengage from the social roles that define who we are, especially in this rapidly changing world in which role exit is becoming commonplace."[2]

In reading Ebaugh, I was particularly intrigued by the confluence of autobiography and theory, by the blend of self-reflection and sociological analysis running through her text. As a doctoral student in the late 1970s, Ebaugh—a Roman Catholic nun—had focused her dissertation research on the growing number of nuns leaving religious orders. She wanted to know what precipitated their exits, how they negotiated their departures, and what their life experiences were as ex-nuns. In my language, she wanted to trace the yearnings in their hearts, the paths they traveled, and the ways these yearnings got translated into choices and actions. In the process of doing the research, Ebaugh became one of her "own statistics,"[3] left the order, and, shortly after leaving, married a divorcé. She was struck by the similarities of their exits—hers from the convent and his from his first marriage. Several years later, in *Becoming an Ex*, she explored the ways in which a "stage theory of role exit" might apply more generally to a variety of exits: from careers, from political and sectarian groups, from families, relationships, and organizations.

Ebaugh defines "role exit" as the process of disengagement from a role that is central to your identity and the reestablishment of an identity in a new role that takes into account your ex-role. She also notes that some exits are so common and frequent in society that they have become institutionalized; there are terms for these exiters—retiree, divorcé, recovered alcoholic, widow, alumnus. These institutionalized exits carry certain expectations, privileges, and status. Other, noninstitutionalized exits are also numerous in our society and simply carry the prefix "ex." Ebaugh frames role exit as a basic social process in which, regardless of the role being departed, there are underlying similarities. Every exit, for example, begins with "disengagement" (withdrawing from the role and the expectations associated with it), accompanied by a process she calls "disidentification" (ceasing to think of yourself in the former role), and concludes with resocialization (forming a new identity that includes adapting to the new role and hanging on to the vestigial residue of the previous role).

According to Ebaugh, the role-exit process proceeds forward through four distinct stages. The first stage is that of "first doubts," in which individuals begin to question the role commitment they had previously taken for granted. They start to reimagine, reinterpret, and redefine the qualities and responsibilities they have always seen as central to their identity. Usually, the doubting stage is gradual, often fraught; at other times it may occur surprisingly rapidly. The next stage is the seeking and weighing of "role alternatives." Here the quest for viable paths and attractive possibilities grows from a vague general awareness to a conscious step in the exiting process. Ebaugh calls the third stage the "turning point," when the individual actually leaves the role, often going public with his decision, making it more difficult for him to change his mind or turn back. The last stage of the exit process is "creating an ex-role," where one's previous role identification (a "hangover identity") is incorporated into a future identity. On the other side of the exit, people often struggle with establishing themselves in their new role while they continue to disentangle themselves from the self-perceptions and social expectations of their previous role. The tensions and incongruities between the new self-definitions and the old identity and patterns of behavior ("role residual") can become a big struggle for people during this time.

In many ways, Ebaugh's stage theory offers a useful framework for interpreting many of the narratives I heard, particularly those tales people told of exiting from their careers, from the organizational anchors and professional roles that had defined their work identities. Her analysis helpfully traces the sequence and order of exiting, the difficulties of letting go and leaving, the moment when we decide to take the leap of faith, and the tensions and ambivalence we experience defining ourselves in the new role when we still feel the vestigial residue from the old. I particularly like the way she helps us see that we never fully exit; we never fully escape our former selves. Those qualities and experiences "hang over" and become embedded in the reconstructed new role.

But as in most stage theories, there is a lot missing, a lot that gets masked by the discrete stages and categories that Ebaugh lays out. The progression of stages she presents as a unidirectional, relatively straight road misses the twists and turns and the retreats and regressions of our exits. Likewise, the sociological concept of "role" (a person's place in the normative structure of a group or organization) distorts our view of the individual characteristics and agency of the exiting person. We do not see the various and idiosyncratic ways in which people take leave; neither do we get to glimpse the universal patterns that are found in their unique stories. And although Ebaugh recognizes the ambivalences and apprehensions that make exiting hazardous, her framework does not resonate with the haunting sound of yearning, the melancholy of desire, the undertow of regrets that echoed through the stories I heard.

The two narratives in this chapter pulsate with yearning. Joe Rosario, an ex-priest, tells a long and arduous story of his exit from the Roman Catholic Church—a journey away from work that he loved, the parishioners to whom he was devoted, and the church in which he had grown up, a leave-taking full of ambivalence, procrastination, and caution, desire and yearning. After weighing the alternatives and balancing the pros and cons, after consulting with mentors and rationalizing the risks, Joe finally takes the plunge into medicine—a field he had been drawn to when he was an adolescent, a field that appeals to many of the same values and strivings that shaped his priesthood. But even though he ultimately finds deep satisfaction and reward in being a physician, the yearning continues to burn in him, a wistful yearning for what he has left behind.

By contrast, Josh Arons's decision to leave his job as the CEO of a major philanthropy is sudden and impulsive, arriving like an epiphany, surprising even him. But in the midst of his quick exit he discovers the yearning that has been in him for a long time, a deep desire—after twenty-five years at the helm—to find something different, meaningful, and creative; a yearning to have the inspiration for his next chapter come from within, "organically," and not feel compelled to rush into something that would feel like "more of the same in a different guise."

THE BURN OF YEARNING

"The ache became consuming."

His title is big—chief of internal medicine (at one of the top teaching hospitals in the country)—but his manner is modest and his office is tiny and spare. Except for two photographs of his wife and children on the wall beside his desk, the physical space is unadorned. A computer sits on his desk, and its organized surface contains a telephone, a small pad for jotting notes, and three neat piles of folders. A bulletin board is full of colorless medical charts, scientific graphs, and hospital announcements; and two simple blue chairs are available for patients and visitors. A large window looking out over the city lets the bright sun come in and makes the small space feel less claustrophobic. My eyes land on three pairs of shoes—all brown (much like the ones he has on)—lined up by the door, and I immediately wonder why they are there. Knowing he is a former Catholic priest, I imagine—in their modesty, sameness, and neatness—that they are left over from his monastic life. Maybe they would have been his entire collection of footwear when he lived a more spartan existence; or maybe they reflect the relative bounty of his life now that he does not have to limit his worldly possessions. Throughout our interview, my mind and fantasies return to the look-alike brown shoes.

Joe Rosario is forty-eight years old, but he looks much younger. He is about five feet seven inches tall, lean, and compact, and he moves with the ease and confidence of an athlete. His shiny black hair frames an open face, attentive brown eyes, and a radiant smile that is infectious and disarming. Everything about him—his dress, his gestures, his stories—feels a bit understated and modest. He does not seem to be aware of his handsomeness; he does not flaunt it. He seems to be most comfortable as the listener—responding to others' requests and needs, empathizing with others' struggles and pain—not the talker. There is a shyness and reticence about focusing on himself, and a style that is always slightly—and charmingly—self-deprecatory.

After I give a brief introduction regarding my project, there is an awkward silence. It is hard for Joe to know where to begin his story of exit—his "transition from being a priest"—so he jumps to the end. "I might as well cut to the chase," he says tentatively. "Leaving the priesthood was not complicated. It was celibacy . . . and I knew it would be an issue for me even before I became a priest." I was warned by one of his former patients—now his friend, who described Joe as "the world's best, most empathic doctor"—that I should not "let him get away with the celibacy story." It is not that his friend doubts that celibacy was "a big deal" in Joe's decision to leave the priesthood; it is that she has been curious about the "struggle and ambivalence" that she imagines must have been part of his journey to the exit. But as I listen to Joe's opening words, I do not feel worried by his spare, truncated explanation. I suspect that the single-word motivation for his exit—"celibacy"—is part of a well-worn script that masks years of history and layers of emotion. It feels like a warm-up, so I listen as he pushes on with the script.

"I actually loved the work of being a priest. I was teaching at a Catholic school in rural Virginia, working with teachers and kids, involved in a campus ministry, doing social service, and saying Mass on Sundays at a nearby parish. I was idealistic and stubborn . . . You see, I agree with celibacy in principle . . . and my work was great, but I knew deep inside of me that I was unhappy. I had a yearning—" Joe's eyes look to me for help. He has finished cutting to the chase; now where to begin. So I ask a grounding question: "Where did you grow up?" And he throws me an appreciative smile.

Joe Rosario was the youngest of five and the only boy in an Italian Catholic family who lived in a small town in Virginia. "We were routinely religious, laid-back Catholics," he confesses, as a way of describing how religion was naturally embedded in the routines and rituals of their lives and as a way of emphasizing how nondogmatic his parents were in conveying the principles and practices of Catholicism. "We were not overtly religious . . . we never had God or Jesus conversations. Our life was not rigid or rule-bound." He offers an example. Joe had a gay nephew, just eight years his junior, who was very close to and admired by his parents. When he "came out" in college—the family had really known all along—Joe's parents accepted the announcement without flinching or pulling back. "The Catholic Church is clear about the sinfulness of being gay, but my parents never skipped a beat. They loved him the way they always had loved him," Joe remembers.

Even though he describes his family's laissez-faire approach to Catholicism as laid-back, he also admits that religion was everything. It defined him; it surrounded him. He sums it up. "Catholic was who I was." And Catholicism was deeply linked with his Italian roots. Everyone he knew growing up was both Catholic and Italian. "Forty percent of the town was Catholic, but the circles that I ran in were one hundred percent Catholic," he says. Although both his parents were born in America, their parents were immigrants who settled in small, rural towns about ten miles apart. Joe's father, one of twelve children, grew up speaking Italian at home and only went to school through the eighth grade. His mother, who spoke mostly English as a child, went to college, a rare event for a first-generation Italian American woman during the 1930s and '40s. She dropped out after her sophomore year to marry Joe's dad and "fell into the traditional woman's role," cooking three meals a day, spending her days cleaning the house and taking care of children, and never driving a car.

All five of the Rosario children went to parochial schools, and three went on to Catholic colleges and universities. When Joe traces his early fascination with the priesthood, he actually goes back to his memories of high school, where he admired many of the priests who taught him. "Their good influence sort of opened up that door for me," he recalls wistfully. He liked what they did, the way they combined the spiritual and the practical, and their devotion to service in the community. And he liked the way they responded to their students with a winning combination of friendship and discipline. "The priests were very kid oriented," he recalls. "They did a lot to empower the students, helping us develop our leadership skills, guiding us in service and volunteer work." To Joe, the priests seemed to be living models of goodness, kindness, and grace generously given, and they knew how to really connect with the children in their charge.

Always a disciplined and high-achieving student, Joe was admitted to Villanova, where he immediately declared himself as a premed major, but he had an "interior life that gravitated" toward the priesthood. He remembers, in fact, "living two lives"—one in which he did "all the things kids do in college" and the other devoted to fantasizing about becoming a priest. For the most part, living these dual lives did not make him feel anxious or stressed out. As a matter of fact, he recalls feeling "comfortable and easy" balancing both realities. The two paths reached a point of divergence and some "unease," however, during Joe's junior year, when he studied very hard for the MCAT (medical college admissions test) but then decided at the last minute not to take it.

Even then, he recognized that an "internal decision" to enter the priesthood had taken place, one that he was not fully ready to recognize or talk about with anyone. When I ask him whether there was anyone who knew about his "deep yearnings," he mentions his college roommate, with whom he may have had a brief conversation, and he tells me about one of the priests who taught him in high school and became a "sort of mentor," to whom he sometimes turned for advice and guidance when he was home on vacation. But even after he told folks he had decided not to go to medical school, he did not mention the priesthood. Instead, he talked about going to graduate school in psychology (his minor in college).

Senior year forced his hand. He could no longer sit uncomfortably on the fence, between his two lives. He felt this most powerfully when he was with his girlfriend of two years, a Catholic girl with whom he had developed a sweet and loving relationship. He cared deeply for her; she was his best friend, a person with whom he shared his confidences. But their intimacy was always compromised by "the big secret" that remained hidden from her—his growing interest in the priesthood. Parting was hard, full of sadness and guilt. Even today Joe occasionally fantasizes about the road not taken and feels some remorse for the anguish he might have caused her. Even today he wants to protect her by not telling me the details of their relationship and separation.

The phone rings, startling both of us back into the present, and Joe excuses himself as he turns away from me and the past and answers it. One of his patients, a man in his mid-fifties, whom he saw a couple of weeks ago at the obesity clinic he directs, has suddenly died at home, his final exit. The caller is asking Joe for any information he has on the patient's condition when he was last seen at the hospital, and Joe punches his chart up on the computer. This is surprising, upsetting news, completely unexpected. Joe looks stunned; his voice grows quiet and intense. He tries to piece together the meager information he sees on the chart—obesity, high blood pressure, unemployment, living alone, etc.—and ends the call quickly with a promise to follow up. He shakes his head; there is sadness written all over his face as he tries to bring back the memories of the last time he saw the patient. Were there any signs he might have missed? I listen as his sentences trail off and he finds his way back to the spring of his senior year in college, when finally—"after endless procrastination and processing"—he contacted the Catholic Diocese of Virginia to inquire about training for the priesthood.

"I was completely naïve . . . I had absolutely no idea of what becoming a priest might involve. I did not even know that the priests at Villanova were different from the priests who taught me in high school." Joe's voice is incredulous as he laughs at his ignorance. I ask for clarification of the differences and distinctions. It turns out that the priests at Villanova are part of the Order of Augustine. They are not tied to a particular geographic region. Joe's high school mentors, on the other hand, were called secular priests, who are defined by geography and community, not by a particular order. Even though Joe did not know the various priestly classifications when he first contacted the diocese, he did know that he wanted to be like the priests who taught him in high school. "What I saw in high school is what I wanted to be," he says definitively.

"It was a coming out of sorts," he recalls about the moment when he finally, definitely stopped deliberating and took action. Everyone did not welcome his news. His girlfriend, whom he dated right up to the end of senior year, was hurt and crushed, even though she admitted to seeing the writing on the wall much before and even though she bowed out as gracefully as she could, her quiet retreat a cover for the anguish she must have been feeling. Joe's parents were surprised at his decision and definitely not enthusiastic when their son announced his plans. "They thought I was not making a mature decision," says Joe wanly. And his sisters—all four—were deeply skeptical. As a matter of fact, they did everything they could to dissuade him. Joe grins at the memory. "My sisters are all pretty Catholic, but they all sort of ganged up on me. They kept asking me why I wanted to do this, what my motivations were, and how I could possibly have come to this decision." Joe's oldest sister, a Hollywood costume designer, offered what she considered to be the ultimate seduction. She invited him to come out to Los Angeles for the summer, with the hope of introducing him to some gorgeous girl who would steal his heart. "She wanted to hook me up with someone; then I would be persuaded not to become a priest." Joe, in fact, did go to L.A. for the summer. He even dated a couple of girls while he was there. But when September rolled around, he was on his way back east to begin his "transitional year" of priesthood training.

Joe is quick to tell me that when his parents and sisters finally realized that he was fully committed to the idea of becoming a priest, they were completely behind him, offering him encouragement and support. And on the day he was ordained, they all turned out and cheered him on. "They were extremely proud. They stood there, completely amazed, very gaga. My family is terrific, incredibly supportive," he says about the ways in which his folks have always been there for him, always believed in his capacity to do whatever he sets out to do, always supported his decisions. And he reminds me that being from the community he comes from, becoming a priest is, after all, a big deal, "pretty, pretty cool."

The "transitional year" before actually entering the seminary is a time for asking the hard questions, for raising doubts and testing one's resolve. Through all the teaching, learning, and reading during that year, one question prevails: Are you sure that you want to do this? The theological curriculum at Saint Joseph's Seminary, where Joe was enrolled, had two parts—the first "academic" and the second "formative," dealing with the life of the spirit, community building, and the discipline of celibacy. For Joe, the year went by quickly and relatively smoothly. His answer to the big question about whether the priesthood was the right vocation seemed to be a resounding yes as he made his plans to enter Saint Vincent's in Philadelphia for the four-year march to ordination.

Joe remembers his early training in seminary as a time of spiritual devotion and probing questioning. "I was a practical skeptic," he says, comparing himself with those of his classmates who were unabashed believers. "I would say that I was a non-mystic in my beliefs. Many of my classmates were certain of the existence of God. They believed that miracles were real . . . that God's will was woven throughout their lives in very tangible ways. That was not me. I believed what I believed because I chose to, and I believed that there were legitimate alternative viewpoints that might be acceptable. Mine was not the one and only truth." Not only was he a skeptic and a doubter, he also believed in the pragmatic, real-life implications of religious belief. He wanted to witness—and participate in—making God's imprint on the world around him. "I believed that religion must be applied in a pragmatic way. We must make a difference in the world."

He offers a recent example. This past Easter, for the first time in years, Joe decided to go to church. "I've made several exits from the church," he says sourly. At Easter Mass, he found himself doing what any priest might do while listening to another priest's homily. He made up his own, to himself. "You can't help doing your own homily in your head, and mine was about resurrection giving me hope . . . asking myself the question about how hope overflows in my life . . . searching for a specific story, a real, lived experience, not a theoretical abstraction." Just in case I have not yet understood the contrast he is drawing between his own practical, real-world bent and other believers who turn inward in their devotion to God and the church, he says, "If I was making the distinction between applied and theoretical math, my approach would always be the former."

Luckily, Saint Vincent's was a fairly liberal seminary that offered the space for critical thinking and the questioning of church dogma. "In our discussions, there was always room for skepticism, openness, and discourse, which allowed me to become more comfortable talking about spirituality and my approach to religion," Joe recalls. As a matter of fact, he believes that in general, seminaries have become more rigid and closed-minded in their interpretation of church doctrine than they were when he was a student, and he feels fortunate that he matriculated at a time when progressive thinking and alternative views were welcome.

As we talk, Joe remembers a long-forgotten conversation he had during his third year of seminary, an exchange that presaged a struggle that would haunt his priesthood. He recalls saying to a friend one day, "'If I leave [the priesthood], it will be because of celibacy.' I knew even then this was a big yearning." And by celibacy he meant "the whole thing," not just the sex. He was yearning for the "connection, the intimacy, the closeness" of a relationship as well. And he recalls one evening that same year going to a party with a bunch of old college friends, having a few too many drinks, and going home with a girl. Nothing happened between them; she knew he was a seminarian. But the lingering memory is of feeling the yearning and the guilt, the attraction and the repulsion, and the wish that he had not put himself in such an awkward position.

After seminary, Joe was assigned to a small parish, close to a college campus in a rural town in Virginia, near where he had grown up. "They ask you what sort of work you want to do, but really they assign you . . . plug you in to a place where they think you are needed." The fact that Joe had no real choice in selecting the place for his first ministry did not bother him. "It was the perfect place for me," he recalls with pleasure. "But then I'm the kind of person who feels whatever place I end up is perfect for me." He loved the work—the variety and the meaningfulness of it, the chance to build close relationships and help people, the feeling of appreciation and adulation from his parishioners. He speaks about a paradox of priesthood that most people do not recognize. "The work is great because there are lots of ways of working, and you can do lots of things. Even though the church is a rule-bound and seemingly rigid institution, priests have a lot of autonomy and flexibility." Joe enjoyed the hidden degrees of freedom that were there to be seized and the way he was able to make choices about how he would do his work.

He also began to recognize the value of celibacy in a priest's life, the advantages and benefits that came with not being married, that came with sexual abstinence. "I never really bought into the religious notion of celibacy, the part about giving yourself to God . . . the part about Jesus not being married," he admits. "But there is something about not being married, not being committed to a family life with a wife and children that leaves room for developing close and intimate relationships with the people you are serving. If you are a social kind of person, you can become part of people's families, get connected to lots of people in really deep ways." His voice is wistful. It is clear that now that he is not a priest, he misses the kind of closeness and trust that comes with being free of the responsibilities and expectations of family life. He admits sadly, "I've never found that kind of intimacy since I left the priesthood."

But it is not only that there are opportunities for connecting with people deeply through priestly work; there are also the benefits of being known and appreciated by an entire community, particularly in a rural Catholic town. Joe is still amazed—and slightly embarrassed—by the status and adulation he enjoyed as a young priest. "You were put up on a pedestal. Everybody knew you." He tells me the story of a community fund-raiser for a health center in the small town where he worked, where the big prize they offered was the chance to have the priest over to your house for dinner. The raffles sold out immediately. Folks clamored for the privilege.

The intimacy and the reverence that came with the access and trust afforded priests now makes Joe shake his head in anger and disgust. With the worldwide exposure of abuse and pedophilia by priests and bishops of the Catholic Church, he is outraged by the ways in which people's trust has been betrayed, the ways in which the clergy have taken advantage of their cherished place and high station to do violence to innocent children. The heightened visibility of the rampant pedophilia not only enrages and disgusts him, it also has made him recall and question the motivations and behaviors of some of the priests he admired and revered in high school whose closeness to the students—his classmates and friends—now seems suspect, "even creepy." It makes him wonder, and feel suspicious, about moments of physical closeness and gestures of intimacy he experienced with his high school teachers that he, in his innocence, interpreted as benign and salutary. Recently he heard that a couple of those priests he knew in high school had, without admitting their guilt, quietly resigned under a cloud of suspicion. Again he closes his eyes and shakes his head, glad not to be a part of such a tarnished fraternity, furious at a church that would cover up and protect the abusers.

Even though Joe loved his ministry, loved serving the small community, loved the intimacy and flexibility of his work, and loved the priestly status and adoration from his parishioners, the yearning for a love relationship was always there. It was as if he were living two lives. "On the surface I was the same functioning and happy priest, but inside I was unhappy, and no one knew. Ultimately I couldn't reconcile these parts of me." Finally, when "the ache became consuming," Joe decided to talk about it with his spiritual director, and then he sought help outside of the church. "In the midst of this woefulness I recognized that I was truly depressed, that I needed the emotional support of a clinical psychologist."

The psychologist he saw was, in fact, a practicing Catholic who listened to him with patience and sympathy. During his therapy sessions Joe found himself drawn back time and again to the memories of his girlfriend in college, the one he had left when he decided to become a priest. "In some ways, I felt I had never gotten over her," he recalls. "It is not as if I wanted to erase all the years in between—they had been good—but I wanted to just go back to that time when we were together. She symbolized all that I was missing and yearning for."

Just as he had done before entering the seminary, when he was struggling with his family's worries about his chosen vocation, Joe traveled out to visit his sister in Los Angeles, the place that has over the years come to represent escape and freedom for him. His sister has always been loving and fiercely protective, but she has also offered him the space to express his ambivalence and uncertainty. "She is very unconventional, very different from me," says Joe with appreciation. Her home has always felt far away from the rules and routines of his priest life, far away from the watchful scrutiny of the church.

On this particular visit, his sister introduced him to one of her girlfriends, actually someone who was about Joe's age. They ended up spending all their time together. "We had a great time . . . nothing intimate or sexual. It was just fun and flirtatious . . . sitting close, next to each other. It was sixth-grade kind of stuff," says Joe about a time he still remembers as wonderfully "liberating and carefree." However innocent it was, he left L.A. knowing something for sure. He returned to the East Coast with a new clarity. He was going to leave the priesthood; he could no longer live the celibate life.

Joe returned to face the resistance of his spiritual director, who remained skeptical about his decision and tried to dissuade him, coaching him to "hang in." He even went to see his old mentor from high school, who surprised him with his straightforward, no-nonsense advice. "If leaving the priesthood is what you want to do, then do it." Something about the clarity and brevity of this response was "pivotal" for Joe. It helped to release him, propel him into action. For the first time, he remembers, a whole "new life opened up" for him. Leaving no longer tugged so hard at his heart. Now it was just a matter of jumping the church's hurdles and navigating the exit procedures. The psychologist who had counseled him wrote a letter of support to his bishop. Then Joe met with the bishop and told him "the whole story" behind his decision. Still hedging his bets, he did not ask for a complete separation, but for a leave of absence from the church. The bishop listened attentively and responded supportively. "Take all the time you need," he said gently. "We are here for you."

The bishop made the departure relatively easy, leaving the door wide open for Joe's return. It was harder—much harder—for Joe to say goodbye to his parishioners and the teachers and students he worked with at the local school. He had, by then, become "very good friends" with so many of the people, and he felt that they needed to hear the truth from him. But the bishop had insisted that when he said his farewells at his final Mass, he should "not go into the reasons why." So he stood up in front of the congregation—full of many people he had grown to love—and spoke ambiguously. He "left it enigmatic," giving a stilted presentation that satisfied neither him nor his listeners. It was also a talk that left people wondering and skeptical, perhaps fantasizing that he was trying to cover up something, that he had been "part of a scandal." But mostly Joe hated that he had to lie to the folks who had been so "incredibly supportive and generous." He was not giving them what they deserved—the "real story" of why he needed to leave them. "That was what made me feel the most guilty," he whispers.

With the reassurance of the bishop, Joe explored every option he could think of, from doctoral programs in psychology and education, to M.B.A. programs, to law school and medicine. He visited the campuses, went on tours, had interviews, studied brochures, and filled out applications. There is no one, he claims, who is more methodical and comprehensive—perhaps to the point of being "obsessive-compulsive"—than he is. "I process everything to death," he says about the way he always weighs his alternatives and is never impulsive or rash in making decisions. Finally, after more than a year of casting about, Joe applied—at thirty-six—to a post-baccalaureate premed program at a college near L.A. that was known for its personalized mentoring of students and for getting them admitted to prestigious medical schools. It had been so long since he graduated with an undergraduate premed major from Villanova that there were whole new fields and courses—such as molecular biology—that he had to study.

During the two years there, Joe lived with his sister and worked at a series of odd jobs to earn spending money. Even though he was a full-time student, he was still "officially" a priest, an identity that remained mostly hidden from view. He had saved about $25,000, a "huge sum" that disappeared amazingly quickly. With the savings, he was able to spend the first seven months just going to school. But then he needed to hustle and make a living. Having spent the last decade and a half in religious life, Joe felt frustrated by a job market where his experiences and skills held little value. After applying to—and being rejected by—several low-level service jobs, he finally found work as a courier, driving 150 miles a day on the L.A. freeways, delivering movie scripts and legal documents. One memory—of the humiliation of his new low status—stands out. He recalls delivering a document to a Hollywood agent's office and being treated dismissively by "some eighteen-year-old kid" receptionist. Motioning to the empty chair, he told Joe, "Sit right there. I'll deal with you when I'm ready." In that moment Joe came face-to-face with his fall from grace. "Doesn't feel very good," he says, smiling wanly, "to go from being a big shot to being a thirty-six-year-old delivery boy."

Every night as he left the college library, Joe would call his sister to say that he was heading home. "I come from a family of worriers," he tells me, "and my sister was taking on my mother's role, wanting to know my every move." Not only was his sister committed to keeping him safe; she also was always looking to introduce him to women. She wanted him to relish his new freedom. She wanted him to celebrate his release from the "claws of celibacy." One day she spoke to a former neighbor whose daughter was looking for a job as a costume designer, and she happened to mention that Joe had left the priesthood and was living with her. The neighbor, who recalled having met Joe years earlier, thought he might be an excellent match for one of her coworkers, and she gave Joe's sister the woman's number.

It took weeks for him to get around to calling Angelina, a real estate agent and divorcée who was a single mom of a five-year-old daughter. They met for lunch and "really hit it off." It was several months—of dinners, dates, and adventures together—before Joe met her daughter at a family gathering. For some reason, that moment of meeting her child stands out. The little girl was wearing a red hat, tilted to the side of her head. Joe recalls, laughing, "She was a real charmer . . . she worked the room. It was easy to fall for her in a superficial sort of way." But Joe was aware of some resistance inside of him, some need to not fully succumb to the little girl's wiles. "I sort of stood back and watched, thinking that there was more to this story than I knew or could see . . . feeling that I was not quite ready to take this on."

Over the months, Joe's reluctance slowly melted as he continued to date and enjoy Angelina and as he grew closer to her daughter. But he still did not feel completely sure about his path to medical school; nor was he 100 percent certain about leaving the priesthood forever. "This was still somewhat of an experiment," he says about his romance and his newly chosen vocation. "I was ninety-nine percent sure of pursuing my medical degree, but there was still that one percent possibility that I would return to the priesthood. I'm one of those people who holds on to the possibilities until I finally make a decision. Then I let them go." Since he was still not 100 percent certain of his path, he decided to tell the medical schools to which he was applying that there was a dim possibility that he might return to being a priest. He also dangled his indecision in front of Angelina, believing that it was only fair that she know the truth as well, know about his lingering ambivalence.

As he applied to medical schools, he felt the double edge of excitement and dread. "It was thrilling to be thinking about starting my new life, but I was also worried about not getting into medical school and having nothing that was marketable." Keeping as many options open as possible, Joe applied to scores of schools, had lots of interviews, and "daydreamed often about what it might feel like to receive an acceptance letter." At first he did not put fancy schools on his list, thinking they would be out of his reach, but his professors insisted that with his record, he could get in anywhere. It turned out that he was accepted at almost every place he applied. The letters from Columbia and Yale arrived on the same day. I am surprised when Joe tells me that his sister opened the letters before he arrived home; and as he walked in the door, she handed him the open envelope from Columbia. Rejection. Then, feigning thirst, she walked to the refrigerator and pulled out a bottle of champagne to which she had attached the letter from Yale. Acceptance! Joe was surprised and overjoyed. "It was a no-brainer. Yale has a great program, and I always knew I wanted to come back east," he says, victory still in his voice.

He headed east the following fall, leaving Angelina and her daughter behind—still feeling "on the fence" about their relationship, vowing to "see what happened" once he "got going in school." They kept in touch through the fall and visited back and forth at Thanksgiving, Christmas, and during his spring break. He did not date any other women. "Then," he admits quietly, "I started worrying about her." He furrows his brow, admitting again, "I come from a family of worriers . . . it is a sort of strange way to show love, but that is the way we do it." During the first three years of medical school, there were longer visits between them. He even took a Spanish immersion course so he could do a rotation at a community clinic in L.A. that served Latino patients. And while he was there, he lived with Angelina and her daughter.

After living together, even Joe, the big "processor," the "huge worrier," knew that decision time was near. How long could he string this out? It was his mother who finally said to her son, in a fit of frustration, "Shit or get off the pot! If you're going to marry her, do it now." The next day, Joe and his sister went out to find the ring, and that evening Joe proposed to Angelina. "I'm the least spontaneous person I know," he says with understatement. But once Angelina said yes, life flew by with the speed of lightning. She gave two weeks' notice at her agency, they packed up the rental truck, and the three of them—Joe, Angelina, and her daughter—drove across the country and into the future. They had no jobs, no plan, and no place to live. Something had turned the worry into an adventure.

In many ways, Joe Rosario's long leave-taking from the church resembles the stages of role exit identified by Ebaugh. He goes through a protracted period of "first doubts," keeping his "longings" secret, his "woefulness" under the radar; enjoying—and feeling guilty about—hanging out and flirting with a girl in a "sixth-grade kind of way"; feeling a huge nostalgia for the serious girlfriend he abandoned in college when he decided to enter the priesthood. His mounting doubts make him feel that he is leading a "double life"—on the outside he is the jovial, compassionate priest; on the inside he is aching with anguish. When the dualities and masks get to be unbearable, he consults with mentors, former teachers, a psychologist, and his bishop, explicitly asking for their guidance, implicitly begging them for their permission and blessings. A second summer in L.A.—under the protective and liberating tutelage of his sister—finally convinces him that exit is the only option. But even then Joe hedges his bets and decides to take a leave of absence rather than resign from the priesthood.

Joe plays out the second stage of Ebaugh's theory—weighing "role alternatives"—with his signature caution and meticulousness: casting a wide net, investigating numerous options, holding on to his allegiance to the church even when he submits his applications to medical school, even when he is 99 percent sure that he wants to leave the priesthood and become a doctor. The "turning point"—Ebaugh's third stage—actually comes several years later, when his mother forces his hand ("shit or get off the pot") and his older sister goes with him to buy the engagement ring for Angelina. All of a sudden, after years of "processing and procrastination," a decision that has been waiting to happen propels life forward, a mighty wind that sweeps the family of three across the country in their U-Haul.

As Joe rehearses all these stages of exit, there is an undertow of regret and "yearning," a word he uses more than any other to describe the "ache" that never leaves him, that gets rationalized in his caution and deliberation, in his meticulous listing of the pros and cons, the opportunities and liabilities at every fork in the road. His exit is marked by huge "what-ifs," endless deliberation, and processing, an internal decision that lives for years inside of him, not ready to be revealed, more a response to circumstance than an exercise in agency. His tale shows us how much not being able to exit can hurt, and how we can begin to accept that hurt as part of our lives for a very long time. Some of the hurt seems to be inherited. Joe comes from a "family of worriers"; worrying is the way they show their love. Worrying is embedded in the family's approach to life decisions and in the ways they relate to one another. Being raised in the bosom of the Catholic Church must have added another layer of yearning and hurting, fueling his aching guilt for having abandoned his sacred duties and promises and deepening his wistful longings for the people he left behind.

The path toward exit, Joe claims, "begins and ends" with his unwillingness to live a celibate life forever. He knew that the vow of celibacy would be a problem even before he signed up for the priesthood. But when he yearns to be with a woman, he realizes he is speaking about something more than sex. He wants the intimacy, commitment, and companionship of a "fully realized relationship."

He wants a partnership with a woman that is "liberating and carefree." He wants the pleasure of flirting and playing, feeling the comfort and warmth of her body next to his. But when he meets Angelina's five-year-old daughter—charming in her fetching red outfit and precocious femininity—he is not at all sure he wants to take her on. He wonders whether he is ready for the responsibilities, the compromises, and the risks of embracing family life. He wonders whether he is ready to leave the safe harbor of celibacy.

As Joe tells me about the dark, aching side of celibacy and recounts his years of yearning to break its hold on him, he discovers its silver lining. He has a sudden, surprising epiphany. He doesn't believe that the reason priests should take a vow of celibacy is so that they can give themselves fully to God, or because Jesus never married. But he does believe that the celibate life offers priests the emotional space to be present with the people they are serving, to enter fully into their lives. "I have never known an intimacy like that since I left the priesthood," he admits. There is an irony in Joe's exit search. After long years of yearning for the intimacy and devotion of marriage, he exits the priesthood and discovers what he has lost and left behind, some of the deepest human connections he has ever known.

There is wistfulness in Joe's voice, a sadness that seems to run deep when he tells the story of his saying goodbye to the small parish in Virginia. It was hard enough to leave those people who depended on him, whom he had grown to love, who had loved him back with a purity and adoration he would never experience again. But even harder than leaving was the way he had to muzzle his message, telling his parishioners vague half-truths that left them feeling uneasy and suspicious. By far, the biggest injury was his having to lie to them, leaving a hurt that continues to haunt him today.

Joe's unsettling departure—compromised by lies of omission—helps us understand the importance of truth telling and authenticity and the critical role of ritual in paving the path to successful exits. His last lame sermon, full of ambiguity, did not give Joe the chance to offer his appreciation to and affection for his congregation, nor did it give him the vehicle to express his loss and grief at leaving. And it did not give his parishioners the opportunity to record the sadness in their hearts or their rage at his going. There was no ceremony to hold their overflowing emotions, no way to channel their beautiful/ugly mix of feelings, no way for Joe to bow out with grace.

Rituals that are intentionally and artistically designed, that allow us the chance to revel in our emotions—of appreciation and love, of regret and despair—give us the chance to mark the separation, say our goodbyes, and move on. Otherwise the exit feels incomplete, nourishing a yearning that burns on forever.

YEARNING TO MAKE SENSE

"Stepping out, looking back, measuring myself."

I am witness to the elaborate farewell ritual that marks the departure of Josh Arons from the Beacon Fund, the largest philanthropic organization in New Hampshire, which he has masterfully led for a quarter of a century. Almost a thousand people have come to celebrate Josh's leadership and to mark the growth of the fund that under his stewardship has more than quadrupled its endowment—serving as a safety net for the poorest citizens, offering major grants to community service organizations, lobbying the state legislature for public funds that will contribute to sustainable economic change, and pushing through some of the most controversial and progressive public policy initiatives in the state. Colleagues and friends, politicians and community organizers, and leaders of corporations, colleges, and nonprofits are gathered in the Hyatt Hotel in the state's capital to honor Josh and say their goodbyes. Eight hundred fifty chairs fill the ballroom (with 150 more in an anteroom with a video feed), a glittering space with ornate chandeliers, heavily draped windows, and deep burgundy carpeting. The stage has two huge screens on either side of a giant photograph of a New Hampshire scene, with mountains in the background and in the foreground a bridge over a gushing river. "Bridge" is the symbol and metaphor of the evening. An abstract graphic of a bridge appears on the invitation, the program, and the 2009 annual report, marking Josh's bridging of the past and the future, underscoring his transition and journey.

A planning committee—of board members, staff, donors, and grantees—has worked for almost a year to find a way to honor their leader, hoping to strike a balance between their wish to lavishly celebrate him and his wish to "keep it simple." Finding within him the discipline to "stay out of it," and knowing how important it is for folks to "make a big deal," Josh has made only three requests. He does not want any big speeches, he wants everyone at some point to join in singing "Stand By Me," and he wants everyone to be given a piece of dark chocolate (in this case shaped like the state of New Hampshire). The first request is the hardest to honor, admits the master of ceremonies, but they do manage to finesse it by asking about ten people—longtime friends and colleagues—to speak for two minutes or less on an essential quality they have admired in Josh. And surprisingly, everyone sticks to the time frame, even the governor, who leads the parade of tributes.

While people are taking their seats and greeting one another, a Ghanaian music and dance troop, dressed in the traditional kente cloth, are onstage beating their drums. The sound is loud and thrashing, reverberating through the hall, causing some people to grimace, cover their ears, and shout to hear one another in conversation. For me the juxtaposition is jarring: the dark black musicians—smiling, gesticulating, bodies gyrating, barefoot—and the very white, traditionally garbed audience sitting primly in their seats. It is a black/white contrast that continues to be underscored throughout the evening, signifying Josh's rebel activist days in the civil rights movement in Mississippi and his long tenure as executive director of the Beacon Fund, working with white communities—many of them poor and rural—across the state. I sit there feeling troubled, even sad, as I imagine how the dissonance and distance between these black and white worlds must have required more than bridging, more than compromise and negotiation. I think there must have been some suffering as well, some ways in which Josh has had to dampen his progressive, activist impulses and mask his rebellious spirit in order to be successful at his work in New Hampshire.

The tributes and numbers speak to his amazing success and commitment—the huge growth in resources, endowment, and grants; the initiation and development of new government programs and policies; the outreach to marginalized, impoverished communities; the building of social capital in neighborhoods around the state. The statistics of expansion and growth under Josh's leadership appear on the screens and make people gasp and applaud. But the tributes are a much more poignant reflection of his contributions and the respect, even reverence, in which he is held. Each speaker chooses a word or two to describe him—energetic, imaginative, productive, attentive, creative, hardworking, empathic, visionary, masterful, extraordinary, politically savvy—and several of them choke up as they tell stories of his deep listening, his steady support, his love of ideas, his large and nimble mind, his big embrace.

When Josh rises to make his comments, the audience stands in lengthy applause, and he is clearly moved. His voice is soft and hoarse; he speaks slowly and carefully, from the heart. He speaks mainly about his growing appreciation for the meaning and power of "place"—the way he has come to love this place called New Hampshire, the special qualities of the people and the ways they have worked together, powerfully connected in their collective mission, bridging the differences, nourishing the bonds. At one point he brings up the work of his rebel youth, reminiscing about the ways in which the black folks from rural Mississippi talked about their responsibility to place. "I does where I am," he says, sounding black and southern. But he quickly returns to the Beacon Fund story, the last twenty-five years of labor he has loved in a place he loves, back to his testimony that there is no place he would rather have spent this part of his life. Oddly, there are no comments from his family—children and grandchildren—who are all sitting in their black, white, and biracial splendor in the front row, and no appreciations from old and dear friends who have known him for forty years and have traveled from Rome, Chicago, and Seattle to be here. The celebrants are all closely linked to "place," New Hampshire and the Beacon Fund. The ceremony is intentionally focused on his work community, not his family; it is designed to focus on his public, not his private, life.

The gathering concludes with the song Josh requested. On three huge screens flashes the face of an old black street musician strumming his guitar. With a bag in front of him open for tips, he sings a soulful, raunchy version of "Stand By Me." His eyes are shut; his head sways back and forth to the blues rhythm. Then the video pans to other places where brown and black people are singing "Stand By Me," voices from around the globe joined in a universal anthem. The audience is surprised and delighted when the video turns back to their "place," to groups of folks they recognize, white people from across their state singing "Stand By Me," awkwardly smiling, tentatively swaying, trying to loosen up and catch the rhythm in their bodies. For minutes we take in the contrast— the sensuous, soulful bodies; the raw, husky voices and plaintive calls of the blacks from the United States, Africa, the Middle East; even a Native American group dressed in their tribal costumes . . . and the white folks from the office, community groups, and local churches around New Hampshire giving it their best shot, trying their hardest to find the melody and move to the beat, enjoying themselves. I sit there wondering what Josh feels about all this. How is he taking in this celebration of his good works? Whom does he want to stand by him once he crosses the bridge? Where does he want to stand next?

Josh Arons remembers the exact moment when he decided to cross the bridge. It was December 2008, and he was attending a conference in San Francisco sponsored by Civic Ventures, a non-profit on whose board of directors he sits. Each year Civic Ventures awards a Purpose Prize to a dozen people over sixty who have embarked on "Encore Careers"—visionaries whose ingenious and generous vocational shifts are making a big difference in the world, locally and globally. Even though Josh has attended this annual awards ceremony since it was initiated a decade ago, and even though his own work for the past twenty-five years has focused on public service, this was the first time he felt the powerful impact of the stories he heard in a "deeply personal way."

He was inspired by the sixty-five-year-old perfume baron who left his lucrative spot as the CEO of a major international company to work with men leaving prison, helping them find work and dignity on the outside. He loved hearing from the former cameraman whose Hollywood career had dried up long ago, who had suffered through years of poverty and unemployment but finally, at the urging of an old friend, traveled to West Africa to work with indigenous folks to invent a technically simple and elegant machine that shelled peanuts, increasing the productivity of the rural region tenfold. There were other amazing stories from "ordinary people making extraordinary contributions"—discovering new life paths, taking big risks, learning new skills and disciplines, awakening new passions—and Josh drank it all in.

He recalls the "enormous impact" of those "amazing stories" and the excitement, the provocation, and the urgency that rose up in him. Right then he knew that something had shifted in him; he

felt it in his gut. He knew—with a clarity and poignancy that surprised him—that it was time for him to "move on"; it was time to
"embark on his next chapter." Josh returned to his hotel room that
night and called his partner, Joyce, to tell her the exciting news.
And two days later, when he landed back in New Hampshire, he
sat down with his board chair to tell him that he would, within the
year, be ending his tenure as CEO of the Beacon Fund. Even
though Josh suspects that his decision to exit must have been stir-
ring in him for many years, his "moment of epiphany" came like a
bolt out of the blue. It arrived without warning and required no
rational listing of pros and cons, no calculated deliberation.

Josh welcomes the opportunity to reflect on his exit from the
Beacon Fund. His decision to leave sneaked up on him all of a sudden, but he knows that moving forward—with "purposefulness
and grace"—will require that he revisit his journey and rehearse
the mixture of feelings that have converged in him during this moment of transition. He leans back in his chair and strokes his chin
in thoughtful meditation. He furrows his brow; his voice is almost
a whisper. "What has interested me in leaving . . . is how much I
have loved the work as much as I've ever loved anything. I'm struggling to make sense of it all, wanting to learn as much as I can
from it." He asks me whether I've ever read *Stranger in a Strange
Land*,[4] a science-fiction book that he loves, where the characters
invent a new verb—"grok"—that means to "be at one with some
truth." Josh smiles. "That's what I want to do now . . . grok what it
means to be leaving."

In his effort at meaning making, he begins at the beginning,
sketching out his early biographical route. Adopted at birth, Josh
grew up in New Jersey and attended public schools all the way
through high school, then attended Williams College. After college he earned a master's in foreign policy at Columbia before
heading off to do relief work in West Africa. Within a year he had
returned to the United States, intent on becoming part of the civil

rights movement. "I kept reading about the struggle in Mississippi and Alabama," he recalls, "and I thought, I need to be there." He was right. His work in the South was deeply engaging and formative for him; even now it seems to serve as a touchstone, a reference point against which much of the rest of his life is measured. The stories from Mississippi—his work with sharecroppers, doing voter registration, sitting in at lunch counters, joining the bus boycotts—remain a "huge part" of his identity, giving early definition to his lifelong commitment to social justice. The Selma march stands out as an unforgettable marker: blacks and whites, Christians and Jews, southerners and northerners coming together in collective action, marching side by side, singing freedom songs. These are the songs that still echo through him as he gathers with friends around the dinner table or takes his activist work to the rural regions of New Hampshire; these are the songs he hoped to hear at his goodbye gala.

John Lindsay's campaign for mayor of New York pulled him away from his work in the South, and when Lindsay won the election, Josh, at twenty-five, stayed on in a major policy position, overseeing the antipoverty, welfare, and educational initiatives—a lefty Democrat working for a progressive Republican mayor. It was a heady, even glamorous time. Josh points to the teachers' strike he helped organize, which closed down the public schools from September through November. A recently completed documentary about the Lindsay years stars him as one of the chief protagonists, giving him the opportunity to relive those amazing days of his youth and reflect on the way he shaped and was shaped by the political and cultural landscape. After eight years with the Lindsay administration he moved to New Hampshire to work as a university provost, and twelve years later he was hired as the CEO of the Beacon Fund.

And Josh says that, like the John Lindsay days and his time in Mississippi, his twenty-five years at Beacon have "never felt like a job." Life has been "seamless and deeply rooted in the community"; colleagues have become close friends; public has blended into private; professional relationships have been sustaining and familial. He talks about the "seamless" blending of life's pieces as a way of emphasizing that his exit from Beacon is "not like leaving a job . . . it's like leaving a life." One of the ways in which he has begun to get a "purchase" on his feelings of exiting has been to speak about them in a public forum. "There is a discipline of having to say it publicly . . . having to actually say it, not just write it." In a speech that became his final published piece for the fund's newsletter, Josh examined the long sweep of his work, focusing on the ways he let himself and his constituents down, the ways he felt compromised, the places where "the institutional ways and the individual values were in conflict" and the former won out over the latter. Here are some of his poignant and brave reflections:

> As I leave this job that I love beyond description, my greatest feelings of personal failure, of not rising to the challenge, were where I surrendered to the institutional inertia rather than challenging it. Where I deferred taking actions that may have offended the norms of the institution.
>
> Where my individual sense of what was right would have required me to choose the unconventional: to ask the Fund to weigh in more publicly and directly on behalf of those who wanted change and to go against the broader and accepted norms of our community.
>
> I didn't push hard enough on issues of race. Even on symbolic issues such as honoring Dr. King's birthday, where New Hampshire was among the last states in the country to do so. Nor on immigration reform, though virtually all of us, somewhere in our own family past, came as immigrants to this country. We have not done enough to franchise the disenfranchised.

Although the speech is a self-critical meditation—he quotes Atticus Finch in *To Kill a Mockingbird* when he says, "The one thing that doesn't abide by majority rule is a person's conscience"— Josh's analysis seems neither morose nor self-flagellating. Rather his words offer a gentle, courageous summing-up of a quarter of a century of work that has been at once exciting and unnerving, productive and imperfect, sweet and bitter. Josh avoids the plati tudes, the facile conclusions. He resists the congratulatory voices of all those around him who say that—on the contrary—he took a lot of risks at the fund and showed uncommon courage and brave leadership while he was there. "But I am not lulled by their claims," says Josh quietly. "My efforts were often engaged in trying not to offend. My actions were too often premised on caution and cordiality."

Even though the institutional inertia and norms forced a kind of caution, Josh has always worked hard to move the fund toward the arena of public policy. Now his voice is almost strident. "I believed—and I still do—that you can't make substantial change with grant moneys. You must wade into the political process. In the beginning there was a lot of discomfort about that . . . I had early political battles with conservative governors who pushed back against my efforts to challenge and engage the political system . . . who called me a pushy New Yorker, a code word for my being Jewish." Now, at almost sixty-eight, Josh indulges this kind of "stocktaking," weighing the wins and losses, holding up the balances and tensions between the individual and institutional forces, admitting the compromises and the things left undone. He believes that he would not have been capable of this stocktaking— this "groking"—any earlier in his life. This moment of maturity, slowing down, and leave-taking has forced a new capacity for reflection—"stepping out, looking back, measuring myself." It doesn't matter what others say, claims Josh. "It's what is in me."

Interestingly, this taking stock of his work at the fund came at the same time as a large gathering in New York City celebrating the Lindsay retrospective. All the folks who had worked in major roles in Lindsay's administration—and were still alive—came together to view the documentary, to share memories, to reminisce at a big celebratory event. "It was an amazing convergence," says Josh about how the New Hampshire and New York events made him realize that in the busyness and zest of his life, he had rarely made time or space for self-reflection. "I realized while making the documentary that I had never reflected on those Lindsay years. The journalist interviewed me for hours, and I remember being shocked by the questions he asked, shocked at the fact that I never stepped out of it. I was able to do storytelling—lots of stories—but no analysis, no reflection."

In fact, by the time he got home from the interview, Josh felt depressed and embarrassed by his inability to speak critically and analytically, his sense that he had been caught with his pants down, sounding facile and quixotic. "I was sufficiently unnerved . . . enough to call the reporter back and ask if we could do the interview again. I said I thought his questions were unfair, even hostile." The reporter, who thought the interview had gone well, was surprised by Josh's defensiveness and anxiety and tried to assure him that he had not only made a lot of sense, but he had a prominent place in the film. His words had provided the moving ending of the documentary; his reflections were the perfect coda. Now Josh is shaking his head at his surprising feelings of vulnerability. "I guess I must have been worried about how my peers would see me. I thought, God, I'm going to be exposed . . . and maybe what I said will betray others."

Josh thinks that his inability to "step out of himself" and look at his work may be related to the fact that he does not live his life in parts, separating the personal from the professional, family from work. "I am more and more aware of how much my professional life is embedded everywhere. I am one person. This place is family and life . . . seamless," he muses, spreading his arms to embrace the office space around us. Although he sees the great benefits in living life holistically ("You hope that your children will also find work that they love . . . putting all the pieces together"), Josh also recognizes the possible liabilities. "There could also be solace unlinking these various parts," he says as he thinks about the freedom that might result from drawing boundaries and creating separations.

When Josh returned home from San Francisco—after his "great epiphany"—he was consumed by two warring emotions. "It all felt very exciting and very clear, but I was also hugely sad about leaving this place, and I still have not reconciled these feelings." Since he made the decision to exit, each day has felt like a "countdown." Each meeting, each conference, each speech feels like "the last this or that." But he does not necessarily view these final steps as a path to freedom. "There is no sense of liberation on the horizon," he says. "I don't feel, Oh boy, I will finally be free." As he spends his last year counting down and taking stock, Josh is determined to "keep both feet planted" in the present. "I didn't want to use this last year with one foot in and one foot out of this place," he says. "I did not think that would be honorable or fair to others." So when calls have come in—and many have—from folks who want to feel him out about his next career move or even offer him a job, Josh has told them he will not talk with them until after he leaves Beacon. And even then, he feels as if he does not want to rush on to the next thing. Rather he wants the space and time to "stop and breathe and see what swims up inside" of him.

A big smile covers his face as he remembers the one call he could not resist taking. One of his friends, a big banker and a great guy, who owns the minor-league baseball team in town, called several weeks ago to see if Josh might be interested in joining his organization in some capacity. Immediately Josh's heart began pumping, his mind began racing, so much so that he didn't listen to a word his friend was saying. Now he's laughing at the memory. "I'm thinking

to myself, He sees I've still got it. I could play third base. I could do
it . . . or maybe I could be the designated hitter." It took a while for
Josh to realize that he had gotten swept up in his own fantasies, a
while before his friend's voice finally brought him back to reality.
And then he was embarrassed. "Dummy, he means are you interested in being the manager." Now he can laugh about it all, but at
that moment it felt confusing and humiliating, out of time and
space. He didn't even tell Joyce—with whom he usually shares his
wildest fantasies—until weeks later, when he made it into a big joke.

Now Josh sees the baseball fantasy as "illustrative" of the energy
and imagination he hopes to find in his next work. He is determined
not to do the same old things. He does not want to join any more
boards or manage any more institutions. He wants to go through a
process of discovery, wants the ideas to flow from within. "I want
to find inside myself what I want to do. I do not have a bucket list.
I don't have hobbies I want to expand on . . . But there is something
in me that is confident that I will find something meaningful and
creative to do."

He is reminded of the three-month sabbatical he took in San
Francisco ten years ago. A friend of his had suggested that he go to
one place and plant himself there, not spend his time traveling
from place to place. Josh not only took his friend's advice about
"staying still"; he also decided to separate himself from all things
familiar. He recalls, "I stopped reading *The New York Times* . . . I
let all my friends out there know that I would not be seeing them . . .
I found myself involved in all sorts of things I had never tried." His
San Francisco days were completely different from his New Hampshire ones. Every day, he went to the gym and did karate; he took
drawing and painting lessons; he learned to cook Chinese food.
After three months he came back not only renewed but also feeling that "there was so much more in life." The San Francisco experience seems like a good way to anticipate entering his next
chapter—with an open mind and heart, with curiosity and eager-

ness, with the determination not to fall back into old, comfortable patterns.

Despite Josh's optimism about finding something new and meaningful after the Beacon Fund, he admits to feeling a chronic, low-grade worry about his capacity to live a life without work being at the center of it. His face is pensive, his voice plaintive as he muses about his feelings of unease and vulnerability. "I've never not worked. I don't know whether work actually gives me my sense of wholeness and identity. The traffic in my life has always been tied to work . . . that's been the commerce of my life." Josh's decision to not jump into the next thing immediately—even though he believes he has "one more big piece of work" still in him—adds to his eagerness and his nervousness. "Because I'm doing it this way, counting on sitting still, it all feels unsettled, and I'm scared about waiting for something to come up inside of me." He seems to be talking to himself, or maybe he's trying to convince himself. His voice is soft and searching. "There is, I believe, a new discipline in doing it this way, leaving myself totally vulnerable . . . not interested in being defined by institutional anchors, not measuring my life in comparison to others . . . just wanting to bare myself."

Even though the decision to "sit still" feels scary, Josh is clear that when he leaves Beacon, he will not for a moment regret the decision to exit. He will walk away and never look back. "As soon as I leave," he says without ambivalence, "this will be behind me. It will be done. It will look very distant, and I say this without wanting to betray all the people I will leave behind."

Knowing that he wants to leave space in his life to let the next phase emerge naturally and organically, I ask him what other roles and responsibilities might begin to fill the spaces left empty. Will his fathering and his grandfathering assume a bigger place and pleasure in his life? Josh has three children and four grandchildren, and he has spent a good deal of time telling me about them. But my question seems to come as a surprise, and Josh takes a long time to form his answer. "I don't necessarily see these roles becoming larger or more prominent. There is no doubt about how important they all are to me, but as much as I love these kids, I still see myself as a player in the game. I want to be a part of making change in the world . . . I still want to be a part of the larger struggle." Not only does Josh still want to use his energies to "continue the justice work in some form"; he also believes that his job as a father has changed a lot as his children have become responsible adults. He is not—and should not be—at the center of their realities. "My job as father has been to enable, empower, and love them. Then it is up to them to make their own lives. It is like teaching a child to ride a bike. You hold on for a while; then you let go. They fall and get up . . . and finally ride away from you."

Even though he anticipates that his children—and their children—will not fill a bigger space in his life after he leaves Beacon, he is keenly aware of the "aging part of it." He knows that at any time, his life, or those of his loved ones and friends, might be shattered by illness or death. "We are not free agents," he says, in reference to how much more vulnerable he feels, even though his health is good and his mortgage is paid. He remembers how many funerals he has attended and how many good friends he has eulogized in the past year. He thinks of the folks he has known for forty years who are now in their eighties and growing frailer, of his old mentor whom he visited just last week in Florida who is suffering from Parkinson's, and the one he still visits weekly who no longer recognizes him because of her dementia. More than ever, he is aware of the finiteness of his own life and the urgency of getting on with it.

As he talks of illness and death, his musings shift to the subject of religion and his claim that he "has nothing to say on the spiritual side." His statement surprises me as he "continues taking an inventory, a checklist, of the various domains" of his life. But then he draws a distinction that settles my puzzlement, claiming that he is actually "very Jewish" but his "Judaism" is more about his connection to a community of people, his embeddedness in the culture. The sacred rituals matter a lot. Every Friday evening he and Joyce celebrate Shabbat with candles and prayers, and when his children were still at home, Josh used to bake the challah bread that would grace the table. And for the past fifty years, eighty to ninety members of Josh's extended family have gathered at a restaurant in New York City for the Passover seder, coming from all over the country to be together. In all this time, he has missed only one Passover (when he was in his early twenties working in West Africa), and this year, for the first time, he got to preside at the seder, and he loved it. The uncles have now grown too old to carry on, and he has accepted the mantle enthusiastically. "It is all about affirming and nestling," Josh says with great feeling. "These are my people, and this is who I am." Now he is weeping. "There is a huge sense of peace and connectedness."

As we sit quietly together, the inventory taken, the interview over, I think that despite Josh's claims to the contrary, it is this anchoring and connectedness, this sense of peace that will scaffold and nourish him as he tries on the new discipline of "sitting still and letting the next thing come from within." It is this spiritual source that will help him navigate his exit.

Although I still have not read *Stranger in a Strange Land* (science fiction is not my thing), I do love the verb—"to grok"—that Josh has borrowed from the book's probing protagonists. "To be at one with some truth" is Josh's form of yearning. The "bridge" he is building from the old to the new, from the familiar to the strange, is filled with earnest moments of self-interrogation. He goes public with his self-examination of the last twenty-five years. It is one thing to write down what you believe, another thing to give your views public voice, to hold yourself audibly accountable, to stand up and be counted. His public self-appraisal is followed by some deeply private reflections, strange feelings of uncertainty and vulnerability, and determined efforts to "sit still," feel the spirit, and listen for the "organic" unfolding of the next chapter.

Unlike Joe Rosario's exit from the priesthood—which roughly mimics the four stages laid out in Ebaugh's theory—Josh's departure from his CEO position follows a very different trajectory. One night in San Francisco he listens to the extraordinary stories of brave and generous "social pioneers" who are changing the world, and he has an epiphany—a sudden and surprising surge of inspiration that propels him forward immediately and decisively. And unlike Joe, who spends years in protracted deliberations, seeking out mentors for advice and counsel, weighing the costs and the benefits, hedging his bets until he can no longer, Josh makes the firm decision to exit, announces it to his board chair, and decides to spend the next year fully immersed at the Beacon Fund—"with two feet planted"—turning away inquires from bidders who want to offer him a job or tempt him with predictable opportunities. Purposefully, he does not seek advice or guidance from friends and colleagues; he wants to heed the call from within. His intention is not to make a rational list of pros and cons; he wants to be moved by the spirit.

Even though Josh knows that he wants his next chapter to be different, that he does not want to repeat the patterns and rhythms that have shaped his life at the Beacon Fund, he is clear that he has one more "big" piece of work in him. And he knows that he wants that work to allow him to be more deeply and directly engaged in social change, in the struggle for justice. He does not know what form it will all take, but he is excited by the freedom that comes with not knowing, the liberation that comes with the chance to imagine. The freedom allows for some wild fantasies. His brief moment of thinking that he might play third base for the local minor-league team speaks to his yearning to do something big and energetic, something fun and youthful, something that will recapture the kid in him. As a matter of fact, his wish to bring back the old days, when he might have picked off the runner at first with his perfect throw from third, speaks about the largeness and boldness of his imagination, the strange sensation of looking backward into the future.

Josh's yearning for a new adventure, for risking the unknown and charting a new path, does not surprise me. It marks a critical stage in his developmental journey. I listen to him and hear echoes of the voices of folks who told me their stories for *The Third Chapter*,[5] my most recent book, which focuses on the creative and purposeful learning that goes on for women and men between the ages of fifty and seventy-five. It turns out that for many of us, this is a chapter in life when the traditional norms, rules, and rituals of our careers seem less encompassing and restrictive, when the status and station we've earned no longer seem so important, when we are ready to embrace new challenges and search for greater meaning in our lives. Demographers in fact tell us that in the twenty-first century, the Third Chapter is becoming a distinct developmental stage—mapped into our identities, relationships, and institutions; imprinted on our culture—when those of us who are "neither young nor old" are prepared to exit the old and enter the new, choose change over constancy, and compose a new reality for ourselves. Like Josh, we yearn for adventure and inspiration. For the first time, we see the arc and finiteness of our lives, and that produces urgency in us. If not now, when?

At the huge goodbye gathering, tears spring to Josh's eyes as he speaks about the power of "place." By place, he means the physical setting, the ecology and geography, the towns and cities, the rural countryside, the mountains and lakes of New Hampshire, where he has labored for the last quarter century. He means the people, the relationships he has built, the political networks he has established, the "social capital" he has worked to forge in poor and struggling communities. But place also speaks about his devotion, his attachment, his passion and love—the sense of "wholeness and identity" that he gains through the work. "What has interested me in leaving," he tells me later, "is how much I love the work as much as I've ever loved anything." Place is home, with all the complex layers that bind and constrain, and it is hard for him to leave, even when his friends and colleagues build the bridge for him to walk across. "I does where I am," says Josh, quoting the rural black folks in Mississippi who said it best as they stood on their land—their "place"—looking out over the cotton fields, as they marked their sense of belonging and commitment and traced the boundaries of home. Now, as Josh says goodbye to the place he loves, as he "groks" what it means to sever his "institutional anchors," he leaves himself "totally vulnerable" to the yearning.

Six

GRACE

In a haunting essay, "Of Beauty and Death," from his collection *Darkwater: Voices from Within the Veil* (1920)[1] W.E.B Du Bois philosophizes about the beauty in nature and the relationship of beauty to the finite, of ugliness to the infinite, and of both beauty and ugliness to death. He reminisces about the beauty of Bar Harbor, Montego Bay, and the Grand Canyon and then lets his mind wander over the contrasting terrains of Paris and Harlem as he seeks among the myriad experiences of his recent life for a clue to a mystery he sees as essential to life:

> There is something in the nature of Beauty that demands an end. Ugliness may be indefinite. It may trail off into gray endlessness. But Beauty must be complete . . . whether it be a field of poppies or a great life, it must end and the End is part and triumph of the Beauty. I know there are those who envisage a beauty eternal. But I cannot. I can dream of great and never ending processions of beautiful things and visions and acts. But each must be complete or it cannot for me exist.
>
> On the other hand, ugliness to me is eternal, not in the essence but in its incompleteness; but its eternity does not

daunt me, for its eternal unfulfillment is a cause of joy. There is in it nothing new or unexpected; it is the old evil stretching out and ever seeking the end it cannot find; it may coil and writhe and recur in endless battle to days without end, but it is the same human ill and bitter hurt.

But Beauty is fulfillment. It satisfies. It is always new and strange. It is the reasonable thing. Its end is Death— the sweet silence of perfection, the calm and balance of utter music. Therein is the triumph of Beauty.[2]

With language both searching and defiant, Dubois claims that beauty—whether it is a field of poppies or a great life—must have an end; it must be a complete experience; it is defined by its finiteness. I hear in his words, as well, a bow to the importance of endings well done, exits—as Josh Arons says in the previous chapter— accomplished with "purposefulness and grace." It is not only that ending is "part of the triumph of beauty"; it is also that how we end—with intentionality and care, with music, metaphors, and rituals, with elegance and form, with "calm and balance"—shapes our experience of fulfillment.

In this chapter we hear the stories of two women—Carla Anderson and Gwen Taylor—who care deeply about beautiful endings, exits gracefully done, and the rituals designed to mark and honor our farewells. In her mid-fifties, Carla Anderson has navigated many vocational exits—enjoying the changes, transitions, and movements; relishing the "hunt," the seductions, the new opportunities, and the feeling of being sought after, always poised for the next challenge. Looking back, she now recognizes that her exits—largely defined by the opportunities, expectations, and needs of others, by her own wish to be needed and her desire to be at the center of the action—have not been particularly uplifting or fulfilling. She has left without ritual or ceremony, without experiencing the completeness of her work, without letting people chant their praises or sing their sorrowful songs of goodbye. This time, Carla—like Josh Arons—wants to exit differently; she wants to listen to her own muse and music; she wants to "sit still" and let it all unfold "organically." And she is determined to move through the exit slowly and gently, with intentionality and with "grace."

Gwen Taylor promises her dying husband that the ending will be beautiful and triumphant. They will move his bed into their large, sun-filled living room with the spectacular view of the city. They will welcome a steady parade of family and close friends, celebrate with flowers, fresh vegetables, and music; and every day he will be nourished by "fabulous conversations," rich recollections, and wonderful storytelling. Gwen wants there to be—as Du Bois puts it—"a never-ending procession of beautiful acts"[3] before the final exit. She wants "grace to prevail" every day, in every way, all around them. Her husband's last days will be filled with the best living he—and they—have ever known.

GRACE AND STONES

"Exits matter completely."

The setting is beautiful. The view from the ninth floor looks out in one direction over the tall, stately buildings of downtown, and in the other direction over the neat rows of brownstones with their tiny, pretty backyards. When the sun begins to set, there is a rose glow to the sky until the night suddenly appears and the vista is full of magical lights gracing the city landscape. The apartment is large and elegant, filled with art, with textured spaces designed for cozy comfort and lots of company. Burgundy, magenta, and deep orange are the dominant colors in the living room and the dining room, which has a large square table that can easily seat twenty people. I am not surprised when Carla Anderson tells me later that she loves "convening" people, bringing folks together for fun and conversation, nourishment and intellectual engagement. In fact, Carla spent years searching for this apartment and then years more making it beautiful, wanting a space that would give her pleasure and asylum after her long and busy days, that would also be inviting and enveloping for the collections of people she brings together.

Carla is as elegant as her surrounds. At fifty-six she has her own signature style. She drapes large textured scarves in luscious colors around her shoulders; a wide Afghani silver belt stretches around her middle, emphasizing her lovely curves; and she is bejeweled in silver and stones from North Africa, big bracelets with turquoise and coral and three intertwined necklaces that create a dramatic choker. She sits across from me at the kitchen table, looking out the window for inspiration, choosing her words with care, wanting to convey—with honesty and candor—her feelings, her confusions, her hopes, her "hungers," and her "fantasies." When I ask if I can tape our interview and take notes as she talks, she surprises me by saying, "As my grandmother used to say, I have no secrets . . . I really don't." And she lives up to her claim. She is thoughtful and unscripted, using the opportunity to be self-reflective, to push beyond her earlier thinking, to make connections. By the end of our three hours together, she says, with gratitude, that our session has been "therapeutic" and "provocative." "It has been a deeply honoring time," she says softly.

Carla begins right at the center of her current preoccupations and ruminations, with a succinct description of her essence. "I am a person who is endlessly curious and enthusiastic. I have always jumped into the middle of things with both feet. I've never been planful, envisioning a five-year goal, for example. And things have always come to me unbidden. I haven't had to search them out or chase after them." But recently her life has felt very different. It has not had the same energy or inspiration; it has not been fulfilling or life-giving. Rather than feeling fulfilled, she has felt "overfull"— stuffed with "too many things around, too many e-mails, too many phone calls, too many friends, too much going on." She is no longer feeling energized by her busy, complex days, and her "life has become a check-off list of to-dos" that has begun to make her very uncomfortable. Carla wants me to understand her feeling of being "overfull"—distinguishing the good kind of nourishment and pleasure from the nausea that results from gorging yourself on overly fatty foods or too many sweets. "Sometimes fullness is a very positive thing, a robust way to live," she explains, "but the kind of fullness I feel now makes me hungry . . . hungry to meditate, yearning to go on a silent retreat and make a new space."

In the past when Carla occasionally faced this feeling of over-fullness, she would try to "solve" it, find a way to simplify the complexity of her life, try to unravel the knots of stress and confusion that were tangling her up. But this time—for the first time—she is feeling different. She does not want to "solve" it, make it right so she can keep moving forward in her familiar and comfortable patterns. This time she wants to change directions and create a different reality for herself. She wants to get rid of the tedium of routines that no longer challenge or inspire her, get rid of the to-do list, with all of its compulsions, distractions, and responsibilities.

In deciding that she needs a change, however, she is realizing—again for the first time—that she does not simply want to "shut the door" on her old life and move on. This time she wants to "navigate her way" through the uncertainties and choices consciously and thoughtfully. This requires a "reframing" for her. Rather than just thinking about "how to go on to the next phase," Carla finds herself considering how to leave with "grace and dignity," "without regrets." She is thinking about "saying goodbye" in a way that will liberate her, that will give her the energy and creativity to compose the next chapter. "I want my soul to be free," she says with deep feeling.

Carla believes that the grace she seeks must be accompanied by ceremony and ritual, that we in our culture tend to underestimate the value of ritual, particularly the rituals connected to leaving. But she admits that, aside from the general cultural neglect of rituals, her family of origin was "completely not ceremonial." "We did not mark the moment, either the celebrations or the downsides . . . we did not pay attention to closings and endings." With this "absence of meaningful ritual" in her family, Carla—who has always loved the "art and shape of things"—has had to make it up as she goes along. "Having children has helped me," she recalls as she thinks back on all the ways she tried to embroider rituals into her homelife with her own children, and how these occasions were important "markers" for them, providing moments of anticipation, recognition, celebration, and appreciation.

Carla was trained as a botanist. Her first job after college was in the laboratory at the Botanical Gardens, a job she loved for its scientific exactness and its beautiful surroundings. Although she loved science, even as a young woman fresh out of college she knew that she would not be able to live her life in a laboratory. The lab life was too contained and insular, too removed from the action. More than anything, she wanted to be involved in the world; she was an activist at heart. In an exit that did not require much calculation or deliberation, she left the lab and enrolled in law school, training that she thought would prepare her to participate—with skills, analysis, and argument—in changing the world, fighting for justice, protecting powerless people. Her first job after law school was working as a public defender in the district attorney's office.

After a couple of years on the front lines, she moved on to private practice, where she specialized in trial law. "I loved trying cases," she says with enthusiasm as she recalls the energy and the high, the homework and intense preparation that came with being in court. But it was not just passion that fueled her love for trial law. She also loved the way it "felt"; the way she had to get to know her "audience" and "what would fly" with them; the way she had to figure out how to tell a "story" in order to inspire, inform, and con-

vince the jury. It was the kind of hard work and high-wire act
Carla relished—the risks, the calculations, the ways you needed to
seize opportunities and run with them. But trial practice also absorbed an enormous amount of energy and time, a work life that
was hard to combine with her family responsibilities. With children who were by then five and seven and a husband who was a
hard-driving venture capitalist who traveled all over the globe,
Carla decided to leave her job and leave the practice of law.

For years, she had been on the board of the Global Environmental Research Institute, founded by her father, a scientist and
entrepreneur, and she decided to commit her time to fund-raising
for the institute. "I adored my father," she says wistfully about her
decision to become more fully involved in the family business. Not
only did she—in record time—raise twelve million dollars for the
institute; she also found that she "fell in love with institutions" and
"discovered the world of nonprofits." Soon she was heading the
board of a new start-up company, chairing the local board of
Planned Parenthood, becoming a trustee of a major university,
chairing the board of the city's largest homeless shelter for women,
and continuing to maintain her leadership role on the board of the
institute. The variety of organizational agendas—focused on science
and social service, spanning the theoretical and the practical—
appealed to Carla. It was a professional life that offered her great
responsibility and amazing freedom, accountability, and autonomy.
She was able to craft each day in her own way while still playing a
crucial role in institution building and advocacy. She relished the
busy and eclectic life she had spawned—the rich array of activities,
the wonderful opportunities, the creative challenges, the development of ideas, the convening of people and communities, the networking to build coalitions and raise money. For the last fifteen
years, this way of living and learning has given her "a robust feeling
of fullness."

Part of the reason that Carla is now exploring other career

options and fantasizing about new work ("I have another body of work in me," she says, looking toward the future) is because the "robust feeling of fullness" has slowly turned into an "interior hunger." "The stories are fairly negative," she says when I ask her for an example of how she experiences the hunger. "I find that I can't produce even when I know I am responsible and must be accountable for doing something . . . I feel stuck." She points to her role as chair of the board for the homeless shelters, an organization that she believes in and has generously supported, with colleagues whom she loves and admires. "These are people who are deeply embedded in my life," she explains. "I care about the work, but I find I cannot rally the enthusiasm. It's just not in me anymore . . . and I think it is fundamentally wrong to continue to do it just because I've signed up for it. That is what I am dying not to do." Her voice is determined, urgent.

"Here are some of my fantasies," she says as she considers the possible choices in front of her. She points to a beautiful photograph on the wall next to her, an image she chose for her Christmas card. It shows Carla—unrecognizable from a distance—sitting on top of a huge sand dune with a clear, cloudless blue sky behind her. It is a photograph from a recent trip she took to the Gobi Desert, and she thinks of the picture as a metaphor for the way she hopes to exit this chapter of her life and enter the next. "I am looking forward, feeling the promise and the possibility . . . It is simple, clear, unencumbered." Having shared the image, she spins out three of her fantasies.

"I could run a not-for-profit . . . but the idea feels overwhelming to me, the work too long and hard and demanding. I think I've had too much freedom in my life for the last fifteen years to choose something that requires that kind of daily, unrelenting dedication and devotion.

"It would be great to work overseas and make a significant difference in the world. I fantasize, for example, about finding an Indian entrepreneur who has made a fortune in the U.S. . . . and wants to return to India . . . working together with him or her on a model for social philanthropy there.

"I could become a diplomat. I love to convene people . . . I love entertaining. I enjoy moving a project forward. I like to bring people together to share ideas . . . I want to create salons."

Her eyes get misty as she recalls a loving and admiring comment made by her son, a young journalist working in London. He was pitching a job with *The Washington Post* and telling them about his personal qualities. "I am," he wrote, "one of the most curious people I know and a great listener, both attributes that I have inherited directly from my mother."

One of the qualities Carla likes most about herself is her "fearlessness in bringing people together." A lot of people are afraid of the unease, the combustion, the conflict that can erupt when people come together from different geographies, cultures, and ideologies, when they are likely to disagree with or mistrust one another. But Carla enjoys the whole process—the edgy discourse that engages and incites, the spirited and fiery conversations that lead to arguments and sometimes reconciliation. "It is freeing for everybody when it works, and at least interesting and provocative when it doesn't," she muses. Carla admires President Obama for just that reason; he is a daring and creative convener, an attentive listener, a brilliant synthesizer. He is not afraid of discord. She offers an example. When Obama was recently trying to decide whether to send more troops into Afghanistan, he brought experts—policy makers and politicians, military men, Middle East scholars—to the table who had very different points of view and perspectives. "It was a phenomenal process," says Carla, "whether you agreed with his solution or not. He listened to everybody; he asked great questions; it was a thoughtful and probing deliberation . . . He is an incredible convener."

Ironically, Carla believes that her experience as a trial lawyer turned out to be great preparation for being a convener of people. Not the adversarial part that yields winners and losers, but the part that requires careful listening and the development of a narrative, a story line. Yes, she now yearns for something less black-and-white, more complicated and nuanced than trial law, but she also sees the imprint of her early training in her fantasies of new work.

There is mischief and glee in her eyes as she reveals her most recent fantasy. Her voice unwraps the "secret" as if it is a precious gift. "I love stones," she whispers. "I love the less-refined materials, the colors, the textures, the coolness to the touch." I look around us and notice that her couches are covered in soft velvet, with pillows decorated in ancient hand-embroidered fabrics from North Africa. Her bathroom wall is even covered in a subtle brocade textile that is both soft and rough to the touch. "I'm a completely tactile person," she says with understatement. "The other day a friend of mine said to me, 'You always glow when you talk about this stuff . . . you need to find a way to follow that passion.'" Carla points to the large amber ring on my hand. "I'm deeply drawn to that kind of stuff, big and smooth and luminous."

As recently as a few weeks ago, Carla admits, she would never have talked about her passion for stones, and she certainly would not have had the nerve to even think out loud about "doing something" with them. It would have sounded impossibly trivial, nowhere near as serious as others see her or as she imagines herself to be. But for the last few days she has found herself giving in to her fantasies and "playing" with ideas like getting her certification in gems or going on a fact-finding trip to a place in Denmark that has an incredible collection of stones, where you can be tutored by experts. A smile spreads across her face. "I'm completely wide open. I would have been embarrassed to say this a month ago . . . it might have felt frivolous, somehow ungrounded."

I ask how her love of stones translates to her body, which she drapes with dramatic jewels and gems, and her response is immedi-

ate and exuberant. "My body is all in it. To the extent that life can
be luscious, then live it!" she crows, standing up and dancing around.
But there is another reason Carla is drawn to stones. When she
wears them, she senses something wonderful and mysterious. "Power
isn't exactly the word I'm looking for," she says as she tries to give
the feeling of "excitement and enhancement" a name. The stones
decorating her body seem to have a "dynamic energy" that propels
her forward and settles her down. They are both peaceful and
provocative, "centering and inspiring."

As Carla talks, her fantasies swell with hope and determination, imagination and energy. So I ask her whether there are any
downsides, whether she has any worries, any apprehensions as she
begins to make her exit. "Oh my God, yes," she responds without
skipping a beat.

"Maybe people will think of me—or I'll begin to think of
myself—as a dilettante. That would feel awful.

"Maybe there is no magic IT . . . that I will find that I am pursuing something false or ephemeral.

"Maybe I'm just old and tired and have run out of steam. I do
believe you need to invigorate your life, or else, as you grow older,
you grow stale. I've seen that in some of my friends.

"Maybe I'll fall off of everyone's screen . . . I'll never be invited
to do anything again."

As she races through her list of fears and names the risks that
are inevitably part of "doing the unthinkable," Carla admits that
her apprehensions are amplified by a keen sense of "urgency." She
asks herself, "If not now, when?" "For the first time in my life,
people are dying around me—friends, associates, people my own
age—and that creates a kind of compelling immediacy." She also
recognizes that she has always been reluctant to reach out to people, to let them know what she needs, to tell them when she is
feeling pain. She has been reticent to seek their guidance, support,
and feedback as she tries to chart a new path. "I haven't turned to

people enough," she says sadly. "I'm not afraid to talk to people about what I'm thinking, but it is difficult to examine what might be next on the horizon. It feels more vulnerable for me, but it is probably not as risky as I think." As Carla talks about how hard it is to reach out for help, she notices that she has never approached, nor sought help from, her grown children and that drawing them in might have the salutary effect of making them feel more needed and "empowered." She suddenly laughs, recognizing the similar places they are in their lives, the ways in which they are all facing some form of transition. "You know, the three of us (she and her young adult son and daughter) are in the same spot."

A few weeks earlier Carla had had an extraordinary "earth-shaking experience." She was spending the weekend in Canada with her man at his rustic cabin in the woods, sitting in front of the fire and soaking up the peacefulness and warmth of their rare times alone. She decided to do something she has never done be-fore, listen to the audiotapes of a popular celebrity therapist—a favorite guest of Oprah's—whose books have sold millions of cop-ies and captured the hearts and minds of a huge following. The author had, in her forties, suffered a severe mental breakdown, a disturbing prelude to a kind of spiritual awakening. In her tapes, workshops, seminars, and performances the therapist tells her own story of survival and liberation, narrates the tales of her patients' struggles and healing, and offers her wisdom to those seeking to break bad habits and change their lives. Carla still cannot believe that she brought the tapes up to the cabin and that she decided to listen to them that evening. "This didn't even feel like me!" she says, surprised at herself. She has always considered these kinds of pop psychology testimonials superficial and hokey. But that night, for four hours straight, she stared into the fire, let the tapes roll, and became completely absorbed, captivated by the message and the messenger.

I ask her what in the stories and lessons grabbed her, and her response is immediate. "It is the work of reframing things for people, seeing the world around you—and the relationships you are involved in—in a different way." She offers two examples of the stories of revelation and survival that the therapist told. The first was about a woman whose daughter was a drug addict, whose life had been controlled and consumed by trying to solve her daughter's problems and save her life. Carla was surprised by the therapist's "reframing" of maternal love and responsibility. The mother, said the therapist, should not try to be her daughter's savior or problem solver; she should not try to rescue her from her self-inflicted injuries and abuses. Trying to take control and make things right only weakens and infantilizes her daughter and makes her feel as if she is not strong enough to be in charge of her own life.

The second case focused on a woman now in her fifties who had been raped by her foster father from the time she was four to when she was fourteen. Years later, when she brought allegations against him, her family had cast her aside, refusing to believe her charges of abuse. Carla listened with special interest to the "reframing" of this story, since years ago, as a public defender, she had had a good deal of experience prosecuting sex crimes, and she had an intimate understanding of the fear, guilt, rage, and victimization that tend to be part of the complex web of child molestation. Again, the therapist's words surprised her, disrupting her usual presumptions about the victim's role and responsibility. The therapist urged the rape victim to "forgive herself for letting this happen to her." But then she went on to say that the victim of the rape was the responsible party; she had to stand up and be accountable for her own healing, or she would forever be locked in a prison of guilt and remorse and forever see herself as helpless and hopeless. Carla remembers giving these stories her rapt attention, not missing a word, losing track of time and staying up until past midnight. "I heard it, felt it, took it in."

Almost as if it had been scripted, the next morning, Susannah,

Carla's twenty-five-year-old daughter, called from Chicago to say
that she had—once again—been kicked out of school; she was
begging to be rescued. Her daughter's urgency and desperation and
her pleas for help were not surprising; since early adolescence she'd
had a history of stumbling, getting herself into trouble and asking
to be saved, counting on her mother to make everything right. But
this time Carla felt an unlikely impulse stir inside of her. Right
then, with the morning sun rising in the sky, barely awake before
her morning coffee, Carla responded in a way that felt unfamiliar.
Her voice even sounded strange in its decisiveness. "I knew right
then that this was Susannah's problem, not mine!" she exclaims,
huge relief written all over her face. "I felt as if a gift had been
handed to me."

She could look back and see that her "sympathy, handouts,
and problem solving" were killing Susannah. "I was not letting her
grow up and take responsibility . . . I need to be real and kind, but
I can't solve it for her. Supporting her and giving her money suddenly seemed ridiculous to me." Carla is smiling at what feels like
an amazing breakthrough for her. "This is huge for me . . . huge
and exciting . . . because it leaves me feeling so much less constrained." She looks directly at me, another mother of grown children, still stuck in the problem-solving/rescue mode, still wavering
in my efforts to both help them and support their autonomy and
adulthood. Her voice rises with authority. It all feels very new and
untested, but Carla feels convinced and oddly certain about this
"reframing" of the responsibilities and boundaries of her mother-
hood, and she wants to convey to me the rightness and goodness
of her changing views.

This "huge" shift in perspective—and actions—in relation to
her daughter is becoming a part of Carla's exit narrative. She realizes that in order for her to move on to her next chapter, she must
cast off some of the "primal and primary" obligations and self-imposed
constraints that have limited her imagination and restricted her

movements. She also recognizes that the relationship she has forged
with her daughter—rescuing her whenever she screamed for help—is
part of a larger pattern of family dynamics, forged in her early
childhood and still present fifty years later. "I'm part of a huge
family—two brothers, eight stepbrothers, twenty-five nieces and
nephews—and I have always found myself being the source of advice, problem solving, and support. I'm the convener."

She offers a recent example. "For thirty years, at Christmas,
the whole extended family has always gone skiing together, and I
have always been the convener, planning all of it, making it happen, but this year it turned out that no one could do it. People
were busy with travel or work . . . neither of my kids or the nieces
and nephews could come. I was completely depressed by this. I was
panicked about how I would navigate the season, stave off the
loneliness." Forced to figure it out on her own, Carla created a
much simpler Christmas. She decided not to travel out of town.
Instead, she stayed put, bought a tiny tree that she could carry up
to her apartment herself, spent almost no time decorating it, and
then invited two couples over for a simple, intimate dinner. Everything was a "tiny portion of what might have been, smaller scale
and spare, much quieter, more deliberate." And she found that
she had a great time. "It felt fantastic!"

Susannah's call for help that morning in Canada and Carla's
experience of the foiled Christmas plans have left her with a
clearer path, a more open mind, and many more choices. She is
beginning to feel less encumbered by the constraints and responsibilities of mothering and less burdened by her role as family convener. Recasting these relationships and retreating from the lifelong
expectations will put her, she hopes, "on the path to liberation." As
I listen to her fierce determination and her earnestness, I sense
that the path forward will be bumpier and more treacherous than
she now imagines. She is still experiencing the first blush of new
discovery. I suspect that there will be minefields along the road,

moments of regression to past patterns, even feelings of loss as she unpeels the old personas and tries on new ones. But for now, all she seems to feel is relief and freedom. "I am reclaiming my life," she whispers. "It has been a good life, but it has not all been mine . . . Here is the opportunity to make it mine."

Even though her new take on mothering seems to have washed over her all of a sudden, Carla mostly believes that exits should be done slowly, deliberately, thoughtfully, and generously; and she thinks that her view could well be seen as "countercultural." She muses, "This notion of exit is a very American concept, an abrupt leave-taking." It is also the way she was raised by her father, who would always say to her when she was ending something, "What's next? What's coming up?" He was always urging her to press on and not look back. But at fifty-six, this notion of a quick exit "no longer resonates" with her. She delivers her next lines very slowly, mirroring the sensation that she is discovering within her. "Exiting feels liberating, but only if it is well navigated . . . and that takes time."

Carla feels, for example, proud of the way she got divorced— slowly, carefully, not precipitately, trying to be careful of her husband's needs and feelings. "I love how I got divorced," she says adamantly. "It took us six years between separating and getting a divorce. Many of our friends and family did not approve of the way we did it. But our daughter was not well, and we both needed to offer her our ongoing, collective support. My ex-husband and I both gave each other the space to work it out." And now that they have been divorced several years, Carla feels completely comfortable with her ex-husband's new wife, wanting to keep her "intimately and directly informed" and seeking her counsel about decisions that need making with regard to the children.

She has one last thought about the value of exits "well negotiated." Carla believes that there is a "negative cultural narrative about exiting," that we tend to honor entrances and denigrate leave-takings, that we do not give enough attention to the rituals or ceremony of our goodbyes. Now she is beginning to recognize that "exits matter completely," that they must be "done with dignity and grace," and that it is important to leave feeling "responsible, good, and whole." In fact, it is crucial that those you are leaving behind have the opportunity to express their appreciation, honor your work, and throw a party. Carla is about to depart from a board she has been chairing for the last decade, an organization whose mission she loves, a place to which she has devoted a tremendous amount of her time. At first she imagined slipping away quietly into the night, doing a stealth action, going out under the radar. The thought of a big, ceremonial goodbye made her feel awkward and uncomfortable. Only recently has she begun to recognize how important it is to let those you have worked with, partnered with, and given to have the opportunity to celebrate you in a way that is meaningful to them. "You owe it to them to let them raise a glass and toast you."

But a "well-negotiated" exit includes not only letting people express their sadness about your leaving, their sense of loss and abandonment; it also means giving them the space to express their love and admiration. And Carla believes that you need to be prepared to listen to them, to really absorb their words and feel their meaning. Now she sounds like she is offering up a prayer. "Grace is carried in being open and receptive to the ritual." "Exits matter completely," she says once again as she lifts an imaginary champagne glass and looks into the future.

Carla feels the impetus for her exit in her body, and she uses the metaphor of food to explain the oddly paradoxical sensations. She is feeling "overfull" from trying to manage too much and put together too many pieces in her life, yet she is feeling "hungry" for real emotional and intellectual nourishment. She hungers, as well, for quiet, for the time to meditate, for spiritual sustenance, for grace.

She hates the feeling of being greedy, "overstuffed" with the wrong kinds of food, nauseated from gorging herself; and she is searching for the discipline that will allow her to know when to push back from the table, when she is just full enough—a "fullness that is robust."

As she moves toward the exit, she cares as much about how she leaves as she does about what she is leaving or where she is headed. She wants to "navigate" her way deliberately, slowly, paying careful attention to her own feelings and those of others. She wants to leave with "dignity and grace" and engage in "countercultural" rituals that will give form and substance to the endings. And she wants to leave "without regrets" because she believes that only then will she find the energy and imagination to compose her next chapter. Her exit quest is about setting her "soul free," releasing her from the inhibitions and busyness that have, by now, overtaken her life and limited her fantasies and choices. Like Du Bois, she sees beauty in endings and ugliness in the infinite—the "trailing off into gray endlessness."

In order to exit—and set herself free—Carla must "reframe" many of the presumptions, perspectives, and values that have defined her essence and identity, her place in her family, and her mothering. Refusing to rescue her daughter Susannah and insisting on her independence liberates her from a mother-daughter relationship that has grown exhausting and consuming; it allows her to feel less constrained and inhibited in her choices and helps pave her path to the exit. Likewise, removing herself from her longtime role as family convener releases her from the tangled web of habits and expectations that have by now become presumed and unspoken. Forced to do Christmas without all the holiday artifacts and hoopla, Carla discovers something more satisfying, simple, and salutary; she can begin to see a new reflection of herself in the life she is now free to compose.

Recalibrating her relationships to family and friends helps

Carla carve out the space to imagine, and then welcome, her most far-out fantasies. She is able to "play" with new options and ideas, turn them over in her mind, and project them into the future. But this is not a straightforward or easy process. She is occasionally weighed down by her doubts; she worries about the risks to her professional and personal relationships, her anchoring in the community. Will she be exposed as a dilettante? Is she searching for something elusive and ephemeral, something she will never find? Will her name disappear from people's BlackBerries? Will her cell phone stop ringing? There is an ongoing calculation—of risks and benefits, costs and liabilities—that she needs to hold in check if she is going to set herself free.

Her good friend sees the glow in her eyes when she begins to talk about her love of stones, and their conversation gives Carla the permission she needs to reveal the depth of her passion for them. She loves the varieties and textures of stones, their beauty and resonance, their luxuriousness. She uses them to adorn her body and feels their "dynamic energy" when she wraps them three times around her neck to make a choker. The stones do not weigh her down; they lift her up. She senses the way they help her to "sit still" and propel her forward, the way they make her feel "wide open" to new possibilities. Gems and stones—in all their unadorned natural beauty—become her inspiration and talisman, symbols of her slow and intentional, grounded and graceful journey to the exit.

AMAZING GRACE

"As glorious as possible."

For Gwen Taylor, it is the final exit that matters the most. She has one last shot to make the ending beautiful for her dying husband, one more opportunity to honor and celebrate his completed life.

Her last fervent promise to him—a promise she is sure she can
keep—is that his final weeks and days will be full of abundance
and grace.

It is less than two months after Tom Taylor's death when Gwen
welcomes me into their home. She stands tall at six feet, with a
large frame and an erect posture. She moves slowly, with waltzing
steps. Her bright red dress, hanging loosely, is covered with a hand-
woven multicolored shawl that she wraps around herself for comfort and protection as she tells the hardest, most painful story of
her life. We sit in her elegant, large living room that stretches across
the top floor of one of the city's most stately, and pricey, buildings.
The room has enough space to hold several couches, sideboards,
lamps, tables, and desks, all fine Victorian pieces.

Every surface is cluttered with piles of paper; the huge oval
dining-room table is strewn with an array of photographs, newspaper clippings, books, magazines, and correspondence. Gwen casually apologizes for the mess and claims that she has always created
this kind of chaos, but it has grown way out of hand since Tom
died. "I always struggle with too much paper," she admits. "I'm interested in too many things, but this mess is even more terrible
than usual." Toward the end of our interview she links the mess in
her living room to her description of herself as "a complete emotional mess" since the death of her husband. "I almost can't find
my life anymore," she says finally about the excruciating experience of feeling "unmoored and in so much pain."

We sit at a small table by the window that is, like every other
surface, piled high with papers. Gwen cleans it off enough to make
room for my tape recorder and notepad, and she fishes in the pile
from time to time to show me a photograph or a letter that documents a story she is telling. Before I can ask her an opening question, she begins. "I am assuming that you want me to talk about
Tom's dying—because there are also other exits in my life, ones I
am going through myself that I could tell you about. But the one

with the most emotional power, the richest and most complete experience, is the story of Tom." And it is a long story that begins in 1976, the year they were married. "Tom was fourteen years older than I . . . he had four adolescent children, and I worried a lot about the marriage for three reasons," she starts. First and foremost, she worried about becoming the stepmother of four adolescents. ("And I had good reason to worry." She smiles.) Second, she worried about the age difference between them. And third, she worried about the difference in their "financial circumstances." Gwen had come from a middle-class—"actually barely middle-class"—background, and Tom had grown up "with a lot of money." He was the heir of a huge family fortune, the grandson of the founder of an international cosmetic conglomerate.

Three years after they were married, Tom had his first encounter with a major illness. He was diagnosed with a cancerous melanoma. Thus began a series of medical consultations as they tried to figure out the best option for treatment. At that point, they—and the medical establishment—knew little about the disease, and Gwen recalls that she was "frozen by fear." "I was terrified," she says. "I knew nothing about cancer." In the end, at the recommendation of their primary care physician, they decided to do the surgery to excise the melanoma, but not to follow it up with either radiation or chemotherapy. After the surgery Tom returned to his normal energetic life—his international development work, his philanthropic activities, his travels to East Africa, and his active physical life of sailing, biking, and running. But one day five years later, when he experienced some pain and discomfort in his chest, he drove himself to the hospital and the doctors discovered that he was suffering from heart failure that required immediate surgery and a new regimen of medicines.

Gwen tells the story of Tom's long history of illness, being faithful to the chronology and to the changing, increasingly serious diagnoses. I am amazed by her level of recall, the way in which she remembers not only the month and year of the diagnosis, but often the exact day, the way she chronicles the many competing diagnoses delivered by the several specialists they consulted, the way she remembers pieces of the actual conversations with the doctors, the ways they delivered the bad news, the questions she asked to seek clarification or some measure of hope, the way she can still hear Tom's voice—brave and determined, then resolute and accepting—as they went through years of illness and decline together. During all these procedures and surgeries, comebacks and recoveries, one of their close friends remarked, "Tom actually had nine lives or more," a statement that stuck in everyone's mind as one of the best descriptions of the extraordinary resilience and fortitude he showed after each major assault on his body.

Toward the end of the interview, after hearing the long parade of serious and painful infirmities that stretched over their thirty years of marriage, I ask Gwen whether her experience of their time together was completely shaped by Tom's illnesses, whether doctors and hospitals and medicine and pain and fear and sleeplessness were most of what she remembers. Her response is immediate. No, those are not her primary recollections. Her memories are mostly filled with good and healthy times, with being engaged fully in their worlds, adventurous travel, beautiful times in their house in the country. Life was full, plentiful, and pleasurable for the most part. Yes, there were clearly moments of crisis and fear and trauma, there was panic and worry, and there were periods of profound weakness and excruciating pain. But they would always navigate through those tough times, emerge hopeful and determined, and move on with their lives.

It takes more than an hour for me to hear the details of Tom's nine lives. As Gwen releases the story, her eyes spill over with tears, her face becomes swollen and red, and she uses a whole box of tissues to absorb the tears that seem to come from every pore in her face. She does not try to stop the flow; she makes no apology.

She also seems determined to continue despite the pain that accompanies the narration—almost as if there is something about the flow of tears that is cleansing and restorative.

I hear about the prostate cancer in 1997 that the oncologists treated with radiation (avoiding surgery because of Tom's age, his heart condition, and their wish to "protect sexual functioning"), his many episodes of pneumonia over the years, the terrible fall in 2006 that caused a blood clot on his brain that had to be surgically removed, the scarred bladder in 2008 that made it impossible for him to urinate, when he had to go by ambulance to the hospital to have his bladder emptied—the suggestion, finally, that Tom "self-catheterize" nine times a day. "He was such a trooper," Gwen moans. I hear about the tumor they found growing out of his prostate on June 12, 2009, which had protruded into his bladder and rectum, the endless trips to the hospital emergency room, the scary moments when the pain seemed too extreme to bear, the constant calibrations of medicine, the deliberations and choices following conflicting diagnoses and treatment plans ordered by doctors. And through it all, Gwen recalls never feeling as if Tom was dying. "We were still in our minds fighting to get him well."

But by the summer of 2009 there was too much evidence to avoid the reality of Tom's decline. The doctors could no longer figure out the source of the cancer, it was "so aggressive and undifferentiated." Gwen remembers the moment when one of Tom's trusted doctors suggested to her that she needed to "think about a do-not-resuscitate order." "That was a stark moment for me," she says, recalling it as a clear turning point, a dose of unwelcome reality. She immediately began to check into hospice care and make arrangements for Tom to "come home to die." He had made his wife promise that she would make sure he would die at home. He remembered that both of his parents had died at home, a dignified, honoring death, surrounded by friends and loved ones, comforted by everything familiar in their surroundings. He wanted the same.

On his last trip home from the hospital Tom asked Gwen whether he was going to die. She responded that she did not know, because at that point she had not yet accepted the doctors' warnings that the end was near. But she was able to tell him—with clarity and certainty—that they would make this time "glorious"; they would have a nourishing, caring, beautiful, and loving time together; and they would do that for as long as he had, for the rest of his life. They would be surrounded by friends and family; the house would always be full of beautiful flowers; people would come from far and near to visit with him, to say things that had been left unsaid before this moment.

Gwen soon decided that his hospital bed would be placed in the most prominent place in their home, in the middle of the action, at one end of the huge living room, near the windows looking out over the city. "I couldn't bear for his bed to be set up in the guest room," she says, weeping again. They bought a large Chinese screen to put up around his bed for privacy when he wanted it and for those times when he was too weak to welcome guests. Every day, people flowed through the house to visit Tom, bringing food, memories, photographs, old videos, and yummy corn and fresh tomatoes from their gardens in the country. His older daughter made a magnificent quilt to cover him on his bed. His other daughter bought bright Marimekko fabric and made him long wraps to replace the ugly johnnies he had worn in the hospital, colorful garments that got bigger and bigger as his body withered away. His daughter-in-law wove him a cover for his pillow.

His children—now in their middle years at 52, 50, 48, and 47—were vigilant, attentive visitors, often arriving together, sometimes with the grandchildren, and staying at the apartment in one of the three "big, puffy blow-up beds" Gwen had bought for company to sleep on. Their sibling time together tending to their dad seemed to draw them closer together, closer than they had ever been. One son, who lived nearby, came to fix Tom scrambled eggs every morning; another would read him the newspaper or essays from *The New Yorker*. The neighbor next door—whose name Gwen had barely even known before Tom's illness—several times brought dinner over, enough to feed twelve, and allowed them to keep their overflow food in her refrigerator. The outpouring of love and care was amazing, and as Gwen had promised, the time actually did turn out to be "glorious."

More sustaining than anything else were the "fabulous conversations" Tom was able to have with everyone who came by. This is what seemed to keep him alive—the intense, deep, rich exchanges he was able to have at his bedside. Gwen orchestrated the visits, the dinners, the readings, and the occasional quiet moments of being alone. But Tom got to choose who came, and they invited only people he loved and wanted there. His children used the time to have conversations that had seemed to elude them—perhaps out of conscious or unconscious conflict avoidance—earlier in their lives. They talked to their father about proud and painful moments from their childhood, times of feeling misunderstood or confused, times of feeling overshadowed by his goodness and generosity. They talked to him about how hard it was when their parents divorced. They told him about how his good parenting had helped them to be good parents. They argued with him about politics and art. They held his hand and caressed his brow when he was too weak to talk or when his sudden silence spelled the onset of acute, debilitating pain. Gwen admits that these conversations with his children were often not "easy," but she insists that they were "fabulous" and that Tom was fully and deeply engaged in them. The ten grandchildren provided a welcome lightness; their constant activity—running around, squealing, eating, playing games—brought everyone back to the ordinariness of the day. The cross-generational mix felt warm and somehow hopeful. And their love for their grandfather was so uncomplicated and pure.

Friends came too—friends who had worked with Tom in Africa,

friends who sat on nonprofit boards with him, friends from Human Rights Watch and other causes he was devoted to, longtime friends from the country. Many came several times a week in a constant and devoted vigil. There was always a houseful of guests staying over, fixing food, and sharing stories. Creating this "glorious" occasion was not always easy for Gwen, however. She had never been someone who enjoys the chaos and complexity of a full house, with lots of people underfoot creating a whirlwind of activity. She says with amazement in her voice, "I would never have believed I could tolerate all this invasion of people, and none of my good friends would have believed it about me either, but somehow my wish for Tom to have these fabulous conversations overrode all my need to be in control of what was happening in my surroundings."

Gwen occasionally joined in on Tom's conversations with friends, but most of the time she retreated and let the conversations go on without her. She says, "I do believe that it is important to let people have private conversations, and also I was so exhausted that I would sometimes use these moments to escape and rest or to do the endless errands that needed to get done." She remembers their good friend Julia, a psychiatrist, who visited Tom daily, a woman they had known since she was very young, who had always been "sort of like a daughter" to them. Julia's conversations with Tom were almost always private, and Gwen suspects that he "sort of used Julia to relay messages" to his wife, to say those things that were hard for him to tell her directly. It was from Julia, for example, that Gwen learned that Tom did not want to be "force-fed." He did not like her constant encouragement that he should eat and drink more. He wanted to be left alone to eat as little as he wanted, or nothing at all if he chose to. It turns out that the hospice workers had also recommended that he not be force-fed. They told Gwen not to try to get Tom to eat or walk. "They felt that this was a dying man, and you must let him live out these last days exactly as he wanted," says Gwen with an edge to her voice. "The kids and I clearly violated that part. If that makes us inglorious, then so be it!" The second message Julia transmitted to Gwen was that Tom did not like it when she took so long saying goodbye to people as they were leaving. He wanted her to come to him, to be with him. "Tom was at the center of everything," says Gwen without an ounce of bitterness in her voice. "Everything revolved around him."

As Tom's health continued to decline and his death seemed imminent, another longtime friend, Deborah, a divinity school graduate (although not an ordained minister), helped them plan the burial and memorial services, a collective effort in which the children and grandchildren and Tom's brothers and sisters were all centrally involved. Tom was also a big part of the planning, offering up ideas, expressing his wishes, vetoing those things that did not feel right. "We wanted the services to be as glorious as possible," says Gwen, "as close as possible to what Tom wanted." As a matter of fact, at a certain point, after weeks of deliberation and consultation about the details of the funeral service, Tom said he had had enough. "I'm tired of it. I'm through," he declared. "I do not want to spend any more time on this." I ask Gwen what sorts of things required a lot of discussion, compromise, and resolution. "Tom and I wanted to sing 'America the Beautiful'—we love its simplicity and message—but his daughter, who lives in Paris and works for an international relief organization, thought it was too patriotic, too narcissistic, so we decided on "For the Beauty of the Earth." A second example: "I love Rudyard Kipling and wanted to read one of his poems, but the children vetoed that idea, so we scratched that."

By far the hardest decision for Gwen was deciding on whether Tom would be cremated. Amazingly enough, until the last couple of months they had not discussed a burial plan, nor had they selected a burial site. Without much discussion they chose a plot at Green Hill Cemetery—they had always loved to walk there—and one of their friends took a picture of it and brought it back to Tom so he would know where his ashes would be laid. But when all the children announced that they wanted their father's body cremated, Gwen balked. "I come from Kentucky, where we have embalming and lay people's bodies out in the coffin," she explains. "My initial thought was that I cannot do this . . . I cannot burn him." She struggled mightily with the decision; the family discussions were exceedingly difficult, very painful for her.

But finally, one night, she had a conversation with one of Tom's daughters, who listened to her worries without judgment, let her express herself until she was completely done, exhausted from her purging. By the end of the conversation they decided together that Tom would be cremated. "What changed your mind?" I ask in amazement, having heard her powerful resistance and initial re-pulsion to the idea. "I decided finally that when I die, I will be cremated and our ashes will be combined. That seemed to soothe me . . . I could anticipate being with him again."

Gwen remembers the time exactly. It was 5:00 on Tuesday after-noon when Tom took his last breath. One of his daughters had come to visit that morning and had left at noon after saying what she knew would be her last goodbye. Both of his sons—Simon and David—were there with Gwen, as was Tom's favorite caretaker, a medical assistant named Kosi, a tall Ugandan man with whom he had developed a deep bond over the last several weeks. The four of them all held hands, circling his bed as they watched Tom take his final breath. "Actually," recalls Gwen, "we weren't sure whether he had stopped breathing. It was hard to tell. But Kosi told us that it was so." Gwen's tears turn to full-blown sobbing as she remembers the moment, the end. Simon began singing softly to his father, a final, sweet lullaby. And each of them took a turn offering a bless-ing, some words of send-off. They called Maria, the head nurse who had been in charge for the last several months, and she came over immediately to fill out the medical paperwork that is required when someone dies. "It took a long time," says Gwen about a task that threatened to distract them from the sacredness and immediacy of the moment. But Maria's respectful, loving presence seemed to override her procedural duties, and she became one of the small community of intimates bidding Tom farewell.

Then the most beautiful thing happened. Together Gwen and Simon washed Tom's body—slowly, carefully, lovingly. "I thought of the washing as part of what we thought was glorious," says Gwen when I ask where she got the idea—and the nerve—to do it. It was "glorious," but not all pleasant, recalls Gwen. "We had to turn him over to do his back, and when we did it, all kinds of brown guck came out of his mouth, and it kept coming . . . so we kept mopping it up until it finally stopped. Then we oiled him. Maria said he looked like marble."

RITES AND RITUALS

INTO THE RELUCTANT ARMS
OF THE COMMUNITY

Fulfilling her promise to her dying husband, Gwen Taylor gives him a "glorious" send-off. In the intimacy of their home she creates a monumental exit—fabulous and warm, beautiful and sacred. Tom dies out in the open, in the epicenter of the action, surrounded by the most precious people in his life. He has conversations with his children that were never possible before: hard, revelatory, searching dialogues that fill the spaces between them that had, before now, been inhabited by silences, opaqueness, and fear. The new and raw truth telling summons breakthroughs of understanding and reconciliation between them. The siblings relinquish the traces of competition left over from adolescence and discover the mature bonds of collaborative care. Tom and his grown children trade places; his daughters mother him with beautiful handmade garments to cover his withering body; his sons father him with nourishing breakfasts. They read him the morning newspapers the way he used to read them their favorite bedtime stories when they were children. Tom's friends circle around him, bringing memories and stories, food and flowers, music and musings.

And Gwen orchestrates it all, relishing each day that Tom is alive, interpreting the hospice rules in her own way, tolerating the chaos and constant activity that usually drive her crazy, and finally participating in the sacred ritual of oiling her husband's body. The final death is not perfect or pleasant—but absolutely beautiful.

We see in this story of "amazing grace" a transfigured view of dying and death, rites and rituals of exit that help us reframe our views of other endings, both large and small, ordinary and extraordinary. The dying person does not suffer alone and isolated in the dark shadows of some back ward; he is in the light, at the center, prominent and visible, surrounded by family and friends. Only people he loves are allowed to come near; he calls the shots and makes his wishes known. It is the "fabulous conversations" that seem to sustain him the most—the rehearsal of old memories with Gwen, the declarations of love from his grandchildren, the vigorous political duels with old friends, the spiritual meanderings with the young divinity school graduate. He actively participates in composing his final ritual, seeing a picture of the plot where his ashes will be buried, voicing his choices of the readings and hymns for the memorial service, and telling his wife when he has had enough. In the weeks and days before his death, Tom Taylor lives large.

Ira Byock, the author of *Dying Well* (1997)[1] and a national leader and advocate for palliative care, speaks of his decades-long efforts—to reframe and reshape the medical practices and healthcare policies focused on the final exit—as a "cultural agenda." He begins with his own "countercultural" practices and the "extraordinary rewards" of helping his patients discover the fullness of life as they are dying. "I get to care for people with advanced psychological, existential, and social concerns . . . people who have a chance to reestablish, reconcile, and complete relationships," he says with enthusiasm as he compares his work in palliative care to the other medical disciplines he formerly practiced in family and emergency medicine. "This," he crows, "is life affirming. This is the real stuff."

But the "real stuff" is also painful, searing, and sorrowful, full of yearning, fear, and regrets. "A person with multiple infections, in the fourth stage of cancer, his gastrointestinal tract not working, his liver shut down—there are physical costs, pain, life-quality changes. Mortality will have its way with you." Ira's voice sounds harsh to my ears as he rehearses the inevitable decline. "I can't apologize for mortality any more than I can apologize for gravity.

"As a physician," he says with certainty, "my first goal is the well-being of my patients, to alleviate pain and the deep emotional hurts that contribute to their suffering. When their time is running out, the gentle revisiting of ruptured relationships may help with one area of unresolved suffering. I strive to teach that it is possible to expand the realm of what people consider possible—to imagine, to move beyond our own constraints." Over the years, he has found that even the worst atrocities—such as child abuse, neglect, and abandonment—can be overcome, leading to "a renewal in the relationship." Often these moments of reconciliation—a dying father who has been estranged from his son for twenty-five years and decides he wants to "seek resolution"—start with an apology. Two words, "I'm sorry." "That's pretty benign," says Byock about the courageous work he encourages in his patients.

Like the "fabulous conversations" that sustained Tom Taylor until the end, storytelling and listening are key to nourishing the imagination that paves the way to a gentle ending. "Storytelling expands the realm of what's possible," says Ira. "It offers some tangible example of something that might resonate with people who are dying. We are a death-defying culture, and we have few examples to draw from. Stories allow us to imagine what's possible . . . they become the key to creating the future." Stories, he adds, also help dying people to get to a deeper emotional level, allow them to explore the buried feelings they may have never been in touch with, allow them to feel growth in the midst of decline. "This is a time when you can become newly empowered, even as you know that you are losing so much."

In order to encourage imagining and storytelling, however, doctors and other caregivers have to learn how to listen. Ira laughs at something that sounds so obvious but is often hard to teach. "I tell my residents to breathe whenever possible, and I mean that literally and metaphorically." After all, he explains, in medical school, communication is equated with giving information, with telling, with advice, with offering guidance and direction; but little time and attention is given to learning how to listen, how to probe for stories. If you take time to breathe, then there is space for the patient's voice. "People can discover and hear their voices, and they can feel heard . . . the transaction can be complete."

Taking the breath that opens the space for listening to the stories is an act of intimacy and connection, one that is best when it is wrapped in the surround of a community. "People must die into the reluctant arms of the community," says Byock in one of his many "countercultural" statements. Our cultural tendency is to "silence and marginalize" people who are dying, to withdraw from them, to "pathologize" and fear them. In giving her husband a glorious send-off, Gwen Taylor re-creates community, reestablishing what Byock claims is the connective tissue that is latent in all human communities. He draws the contrast between the political and biological frames, and his voice rises to an urgent crescendo. "Whatever political paradigm emphasizes Jeffersonian independence, biologically, we are connected . . . we matter to one another." He uses an example from the other end of life. "When the baby cries, the lactating mother gets wet, and if the baby cries in the supermarket, three lactating mothers who hear him get wet. When a baby cries in a restaurant, no one can eat—not because it is too noisy (there may be trucks rolling on the highway outside making more noise than the baby), but because we are all connected."

Our sense of community is reinforced and expanded through rituals—rituals that create a structure, form, and medium for emotional and spiritual expression, rituals that mark and make visible our exits. Religious rites and liturgies often serve this purpose. Even though Ira Byock claims that he has a "nonromantic view" of religion, he admits that there is "wisdom embedded" in rituals and that religion is a "way of human beings reaching out to one another, in community, across generations"—that religion offers guidance in facing the "most existential experiences of human life: marriages, births, deaths, graduations, comings-of-age." He smiles at the memory of how he viewed religion—with suspicion and arrogance—as a young man coming of age in the 1960s, and he admits that "we were wrong." Now, especially after working for years with hundreds of dying patients, he is able to see the healing and holding power of religious rituals and the way it has "morphed" over his lifetime and become more relevant to our generation. "We have found a way to rediscover, revise, and renew the ritual."

Byock's reflections on dying well and Tom Taylor's glorious journey to his final exit echo many of the voices and experiences of the protagonists in this book who were seeking and searching for meaningful exits in their lives—exits that would carry them home, heal their wounds, soothe their yearnings, open the door to freedom. Their exit narratives, for example, speak about the importance of rituals that mark and honor endings, that allow for the expression of the joy and grief and the loss and liberation that accompany our departures from the communities and relationships in which we were embedded. Years after leaving the small parish in Virginia where he was priest, Joe Rosario still grieves for the things left unsaid, the purposeful omissions to the story he told to his parishioners that masked the truth and muted his voice. It was a staged stealth exit, an empty form, a bogus platform that did not allow him to exit fully from his priesthood, a leave-taking never fully realized.

Josh Arons helps to design his huge New Hampshire farewell, owning up to his need for a ceremonial send-off and balancing his wish that it be a low-key affair with his colleagues' desire for big fanfare. His request that everyone—the thousand attendees in the gilded hotel ballroom—join in singing "Stand By Me" speaks to Josh's understanding of the power of community as witness to his exit. He exits the "place" he has inhabited—which has defined him, where he has left his large imprint—in "the reluctant arms of the community." And when Carla Anderson feels overstuffed by the multiple and layered demands of her too-busy daily existence, seeking a life with greater focus and simplicity, she understands, for the first time, that she must not steal away in the night. She must leave in the light; her exit must be visible, offering herself and those she is leaving a chance for ceremony and grace. She recognizes the challenge of naming and honoring exits through rituals—the "countercultural" events in a society that tends to devalue and mask endings. And she also reflects on the ways in which her own family rarely marked the moments of completion, always poised for the next move, always tilting toward the future before honoring the past.

This book, then, points to a radical reframing of the meaning and worthiness of exits, moving exits from the shadows to the light, from the invisible to the visible, recognizing the ways in which exits are enhanced and expressed through ritual—the ceremonial moments that give us a chance to channel our conflicting emotions of joy and sorrow, a chance to stand up and be counted, an opportunity for bonding and community building—witnessing the ways in which exits can become moments for listening, storytelling, imagining, and creating choices that were unimaginable before. These productive dimensions of exit can be true whether we are talking about ordinary, everyday goodbyes or large public farewells. As a matter of fact, I think the micro and the macro are inextricably linked. Learning to name and navigate the daily leavetakings—a hug at the door, a lullaby at bedtime, a thank-you as you leave the office—helps us design and enact the grander public send-offs with intentionality and authenticity.

I want to borrow Ira Byock's notion of a "cultural agenda" (as opposed to an ideological or intellectual one) to underscore my wish—no, my strong proposal—that the practice of exiting with visibility and voice should not only be privately enacted in our relationships and within our families; it should also be braided into the policies and practices of our institutions, schools and colleges, hospitals and community organizations, corporate and political structures. I am, of course, not talking about the empty ritual of awarding gold watches to veteran employees at the end of twenty-five years of service, a sorry sign of their time having elapsed. I am referring to the ways in which organizations and communities might honor endings in a way that is substantive and inspirational, creative and collective, structured and improvisational, that speaks to the heart and the head and allows people to walk away with their heads held high rather than slink off in the night.

EXIT SIGNS: BOLD AND BLURRED

There is a central paradox in most people's recollections of their journeys to the exit. On the one hand, they can recall the exact moment—in bold relief, like the bloodred exit sign in a darkened movie theater—when they decided to leave, when they felt they no longer had any choice, when all the forces and sensations came together in a perfect storm and they said to themselves, "I'm out of here." On the other hand, their retrospective gazes allow them to see the long process of retreat that came well before the marked moment of announced leaving and the many aftershocks of exiting that followed. The protagonists in this book speak about the paradoxical sensation of exits—the moment frozen in time like an old Polaroid photograph, the long, arduous road to the exit, and the fallout and reverberations that inevitably follow—as "iterative" and "messy."

Andrew Connolly remembers every detail of the moment when he could no longer lie to the young woman he was "pleasantly" dating in graduate school as a "cover" for his real feelings of attraction for the "men with muscles" whom he longed to be with openly. He recalls her not-so-veiled hints about marriage as they sat across from each other at dinner that night; her earnest, blushing face as she stumbled awkwardly on her words; the knot in his belly when he realized how unfair he was being in hiding out from her; and how he was finally forced to confront his unkindness and cowardice. Although he did not announce to her that he was gay that evening, he knew in his heart that he could not mask his homosexuality any longer, that beginning the next day, he was going to live a life in which he was "out."

But even though that exit encounter—which Andrew remembers in vivid Technicolor—is clear, he is quick to point out that his coming out of the closet was not a "binary" experience. There were many exits, public and private, and it took several years to come out fully—years of determination, patience, and resolve; years that allowed for a deepening self-understanding. He uses the metaphor of "peeling the onion" to refer to the uncovering of each layer of his emerging identity; to reflect the exciting unmasking of his "authentic" self; and, I believe, to make sense of the tears of joy and relief that flowed when he stood high up in the San Francisco hills, looked down on the fog lifting, pierced by the glistening sunlight, and finally knew he was "home."

Although Andrew names the paradox of exit—of recalling "the moment" and living the "journey"—he also makes a distinction between those exits that were publicly announced and those that were privately experienced; and he tells me that the latter were generally more difficult and messier than the former. As a gay rights activist, he was surrounded by a community of comrades fighting together for a cause. They stood side by side and watched one another's backs, waging war on homophobia in all of its institutionalized and interpersonal guises, celebrating the occasional victories they won. The public exits—marching in gay rights parades, engaging in political campaigns, even being blindsided and "outed" in the newspaper after unknowingly sharing his story with a journalist—were all easier and less fraught than the private ones. Opening up to his parents, who "silenced the conversation" and refused to talk about his homosexuality, who would not even attend the funeral of his beloved spouse, was the hardest and most intimate exit of all. But he also understands how his parents' unconditional love, their unerring support, and the "happy childhood" he enjoyed were the bedrock of the self-confidence that allowed him to take the journey to the exit and emerge from the closet strong and whole.

Theresa Russo also draws the contrast between exit moments vividly and publicly expressed and the long years of private, "iterative" goodbyes. She recalls how relatively easy it was for her to decide—after twenty-five years of leading the nonprofit she founded—that it was time to leave, a decision that she believed would be good for the organization, which had become too "personality driven," and a decision that would ultimately support her individual growth, allow her to raise up her "solo voice" and establish her identity separate from the institution she had spawned. Even writing her letter of resignation to her board, her staff, and the community of kids and parents she had known for more than two decades did not seem terribly onerous. She found the words and sentiments and composed a letter that was both heartfelt and professional, expressive and restrained. And her speech at her farewell party seemed to flow with an elegance and alacrity she had never before experienced when presenting publicly to a large gathering. But the reality of leaving was much "messier," much more difficult and emotionally searing. She wept as she packed up her life in boxes; she felt marginalized and dismissed by the staff who no longer came to her for advice and counsel; and she hated the way she felt, needing them so much. Although she tried to resist the metaphor, it almost felt as if she had lost her baby, the one she had no time to have or care for during the time she was growing the organization. Her neediness and sadness left scars on her body. In the midst of it all, she contracted Graves' disease, an infirmity that lived up to its name.

Theresa's and Andrew's narratives and several of the other stories in this book trace the longitudinal and messy undercurrents of our leave-takings and challenge Albert Hirschman's theoretical framing of our exits. Hirschman speaks about exit—from institutions, and by extension from identities and relationships—as a clean, open-and-shut process whereby people decide that they can no longer be engaged in or tolerate the values, norms, and processes of the organization; neither do they see any way to change them. So they leave and never look back. "Voice," he claims, is messier; it is the "art" of staying put and making your views and criticisms known in an effort to improve the functioning and productivity of the organization. In his view, exit and voice are binary paths, divergent ways of responding to the inevitable decline in mature organizations.[2]

But the tales of exit told in this book point to the ways in which voice and exit may converge and the ways in which both processes are messy and artful. Theresa, in fact, needs to exit her nonprofit in order to begin to develop her voice; she needs to draw clearer boundaries between herself (the solo voice) and others (the choir) and establish the outlines of her singular identity in order for her to successfully end one chapter and begin the next. Her emerging voice gives fuel to the exit. Anthropologist Shin Wang relishes the messiness of exits, enjoying the refracted, layered interpretations of the folks who are leaving and those who are being left; finding intentional, caring ways of ritualizing her departures from the "field"; and joining her voice with those of her "subjects" to create a collective story, owned and authored by all of them.

Not only do the protagonists in this book talk about their exits as iterative and messy, a few of them are even intentional in slowing the exit process, not wanting to accelerate it, force it, or push it toward a decisive conclusion. Rather they want it to emerge "organically"; they want to witness its evolution, watch themselves facing the inevitable moments of ambivalence, fear, and emptiness that anticipate the leap of faith, the new opportunity or adventure. Carla Anderson, for example, tries to hone this "discipline" of slowing down and waiting for the muse, making a space for her imagination and fantasies to emerge, offering her options she would never consider if she rushed ahead in decision mode. She is proud of the way she and her ex-husband managed their divorce, slowly and respectfully, making sure they were not causing undue hurt to each other, wanting to be there, apart and together, to provide a safety net for their troubled child. Josh Arons also slows down his exit from his CEO position at the Beacon Fund. On purpose, he decides not to calculate the pros and cons or weigh the opportunities and liabilities of a rational plan. Rather he wants to listen to his internal "yearnings," which he will be able to hear only if he "sits still" for a moment. He wants to leave himself "vulnerable" and exposed to possibilities he might never have considered before in his life.

In her large-scale sociological study of "role exits," Helen Rose Fuchs Ebaugh identifies four distinct stages of disengagement from a role that is central to a person's identity and the reestablishment of an identity in a new role—a process that includes entertaining "first doubts," weighing "role alternatives," and coming to a "turning point" where the person makes the move, often announcing it publicly as a way of deterring retreat. Ebaugh's fourth stage— "creating an ex-role"—however, is a subtle recognition of the messiness that can protrude even into a neat and linear stage theory;

one identity bleeds over into the next. During this fourth and final stage, people struggle with incorporating their "hangover identity" into their future identity; seeking to find a balance between who they were and who they are becoming; working to find the skills, experiences, and perspectives that are translatable from one identity to the next and the ones that must be discarded; and, most important, struggling to establish themselves in their new role while they continue to disentangle themselves from the social expectations of their previous one.[3] Here Ebaugh, like Andrew Connolly and Theresa Russo, underscores the nonbinary quality of exits—the ways in which the former identity gets merged, mingled, and balanced with the new one; and the difficult work of developing and shaping the new identity when the gravity of the vestigial continues to pull us back and weigh us down.

Coming from a very different disciplinary perspective that considers the person and psyche behind the "role," psychotherapist Linda Gould recasts our interpretation of the language of "termination" that marks, but does not end, the therapeutic relationship. When Linda and her patients say farewell, they go through the ritual steps of celebrating their progress, reflecting on the process, and anticipating the work that still lies ahead. The ceremonial exits of "honoring the work" are both structured and idiosyncratic, predetermined and highly individualized, but they are always unfinished and imperfect. It is not as if the therapy has vanquished the pain or erased the wounds; nor is the exit a sign that people are cured. Rather, Linda hopes that when they depart from the protective asylum of her office, her patients will have developed a deeper understanding of the roots of their addictions and neuroses, the courage to tell themselves the truth about their pain and the ways in which they are implicated in their own unhappiness, and a way of seeing and a set of skills that will put them on a path to a healthier daily existence. When she says goodbye to her patients, she knows that their way forward will be messy and uneasy, that there will still be minefields and rocky roads ahead, and that their wounds will reappear from time to time in new and ancient guises.

In recasting our views of exits—big and small, minute and momentous, public and private—it is, I believe, important to see the double image: one, of a moment in time sparkling with colorful details, of a clear decision, a sudden, edgy action; and the other of a messy, nonlinear journey, a process of forward and retreating moves, uncertainty and resolve, ambivalence and clarity. And it is important to recognize that at least for voluntary exits, we have it in our power to be intentional and reflective about our leave-takings, to see ourselves as the authors of the exit narratives we are composing, listening for the emergence and expression of our "voices," doing the "artful" work of defining a new identity that honors the losses and the liberation of crossing the exit line.

DEVELOPMENTAL AND GENERATIONAL MARKERS

Exits are also deeply embedded in our developmental journeys. Again I turn to the signature work of psychologist Erik Erikson, who charts eight developmental stages across the life cycle, from birth to death. At the very center of each life stage is the choice each of us must make—consciously or unconsciously—between change and constancy, progression and regression, counterbalancing forces pulling us in opposite directions, demanding our allegiance and attention. In order to grow, people must resolve the contrary, competing pulls by ultimately exiting, resisting and surmounting the gravitational pulls that would maintain stasis and keep us in the same place.[4] Exits, therefore, are part of our biological, emotional, and social trajectories, part of the fabric and shape of our life journeys, projecting us forward, helping us evolve as developing human beings. As a matter of fact, one way of mapping our developmental milestones might be by tracking the exits. Not seeing them as negative spaces in between positive launches forward, but by regarding them as the necessary, preparatory steps of progress. If we are able to successfully exit this stage, this place, this identity, we will be able to see and seize the shape and opportunities of the next chapter.

The stories in this book also reveal the exits that are part of the way our cultural scripts shape the developmental sequence. Bijan Jalili's tale of leaving Iran is at its core a narrative about an adolescent separating from his parents—his excruciating first steps away from their embraces at the airport and his yearning, as soon as he touches down at Kennedy Airport, to race home to the warmth and protection of his mother's bosom; his continuing telephone duels with his father, desperately pleading to come home, playing their "brain games," the approach/avoidance dance that is part of the cultural script of adolescent exits. The struggles of separation and self-definition are played out in bold relief in Bijan's story of flight from his family—a teenage tale made more dramatic because of the backdrop of warfare, social dislocation, and geographic distance. But the exit is embedded in and shaped by the unfolding of a developmental journey taking him from childhood to manhood.

We also see the developmental markers in Josh Arons's decision—at sixty-five—to leave the Beacon Fund. After a quarter century of guiding and growing the organization, after "loving" his work and the "place" he has established and imprinted on the philanthropic landscape of New Hampshire, he is inspired to change his life in one of those paradoxical experiences of exit that seems both "all of a sudden" and long anticipated. He wants his next chapter to emerge "organically"; he wants to "sit still" and listen to the stirrings from deep in his "soul"; and he wants to do the unexpected—all in search of something fulfilling and meaningful. As I listen to Josh's "yearnings," I hear the echoes of other Third

Chapter folks[5] between the ages of fifty and seventy-five, whom I have interviewed, who are ready to risk the uncertainties of the unknown, embark on bold adventures, and learn something new. This developmental stage, whose contours have been given new definition in our contemporary culture, is becoming a time when those of us who are "neither young nor old" face the finite years we have left with eagerness and urgency, when we finally proclaim, "If not now, when?" The exits we take from the places we have worked, the relationships that have sustained us, and the institutions that have constrained us are departures written into our developmental scripts.

These developmental exits are also shaped by our families of origin and by the relationships forged across generations that have an impact on how we navigate our leave-takings. Carla Anderson, for example, not only points to our "very American" cultural neglect of ceremonial exits and the ways in which our society tends to denigrate and diminish the important rituals of exit; she also recognizes the ways in which her family never honored farewell moments, never celebrated acts of completion, never recognized the beauty in endings. Her father's first, and urgent, message to his offspring was always focused on the future, what was coming up on the horizon, what was next. When Carla became a mother, she found herself actively resisting the echoes of her father's voice urging her on to the next thing. She was intentional in trying to design family rituals for her own children that would mark both endings and beginnings, successes and failures, moments for coming together face-to-face in thanks and gratitude, in sadness and disappointment. When she is now faced with exiting from her too-busy life, overstuffed with meetings, commitments, travel, schedules, even friends, she understands—in a way she never did before—the meaningfulness of exits gracefully accomplished; and she sees beauty and wisdom in those "countercultural" events.

We also hear the generational echoes in Neda and Ehsan's fragile freedom from the assaults of the school bullies and the abuses of their "kiss-ass" mothers. From the very first day of kindergarten Ehsan is targeted by Ricky and his gang, who turn him into their "soldier" and insist that he carry out their violent orders. When Ehsan resists or tries to hide out, they threaten him and beat him up. Despite Neda's constant vigilance and her aggressive efforts to seek protection for her son, the teachers and principals are never able—or willing—to offer Ehsan a safe asylum. Even when Neda has had enough; even when she can no longer bear to see the lesions and bruises he is suffering at the bullies' hands and begs him to withdraw from school, Ehsan asks for one more chance to face his predators and prevail, one more chance to make it right. He has begun to see himself as his predators see him; he has begun to accept his unworthiness. His endurance, his courage and self-sacrifice, his willingness to withstand the abuse, even his gratitude for being an American have been passed down across the generations.

His mother before him was also bullied at school, singled out and emotionally tortured for being the only brown immigrant child in an all-white small town that felt threatened by her family of foreign interlopers. And as a child, she learned not to whine or complain; she learned that the abuse was the price she paid for the privilege of being in America. She listened to, and heeded, her father's litany—"the Kermanians never, ever give up"—and she passed the message on to her son, who whispered it to himself as he withstood the blows of the big bullies. The final straw, the photo finish that will always be imprinted in Neda's memory— Ehsan kicking the side of their car with his big winter boot—was an act of desperation, rage, and resistance. In exiting from Sartre's hell,[6] Ehsan was resisting the generational imperatives; he was resisting the voice of his grandfather that had insisted that he hang

in and endure the pain, that he trade his gratitude for their abuse
of him. His exit, an act of bold defiance against the gang of bullies
and against his immigrant inheritance, led him to freedom and
saved his life.

THE BEGINNING LEADS TO THE END

There is something overwhelming and awe inspiring about finding
an ending—a beautiful ending—for a book about exits. A self-
consciousness overtakes me as I try to conclude with words that
hold the wisdom and passion, the intentionality and care, the visibility and voice of the protagonists whose exit stories populate
this book; and I find myself searching for the most primal and innocent expression of the power of exits. I think about myself at six
years old being offered a chocolate almond ice-cream cone—my
favorite flavor—and not wanting to yield to the pleasure of licking
it, because once I started, I would already experience my disappointment when it would all be gone. Or I reflect on my grown-up
version of going to Symphony Hall to hear Bach's Mass in B
Minor—a rich and profound piece of music that always moves
me—and feeling the melancholy of arriving at the last chord of the
final chorale even as I listen to the opening phrases of the Mass.

In an evocative short story, "Getting Closer," published in *The
New Yorker* (January 2011), Steven Millhauser[7] tells about a nine-
year-old boy who goes with his family on a picnic by the side of the
river, a treat he has been looking forward to all summer. He arrives
at the riverbank; he is ready to begin.

> But who's to say when anything begins really? You could
> say the day began when they passed the wooden sign with
> the words "INDIAN COVE" and the outline of a tomahawk, on
> a curve of road with a double yellow line down the middle

and brown wooden posts with red reflectors. Or maybe it all started when the car backed up the slope of the driveway and the tires bumped over the sidewalk between the knee-high pricker hedges. Or what if it happened before that, when he woke up in the morning and saw the day stretching out before him like a whole summer of blue afternoons? But he's only playing, just fooling around, because he knows exactly when it all begins: it begins when he enters the water. That's the agreement he's made with himself, summer after summer. That's just how it is. The day begins in the river, and everything leads up to it.

Not that he's all that eager to rush into things. Now that he's here, now that the waiting's practically over, he enjoys prolonging the excitement of moving toward the moment he's been waiting for. It isn't the swimming itself he looks forward to. He doesn't even swim. He hangs on the inner tube and kicks his legs. He likes it, it's fine, he can take it or leave it. No, what he cares about, what thrills him every time is knowing that this is it, the beginning of the long-awaited day at the river, as agreed to by himself in advance. Everything's been leading up to it and, in the way of things that lead up to other things, there's an electric charge, a hum. He can feel it all over his body. The closer you get, the more it's there.[8]

We see the young boy's rapt anticipation, his intentional stalling, putting off the beginning by playing a game with himself about how to measure the day's start. Tingling with excitement, he savors the waiting, the luscious lingering before heading into the water—for to begin the swim would be to face the end, the inevitable disappointment that is just waiting there once he commits his body to the river.

Exits hold that power, that inevitability. If we begin our journey toward home, our quest for freedom, our yearning for a meaningful life—if we choose to lift up our voices in celebration and protest, if we survive the exit wounds and walk forward with grace, we will move inexorably to the exit. In seeing our lives through the lens of the exit, we transfigure the journey, we feel the "electric charge" of anticipation, we learn to celebrate completion, and we witness the "triumph of beauty" that is the end—whether it is a refreshing dip in the water, the sweet taste of ice cream, or the radiance and resolution of the final chord in Bach's B-Minor Mass.

Notes

INTRODUCTION: EXITS: VISIBLE AND INVISIBLE

1. For statistics on divorce rates, see National Center for Health Statistics, www.cdc
.gov/nchs/fastats/divorce.htm and U.S. Census Bureau, www.census.gov/hhes/socdemo
/marriage/.
2. For recent statistics on the numbers of legal permanent residents, naturalized citizens, and refugees, see U.S. Department of Homeland Security, www.dhs.gov/files
/statistics/publications/yearbook.shtm and U.S. Census Bureau, www.census.gov
/population/www/socdemo/immigration.html.
3. For statistics on employment and career changes over a lifetime, see Bureau of Labor Statistics, http://www.bls.gov/oco/ and *Wall Street Journal*, September 4, 2010,
http://online.wsj.com/article/SB10001424052748704206804575468162805877990
.html.
4. For recent unemployment statistics, see Bureau of Labor Statistics, www.bls.gov/bls
/unemployment.htm.
5. For more on "boomerang kids" or the phenomenon of college graduates moving
back home, see *CNN Money*, November 15, 2010, http://money.cnn.com/2010/10/14
/pf/boomerang_kids_move_home/index.htm.
6. See Howard Zinn, *A People's History of the United States* (New York: Harper & Row,
1980).
7. Albert O. Hirschman, *Exit, Voice, and Loyalty: Responses to Decline in Firms, Organizations, and States* (Cambridge, MA: Harvard University Press, 1970).
8. Ibid., 112–13.
9. Sara Lawrence-Lightfoot, *The Third Chapter: Passion, Risk, and Adventure in the 25
Years After 50* (New York: Sarah Crichton Books/Farrar, Straus and Giroux, 2009).
10. Erik H. Erikson, *Identity and the Life Cycle* (New York: W. W. Norton, 1959).
11. Sara Lawrence-Lightfoot, *Respect: An Exploration* (Cambridge, MA: Perseus Books,
2000).

12. For more on the effects of technology on intimacy, relationships, and private/public boundaries, see Max van Mannen, "The Pedagogy of Momus Technologies: Facebook, Privacy, and Online Intimacy," *Qualitative Health Research* 8, no. 20 (August 2010): 1023–32; Sonia Livingston and David R. Brake, "On the Rapid Rise of Social Networking Sites: New Findings and Policy Implications," *Children and Society* 24, no. 1 (January 2010): 75–83; Paul Benjamin Lowry, Jinwei Cao, and Andrea Everard, "Privacy Concerns Versus Desire for Interpersonal Awareness in Driving the Use of Self-Disclosure Technologies: The Case of Instant Messaging in Two Cultures," *Journal of Management Information Systems* 27, no. 4 (spring 2011): 163–200; and Marist Poll, December 18, 2009, http://maristpoll.marist.edu/1218-technologys-impact-on-relationships/.

1. HOME

1. Joan Didion, "On Going Home," in *Slouching Towards Bethlehem* (New York: Farrar, Straus and Giroux, 1961).
2. Robert Pack, *Wallace Stevens: An Approach to His Poetry and Thought* (Piscataway, NJ: Rutgers University Press, 1958).
3. Paule Marshall, *Brown Girl, Brownstones* (New York: Random House, 1959).
4. Paule Marshall, "From the Poets in the Kitchen," *New York Times*, January 9, 1983.
5. Didion, "On Going Home," 166.
6. Marshall, "From the Poets in the Kitchen," 3.

2. VOICE

1. Carol Gilligan, *In a Different Voice: Psychological Theory and Women's Development* (Cambridge, MA: Harvard University Press, 1982).
2. Hirschman, *Exit, Voice, and Loyalty.*
3. Ibid., 115.
4. Ibid., 15.
5. Ibid., 43.
6. For more on Hirschman's theory of exit-voice-loyalty, empirically explored in the fields of psychology, management, and politics, see C. Rusbult, I. Zembrodt, and L. Gunn, "Exit, Voice, Loyalty, and Neglect: Responses to Dissatisfaction in Romantic Involvements," *Journal of Personality and Social Psychology* 43, no. 6 (1982): 123–24; D. Farrell, "Exit, Voice, Loyalty, and Neglect as Responses to Job Dissatisfaction: A Multidimensional Scaling Study," *Academy of Management Journal* 26, no. 4 (1983): 596–607; and W. Lyons and D. Lowery, "The Organization of Political Space and Citizen Responses to Dissatisfaction in Urban Communities: An Integrative Model," *Journal of Politics* 48 (1986): 321–46.
7. Hirschman, *Exit, Voice, and Loyalty*, 15–16.
8. For more on the methodology of entering the field and gaining access as a qualitative researcher, see R. Bogdan, and S. K. Biklen, *Qualitative Research for Education:*

An *Introduction to Theory and Methods* (Needham Heights, MA: Allyn & Bacon, 1992); C. Glesne and A. Peshkin, *Becoming Qualitative Researchers: An Introduction* (White Plains, NY: Longman, 1992); C. Marshall and G. Rossman, *Designing Qualitative Research* (Thousand Oaks, CA: Sage, 1989); J. A. Maxwell, *Qualitative Research Design: An Interactive Approach* (Thousand Oaks, CA: Sage, 1996); J. M. Nielsen, ed., *Feminist Research Methods: Exemplary Reading in the Social Sciences* (Boulder, CO: Westview Press, 1990); and I. E. Seidman, *Interviewing as Qualitative Research* (New York: Teachers College Press, 1991).

9. For more on rebalancing the scales of give-and-take between the researcher and the researched and on reciprocity, see chapter 5: "On Relationships," in Sara Lawrence-Lightfoot and Jessica Hoffmann Davis, *The Art and Science of Portraiture* (San Francisco: Jossey-Bass Publishers, 1997), 153–55, 165.

3. FREEDOM

1. Jean-Paul Sartre, *No Exit and Three Other Plays* (New York: Vintage Books, 1943).
2. Ibid., 5–6.
3. Ibid., 17.
4. Ibid., 45.
5. Ibid., 43.

4. WOUNDS

1. For more on bullying, see Christine Barter and David Berrige, eds., *Children Behaving Badly? Peer Violence Between Children and Young People* (Malden, MA: Wiley-Blackwell, 2011); Monica J. Harris, ed., *Bullying, Rejection, and Peer Victimization: A Social Cognitive Neuroscience Perspective* (New York: Springer, 2009); and Dorothy Espelage and Susan Swearer, eds., *Bullying in American Schools: A Social-Ecological Perspective on Prevention and Intervention* (Mahwah, NJ: Erlbaum Associates, 2004).
2. For more on the intergenerational transmission of trauma, see Carol Whatman et al., eds., *Formative Experiences: The Interaction of Caregiving, Culture, and Developmental Psychobiology* (New York: Cambridge University Press, 2010) and Yael Danieli, ed., *International Handbook of Multigenerational Legacies of Trauma* (New York: Plenum Press, 1998).
3. For more on termination practices in therapy, see William O'Donohue and Kyle Ferguson, *Handbook of Professional Ethics for Psychologists: Issues, Questions, and Controversies* (Thousand Oaks, CA: Sage Publications, 2003) and Jeffrey Barnett and Brad Johnson, *Ethics Desk Reference for Psychologists* (Washington, DC: American Psychological Association, 2008).
4. See Sigmund Freud, *The Interpretation of Dreams* (Oxford, UK: Oxford University Press, 1999).
5. For further reading about the art and science of clinical practice, see Atul Gawande, *Complications: A Surgeon's Notes on an Imperfect Science* (New York: Metropolitan

Books, 2002); Atul Gawande, *Better: A Surgeon's Notes on Performance* (New York: Metropolitan, 2007); Oliver Sacks, *The Man Who Mistook His Wife for a Hat* (New York: Perennial Library, 1987); Oliver Sacks, *An Anthropologist on Mars: Seven Paradoxical Tales* (New York: Knopf, 1995).

6. For more on the culture of medical training and medical education, see Robert Rogers, Amal Mattu, Michael Winters, and Joseph Martinez, eds., *Practical Teaching in Emergency Medicine* (Hoboken, NJ: Wiley-Blackwell, 2009); Commonwealth Fund Taskforce on Academic Health Centers, *Training Tomorrow's Doctors: The Medical Education Mission of Academic Health Centers* (New York, Commonwealth Fund, 2002); Stephen J. Miller, *The Medical Elite: Training for Leadership* (New Brunswick, NJ: Aldine Transaction, 2011); and Tim Swanwick, ed., *Understanding Medical Education: Evidence, Theory and Practice* (Chichester, West Sussex, UK: Wiley-Blackwell, 2010).

5. YEARNING

1. Helen Rose Fuchs Ebaugh, *Becoming an Ex: The Process of Role Exit* (Chicago: University of Chicago Press, 1988).
2. Ibid., 206.
3. Ibid., xvi.
4. Robert Heinlein, *Stranger in a Strange Land* (New York: G. P. Putnam, 1961).
5. Lawrence-Lightfoot, *The Third Chapter.*

6. GRACE

1. W.E.B. Du Bois, "Of Beauty and Death," in *Darkwater: Voices from Within the Veil* (New York: Harcourt, Brace, and Howe, 1920).
2. Ibid., 246–47.
3. Ibid., 247.

CONCLUSION: RITES AND RITUALS

1. Ira Byock, *Dying Well: The Prospect of Growth at the End of Life* (New York: Riverhead Books, 1997).
2. Hirschman, *Exit, Voice, and Loyalty.*
3. Ebaugh, *Becoming an Ex.*
4. Erikson, *Identity and the Life Cycle.*
5. Lawrence-Lightfoot, *The Third Chapter.*
6. Sartre, *No Exit and Three Other Plays.*
7. Steven Millhauser, "Getting Closer," *New Yorker*, January 3, 2011, 58–61.
8. Ibid., 59.

Selected Sources

Byock, Ira. *Dying Well: The Prospect of Growth at the End of Life*. New York: Riverhead Books, 1997.

In failing to deal with that ultimate of exits—death—Ira Byock, in *Dying Well*, argues that Americans have "paid dearly . . . and are culturally poorer for failing to explore the inherently human experience of dying" (p. xiii). In telling ten stories of death, including that of his own father, Byock enacts healing and connection, and builds a theory of death as a time of growth and potential for both internal understanding and interpersonal relationships. It was the experience of his father's death that led Byock to reexamine his experiences as a hospice doctor and to question his assumptions about dying and the care of those dying. Rather than conceptualizing death as a problem, and rather than classifying some deaths as "good," he coined the term "dying well" to evoke a sense of living, engagement, process, and action. This reframing is analogous to the reframing of exit as essentially a positive development rather than a mere ending, absence, or leaving. In addition to these developmental and interpersonal aspects, Byock addresses health-care policy, medical education, assisted suicide, financing strategies, and other large-scale issues, and offers advice for clinicians, families, and policy makers. He ends the book with a set of questions a family could use to begin a conversation about dying and how to treat it with the respect, reverence, and involvement it deserves.

Didion, Joan. "On Going Home," in *Slouching Towards Bethlehem*. New York: Farrar, Straus and Giroux, 1961.

"The question of whether or not you could go home again" (p. 167) raised by Joan Didion in this short essay evokes the archetypal exit from home upon reaching adulthood, and the way that such an exit redefines home. Recounting visiting her childhood home with her husband, Didion draws the distinction between being privy to the secret rituals and language that are open only to the people who grew up in her family, and the misunderstanding and non-understanding experienced by her husband, who is welcomed into the home, but not of it. Didion also defines home and belonging through a generational lens—growing up is an exit in itself. Looking at her sleeping daughter, Didion says she "would like to give her *home* for her birthday, but we live differently now and I can promise her nothing like that" (p. 169). As she comes back home, the separation between the past and present becomes evident, as well as the inevitable exit of the future generation.

Du Bois, W.E.B. "Of Beauty and Death," in *Darkwater: Voices from Within the Veil.* New York: Harcourt, Brace and Howe, 1920.

W.E.B. Du Bois argues that endings—because they are complete and finite—usher in beauty, which "lies implicit and is revealed in its end" (p. 120) and is the antithesis of eternal, incomplete, indefinite ugliness. To the extent that endings are embodied in exit, beauty becomes a component of exit. Juxtaposing the beauty of "sea and sky and city" with the least of the world's ugliness—the "little hatefulness and thoughtlessness of race prejudice" (p. 111)—Du Bois expresses the relationship between beauty, life, and death in this essay. The stories of ugliness include riding on the "Jim Crow" car on the train, the experience of buying a movie ticket in a segregated theater, and the degradation endured by black men volunteering for armed service. The rapturous images of beauty show the mountains of Maine, the Grand Canyon, and "the bugles of Harlem" heard by the town pump in a French village. Weaving among these moments of ugliness and beauty—indeed, entering and exiting each one—Du Bois's writing demonstrates the completeness, satisfaction, and fulfillment of experiencing beauty.

Ebaugh, Helen Rose Fuchs. *Becoming an Ex: The Process of Role Exit.* Chicago: University of Chicago Press, 1988.

Helen Ebaugh's interest in role exit began when she was a sociology student—and a Sister of Divine Providence—at Columbia University, studying with Robert Merton in the late 1960s and early 1970s. Her doctoral research project explored the relationship between changes in religious orders and exit rates and the reasons "why nuns left, the factors that precipitated the exit, what the exiting process was like, and the experience of life as an ex-nun." During the course of her research, she became fascinated with the personal accounts of role exiting that she was hearing, and she began to notice similar patterns and operating influences, which she later defined as stages or sequential events of role exit. Doing this work, Ebaugh herself made a transition and was struck by the similarities of her exit as an ex-nun and her fiancé's exit as a divorcé. She began to wonder how the process or stage model of role exit might apply to other kinds of voluntary exits, such as career changes, departures from ideological and sectarian groups, etc., and she assembled a research group to study the role-exit process across a variety of social roles, with the goal of discovering similarities and differences in the exiting process as experienced by people exiting roles they defined as central to their lives.

Ebaugh defines the term "role exit" as the process of disengagement from a role that is central to one's self-identity and the reestablishment of an identity in a new role that takes into account one's ex-role. She points to a lack of general theory that views role exit as a generic social process, and she frames her book as an attempt to explore and suggest basic issues involved in conceptualizing a theory of role exit. She ascertained a strong pattern in the sequencing of events in the role-exit process. The first stage is that of *first doubts*, in which individuals begin to question the role commitment they had previously taken for granted. The next stage is the seeking and weighing of *role alternatives*. The third stage is the *turning point*, when the individual actually leaves the role, followed by the last stage, which concerns the establishment of an *ex-role identity* during post-exit. Ebaugh also names eleven properties—or variables—that influence the nature and consequences of the role-exit process. These variables are voluntariness, centrality of the role, reversibility, duration, degree of control, individual versus group exit, single versus multiple exits, social desirability, degree of institutionalization, degree of awareness, and sequentiality. Her argument—that role exit be inserted into the broader landscape of sociological literature on role theory and become as central as the traditional concept of socialization into new roles—is an empirically based, unique contribution to the field. There seems to be little that followed her 1988 book theorizing exit as a staged phenomenon, generalizable to most social roles.

Erikson, Erik H. *Identity and the Life Cycle*. New York: W. W. Norton, 1959.
    Erik Erikson defines the stages of development of a healthy personality as the progression through critical psychological conflicts, from childhood to adulthood. Movement from one stage to the next is marked by a radical change in perspective, or an exit from seeing and accepting things one way to seeing and acknowledging another way of being. These developmental stages, in Erikson's terms are: (1) basic trust vs. basic mistrust (infancy); (2) autonomy vs. shame and doubt (early childhood); (3) initiative vs. guilt (play age); (4) industry vs. inferiority (school age); (5) identity vs. identity diffusion (adolescence); (6) intimacy vs. isolation (young adulthood); (7) generativity vs. self-absorption (adulthood); and (8) integrity vs. despair and disgust (mature age). These psychosocial crises occur within relationships with significant people and structures—such as family, school, peer groups, and partners—and therefore are locations of development influenced by both biology and society. Exit from one stage into the next, then, is growth into a healthy self.

Harper, Hill. "Quitting versus Changing Your Mind" in *Letters to a Young Brother: Manifest Your Destiny*. London, UK: Penguin Books, 2006.
    In this series of letters influenced by Rilke's *Letters to a Young Poet*, Hill Harper delivers mentorship and advice to young men. Letter 6, "Quitting versus Changing Your Mind," is on the topic of quitting (a young man wants to quit the track team), and Harper develops a nuanced difference between "quitting" and "changing your mind/ doing something else/moving on." Quitting is performed out of fear, discomfort, and difficulty. Changing your mind, however, means stopping doing something that is holding you back from realizing your true potential. Harper recalls his own experience with changing his mind versus quitting when he graduated from Harvard Law School and

was expected to start his career as a lawyer; instead of following this path, he decided to pursue his love of acting and moved to Los Angeles. In this exit, he enacts serious commitment to be an active architect of his life. Though he positions quitting as a negative response and changing your mind as a positive one, both seem to require justification; in this regard, he confirms the normative stance that exit is something that needs to be explained and rationalized rather than accepted and celebrated like entrances and beginnings. His counterpoint is that both quitting and changing one's mind can be purposeful, productive, powerful moments in the arc of a person's life, exits that beget success.

Hirschman, Albert O. *Exit, Voice, and Loyalty: Responses to Decline in Firms, Organizations, and States.* Cambridge, MA: Harvard University Press, 1970.
    Albert Hirschman's seminal work of economic theory paints exit as a neat, terminal, impersonal, quantifiable, and discernible action that is highly efficient. It is the most direct way of expressing dissatisfaction. A customer resorts to exit, rather than voice, when he/she no longer attempts to change an objectionable state of affairs—whether through individual or collective petition, appeal to a higher authority, or various actions and protests—although Hirschman admits the possibility of acquiescence or indifference as the space between voice (articulation) and exit. Though the exit option is widely held to be uniquely powerful, he states that the "precise modus operandi of the exit option has not received much attention." He attempts to explicate the phenomenon of exit by comparing it with voice, which is not only the opposite but also a complement to and a substitute for exit. The seesawing, complementary, yet unequal options of exit and voice are further complicated by Hirschman's addition of loyalty into the theoretical mix. Loyalty, or a special attachment to an organization, helps group members resort to voice when exit is possible; loyalty holds exit at bay and activates voice. In addition, loyalty calls into question the voice/exit dichotomy by posing a different dilemma: How does *voice from within* differ from *voice from without* (after exit)?
    Hirschman supports the idea that exit is a ubiquitous cultural experience and indeed a hallmark of American society. He also positions exit as a regenerative force in the face of inevitable deterioration and decay, even as he warns of the high cost exit can bring to both the individual and the organization. Though he favors voice as a response to dissatisfaction, he nevertheless portrays exit as a powerful force and is respectful of exit as an entity necessary for the functioning of businesses, economies, and nations. For him, exit doesn't feel like a "problem," but rather a powerful and complex action. For example, he challenges the idea that full exit is ever possible and questions the balance of power between the one who exits and the one who stays. In portraying exit as a fluid, complex, and contradictory experience, Hirschman values this component of our culture and economy through his multidimensional theory.

Lawrence-Lightfoot, Sara. *Respect: An Exploration.* Cambridge, MA: Perseus Books, 2000.
    This book illuminates the roots, development, and expressions of respect, a con-

cept, idea, and practice that in its presence—or absence—marks the essence of public and private lives. It is an exploration that regards respect in ways contrary to the traditional perspectives: respect as empathetic and connective rather than submissive and boundary marking; respect as developing and growing over time rather than a static quantity; respect as commitment and desire rather than compliance and duty. The six portraits of respect in this book also highlight the ways in which respect is tied with exit, especially when considering boundaries, taking risks, relationships and connections, the symmetry of movement back and forth, the beauty of completion, and the way that exit—with and in respect—can be a generative force.

Lawrence-Lightfoot, Sara. *The Third Chapter: Passion, Risk, and Adventure in the 25 Years After 50.* New York: Sarah Crichton Books/Farrar, Straus and Giroux, 2009.
　　The Third Chapter redefines the period of life that has traditionally been limited to post-career aging and decline, and positions it as a developmental stage full of possibility, challenge, and transformation. It is perhaps not surprising that exit—from work, from established roles, from comfortable identities and relationships—is what grounds the contours and experiences of this stage of life. Exit—from the "old" life into the new—is the catalyst for learning, creativity, and risk taking undertaken by folks in their fifties, sixties, and seventies who yearn for challenge and meaning not yet experienced. In fact, exits can be regarded as a necessary condition of development at this stage of life, developmental in their very essence. Most profoundly, exit enables being and becoming at this stage of life; exit is the transition that propels people toward achieving their fullest self at an age long regarded as the time to retreat and disengage.

Lawrence-Lightfoot, Sara, and Jessica Hoffmann Davis. "Chapter Five: On Relationships," in *The Art and Science of Portraiture.* San Francisco: Jossey-Bass Publishers, 1997.
　　In this seminal methodological text, which breaks open the boundaries of aesthetics and empiricism, relationships are at the heart of developing understanding and knowledge. These relationships are marked by the challenges of reciprocity and responsibility; recognizing, sustaining, and negotiating boundaries; and, of course, exit. The importance of exit is especially vivid when considering reciprocity; in respecting the contribution of the research participants to the researcher's work, and in acknowledging that the relationship between the researcher and the research participants is delimited, exit becomes a vehicle by which to act responsibly, ethically, and with goodness. Seldom considered, the idea and practice of exit in research relationships is critical for social scientists.

Marshall, Paule. *Brown Girl, Brownstones.* New York: Random House, 1959.
　　The story of immigration is a classic exit story, the story of leaving the home of one's native land to make another home on foreign soil. Paule Marshall published this novel at the age of thirty, exploring her own childhood and adolescence growing up in the Barbadian immigrant community in 1930s Brooklyn. She captures the fullness and contradictions of home and community as well as the love and the hurts that define her

family's experience after exiting their homeland. The rich language of the novel's characters transforms their particular experience into the universal themes of tradition, history, spirituality, and identity; for Marshall, the texture and sound of this language is what defines home, both before and after the exit of immigration.

Marshall, Paule. "From the Poets in the Kitchen." *New York Times*, January 9, 1983.

In this widely cited *New York Times* article, Paule Marshall writes about the language of home—the legacy of language and culture—that she learned in "the wordshop of the kitchen." Writing about her mother and her mother's friends who, after their long days as housecleaners, gathered around a kitchen table to talk about life, politics, and home, Marshall acknowledges these women and their talk to be the literary giants who taught her narrative art, trained her ear, and set a standard of excellence. The poetry and beauty of this everyday language was found at the kitchen table and within the books, stories, and poems by West Indian and black Americans. For Marshall, this language was home—and her home was this language; within the embrace of the kitchen and her mother's talk, she began to think of someday being a writer herself.

O'Kill, Brian, ed. *Exit Lines: Famous (and Not So Famous) Last Words*. Essex, England: Longman Higher Education, 1986.

This is a collection of accounts of the various ways famous figures in history—from six continents, across two millennia, and including Beethoven, Julius Caesar, Chekhov, Descartes, Isadora Duncan, Goethe, Hobbes, John Lennon, Molière, Napoleon, Isaac Newton, Picasso, Socrates, Gertrude Stein, Thoreau, and Richard Wagner, to name a few—have died and the words they have spoken at their end. Brian O'Kill explains popular fascination with dying words through the commonly held belief that one's manner of dying mirrors one's manner of living. In this ultimate exit—death—O'Kill brings up the possibility that how one dies—expressed in the words one utters—matters. Related to this is also the idea that in the act of leaving life, a person can reveal some essential characteristic or give some meaning to the ones who are left living. Though death is an unplanned exit, it is an inevitable exit; that there is considerable cultural variation regarding rituals and understanding of death points to the possibility that human beings have long grappled with the mystery the exit of death represents.

Sartre, Jean-Paul. *No Exit and Three Other Plays*. New York: Vintage Books, 1956.

The play *Huis Clos* (No Exit) was first performed in a theater in Paris in 1944 and presents a version of hell—a place from which it is impossible to exit, a place that is surprisingly banal, and a place of interminable suffering through the torture of self-reflection and relations with other human beings. The three condemned souls—Garcin, Inez, and Estelle—learn what each of them did in life to deserve hell after death, and they attempt to tolerate one another's presence. They fail, provoking Garcin to exclaim that famous line, "Hell is other people." When given the opportunity to exit the room in which they are confined, they are unable to leave. Hell, therefore, is not only other people, but one's self too; symbolizing potentiality, possibility, movement, and life itself, exit is the ultimate freedom. It is through the ability to exit present circumstances into the abyss of the unknown—to imagine another way of existing that is reachable through leaving what one knows—that Sartre offers a vision for a full and meaningful life.

Weiss, Robert. *The Experience of Retirement.* New York: Cornell University Press, 2005.

Robert Weiss offers a carefully researched sociological perspective on the experience of retirement, characterized as an exit from working or from an occupation, generally defined by age. Weiss's descriptive work supplements the mostly survey and policy analyses of retirement and attends to this social rite of passage through three perspectives—the economic, the sociological, and the psychological. Observing how people exit their professions, their working routines, and their job-related identities, Weiss finds this exit to be multifaceted, complex, and sometimes perplexing. He notes that in planning for retirement, people consider the financial realities of their exit much more than the social and psychological changes that accompany leaving the sphere of work and occupational engagement. He recommends preparing for this exit, especially regarding transitions, activities to replace work, and sustaining relationships. As with some of the folks in the present book, the rituals of retirement are both essential and incomplete.

Acknowledgments

This project required that I ask folks to take a difficult, counterintuitive journey; to begin at the end, to reflect on, and to make visible the exits in their lives, to honor the departures that are so often shadowed by guilt or diminished by inattention. I want to express my appreciation to the nearly forty people whose insights and observations helped shape the arc and argument of this book, most especially the dozen women and men whose solo voices and life-giving narratives are braided through the text, allowing us to hear the resonant and dissonant soundings of their stories, offering us the chance to see the universal in the particular. The storytellers were heroic, openhearted, and authentic in expressing their mix of emotions of loss and liberation, pain and joy, laughter and tears. They were brave in reliving ancient tales, turning old scars into badges of courage, using our conversations as opportunities for discovery, celebration, and healing. I am awed by their trust, inspired by their witness, and forever grateful for their wisdom. Although their voices, experiences, and journeys have been faithfully documented and recorded, I have—by mutual agreement—altered all the names, a few of the narrative details, and most of the places to protect their privacy and that of their families.

Wendy Angus, my extraordinary assistant, was once again by my side, with steady encouragement, probing observations, sage counsel, and discerning attention to things big and small. Irene Liefshitz, my brilliant research assistant, brought her rigor and imagination, her lightness and laughter, her soulfulness and sophistication to our conversations. Her writings, reviewing the literature and musing on the metaphors, were lucid, her analyses penetrating. I am so grateful for Wendy's and Irene's generous contributions to this work.

My magnificent friends Susan Robbins Berger, Andrea Fleck Clardy, Jessica Hoffmann Davis, Mary Graham, Marita Rivero, and Marti Wilson were my confidants and coconspirators as we took our long walk/talks around the Jamaica Pond, along the Muddy River, on the beaches and through the marshes in Woods Hole, as we watched the sunrise over Gilmore Pond and the sunsets on Squam Lake . . . rich conversations inspired by the water. I am thankful for their deep listening and spirited talk, their intelligence and truth telling, their abiding love.

My family, bless every one of them, nourished me with food for my body and my soul. My mother, Margaret, who, at ninety-seven, has seen it all, offered me her spiritual countenance and amazing grace. My sister, Paula, a fearless sojourner, asked the gentle/hard questions that lead to new discoveries. My brother, Chuck, loved the conceit of this book, immediately challenging and stretching my nascent understandings. And my children, now young adults, stuck to the family script: Tolani seeing the art and imagery, the metaphors and poetry in exit journeys, and Martin offering his funky wit and heartfelt encouragement, rescuing me from computer disasters. Irving Hamer sustained me with his fierce love, his huge heart, and his unyielding belief in me.

As always, my agent, Ike Williams, shepherded this project forward with his signature blend of cool and passion. I am always grateful for his friendship, his strategic guidance, and his unerring support. Still rivers run deep with Hope Denekamp, who is always there, holding down the fort, graceful and tough in her advocacy on my behalf. I thank my smart, savvy, and sophisticated editor and publisher, Sarah Crichton, who pushed just enough, practicing her delicate mix of demand and restraint. She was ably assisted by the steadiness, intelligence, and welcome humor of Dan Piepenbring.

A NOTE ABOUT THE AUTHOR

Sara Lawrence-Lightfoot, a MacArthur prize–winning sociologist, is the Emily Hargroves Fisher Professor of Education at Harvard University, where she has been on the faculty since 1972. An educator, researcher, author, and public intellectual, Lawrence-Lightfoot has written ten books, including *Worlds Apart: Relationships Between Families and Schools* (1978), *Beyond Bias: Perspectives on Classrooms* (1979; with Jean Carew), and *The Good High School: Portraits of Character and Culture* (1983), which received the 1984 Outstanding Book Award from the American Educational Research Association. Her book *Balm in Gilead: Journey of a Healer* (1988), which won the 1988 Christopher Award, given for "literary merit and humanitarian achievement," was followed by *I've Known Rivers: Lives of Loss and Liberation* (1994) and *The Art and Science of Portraiture* (1997; with Jessica Hoffmann Davis), which documents her pioneering approach to social science methodology, one that bridges the realms of aesthetics and empiricism. In *Respect: An Exploration* (1999), Lawrence-Lightfoot reaches deep into human experience to find the essence of this powerful quality. *The Essential Conversation: What Parents and Teachers Can Learn from Each Other* (2003) captures the crucial exchange between parents and teachers, a dialogue that is both mirror and metaphor for the cultural forces that shape the socialization of our children, and *The Third Chapter: Passion, Risk, and Adventure in the 25 Years after 50* (2009) explores new learning during one of the most transformative and generative times in our lives.

Lawrence-Lightfoot has been the recipient of twenty-eight honorary degrees. In 1993, the Sara Lawrence-Lightfoot Chair, an endowed professorship, was established at Swarthmore College, and in 1998, she was the recipient of the Emily Hargroves Fisher Endowed Chair at Harvard University, which upon her retirement will become the Sara Lawrence-Lightfoot Endowed Chair, making her the first African American woman in Harvard's history to have an endowed professorship named in her honor.

Lawrence-Lightfoot did her undergraduate work in psychology at Swarthmore College and received her doctorate in the sociology of education at Harvard.